THE NEW EMERGING JAPANESE ECONOMY

OPPORTUNITIES AND STRATEGIES FOR WORLD BUSINESS

Panos Mourdoukoutas

THOMSON

SOUTH-WESTERN

Australia · Brazil · Canada · Mexico · Singapore · Spain · United Kingdom · United States

The New Emerging Japanese Economy
Panos Mourdoukoutas

COPYRIGHT © 2005 by Texere, an imprint of Thomson/South-Western, a part of The Thomson Corporation. Thomson and the Star logo are trademarks used herein under license.

Composed by: Interactive Composition Corporation.

Printed in the United States of America by R.R. Donnelly–Crawfordsville, IN

1 2 3 4 5 08 07 06 05

This book is printed on acid-free paper.

ISBN 0-324-20712-3

For permission to use material from this text or product, submit a request online at http://www.thomsonrights.com.

Library of Congress Cataloging in Publication Number is available. See page 242 for details.

For more information about our products, contact us at:

Thomson Learning Academic Resource Center 1-800-423-0563

Thomson Higher Education
5191 Natorp Boulevard
Mason, Ohio 45040
USA

TABLE OF CONTENTS

Preface   xi

1   Introduction   1

PART I   FROM THE OLD ECONOMY TO THE NEW   13

2   Economic Dualism   15

3   Government Activism   35

4   Economic Frictions   49

5   Deregulation and Competition   69

6   Business and Political Restructuring   89

PART II   HOW JAPAN'S NEW ECONOMY BENEFITS
WORLD BUSINESSES   107

7   Japan's Market Opens to World Businesses   109

8   Trends and Opportunities in Japan's Market   123

9   Foreign Affiliates in Japan   137

PART III   STRATEGIES FOR WORLD BUSINESSES   159

10   Adapt to the Japanese Business Conditions   161

11   Develop New Products   173

12   Promote Products Aggressively   187

13   From Here to the Future   203

Bibliography   209

Index   233

About the Author   241

About Texere   242

To my children, Georgios and Anastasia

ACKNOWLEDGEMENTS

Part of the book was completed during the author's stay at Nagoya University and Chukyo University. The author is indebted to professors Nobuhiro Okuno, Akira Yakita, Tadashi Yagi, and to Mr. Dimitris Triposoitis. The author is also indebted to Mr. Ken Aoshima, President of TDK Corporation of America, and his students Natalia Higashi, Larry Collins, and Abraham Stefanidis.

EXHIBITS

2.1 Share of Regulated Industries in the Japanese Economy 18

2.2 Selective Characteristics of the Noncontractual and Contractual Sectors 29

4.1 Highlights of the US-Japan Trade Friction 50

4.2 Highlights of Structural Impediments and Results-Oriented Initiatives 59

4.3 Highlights of the EU-Japan Trade Friction 60

5.1 Average Tariff Rates for Selected Countries 73

5.2 Selected Foreign-Affiliated Distributors That Entered the Japanese Market in the 1990s 81

5.3 Cost of Living in Tokyo Compared to Other Major Cities Worldwide by Item (2000) 81

6.1 Declining Share of Companies with Lifetime Employment 98

6.2 Rising Share of Part-time Female Workers in Japan 99

6.3 Share of Companies Offering Merit System 100

6.4 The Koizumi Agenda 103

7.1 Real GDP, Imports, and Exports (1986–2001) 111

7.2 FDI Inflows 1993–2002 112

7.3 Selective Foreign Stakes in Japanese Companies as of 2002 113

7.4 Foreign Company Market Shares in Selective Japanese Industries in 2000 114

7.5 Household Disposable Income and Expenditures 1984–2000 116

7.6 Revenue Growth in Japan and Asia Pacific (Percent of Xilinx Revenues) 117

7.7 A Sample of Foreign Corporations with R&D in Japan 119

8.1   Manufactured World Imports Entering Japan   125

8.2   Manufactured Imports Entering Japan   126

8.3   Changes in Household Composition   127

8.4   Japan's Graying Population: % of Total Population
      65 and Over   129

8.5   GDP and Employment by Sector in 2002   129

8.6   The Contribution of Various Types of Services to GDP
      in 2002   130

9.1   Start-up Costs in Major Industrial Countries in 2000   139

9.2   Advantages and Disadvantages of Different
      Entry Strategies   140

9.3   Entry Mode of Selected Foreign Subsidiaries   142

9.4   Distribution of Foreign Capital Companies by Industry in
      FY2000   144

9.5   Comparison of Productivity of All Corporations and
      Foreign Affiliates in Japan   145

9.6   Trends in Ordinary Income to Net Sales Ratios   145

9.7   Foreign-Affiliate Companies: Competitive Strategies   146

9.8   AFLAC Japan Sales Results   148

11.1 Top Ten Automobile Brands   174

11.2 Apple Computer's Top-Selling Products in Japan
      as of 2000   175

11.3 Apple's Market Share in Japan   175

11.4 Business R&D for Selected Countries in 2000   178

11.5 Research and Production Operations in Japan   181

12.1 Japanese Versus Western Commercials   188

12.2 History of Advertising in Japan   188

12.3 Advertising Expenditures by Medium
      (1990 and 2001)   189

12.4 Proportion by Expense Item and Place of Purchase   195

12.5 Internet Access Modes   199

12.6 Utilization of Internet for Purchasing Goods and Services
      (Total Households)   199

PREFACE

This book is the product of a long study of the Japanese economy that began in the late 1980s with my first visit to Nagoya University, and continues up through today with several subsequent visits to a number of other universities, including Nagoya University, Kobe University, Mie University, and Chukyo University, as well as visits to several Japanese corporations, including Toyota Corporation, Eisai Pharmaceuticals, and Yamazaki Corporation. These visits led to the co-authorship of a book on the Japanese banking crisis, and several papers published in academic and professional journals, including "The Japanese System: A Study in Labor Markets Adjustment to Automation"; "Economic Barriers for Foreign Affiliates in Japan: The High Cost of Local Labor"; "Do Japanese Companies Have a Strategy?"; and "IT and Competitive Advantage: the Case of Japanese Manufacturing Companies."

As reflected in these publications, my impression of the Japanese economy has been mixed and changing over time. In my early visits, I was enchanted by the country's vigorous economic growth, their new electronic products, their management system, the Japanese people's passion for hard and detailed work, and the aggressive acquisition of American trophies, such as movie studios, landmark buildings, and golf courses. I was disenchanted, however, with the country's living standards that lagged behind those of America and Europe. Japanese consumers had few product choices, especially hard-to-find-in-the-neighborhood-store foreign products; paid dearly for basic goods and services such as rice, beef, fruits, electricity, and telephone services; lived in small houses; and shared a poor infrastructure. Japan was the land of an economic paradox: a rich county with poor consumers.

A number of factors explain this paradox, most notably trade protectionism and government regulation that limited domestic and foreign competition and kept prices of everyday goods above world levels. Import quotas and tariffs, for instance, limited rice and beef imports. Government regulations limited the entry and expansion of large-scale stores in the retailing sector. Layers of wholesalers placed a wedge between world business and products and Japanese consumers. *Keiretsu* groups formed an iron web that kept outsiders off the electronics sector, while government monopolies kept the telecom and the utility sectors off limits both for foreign and domestic competitors. Compounding the problem, high real estate costs and the reluctance of Japanese career employees to work for foreign employers made entry and expansion of foreign business an almost impossible task, especially for the smaller and medium companies that lacked deep pockets to pay for the high start-up costs.

In my subsequent visits, especially in my most recent 2002 visit, I became less enchanted with the country's economic growth, electronic gadgets, and management system, but I was impressed with the progress the country has made in bringing living standards closer to those of other industrial countries. Japanese consumers had more choices and paid much less for basic goods and services, while foreign products were abundant in local supermarkets, foreign wholesale clubs, and discount retailers.

The catalysts for this epic shift from the "Old" to the "New" Economy are competition, deregulation, and corporate and industry restructuring. Under pressure from trade partners, Japanese governments have been shifting their economic priorities—from producer prosperity to consumer prosperity—by reducing working hours, stimulating domestic demand, removing trade barriers, letting the yen appreciate, and deregulating the distribution, retailing, telecommunications, and finance industries. Slowly, Japan is being transformed from a producer nation to a consumer nation in line with other developed nations.

Japan's transformation from the Old to the New Economy has allowed foreign companies to make significant inroads into the Japanese market. IBM, P&G, Disney, AFLAC, Pfizer, Apple Computer, Starbucks Coffee—to mention but a few—derive a substantial portion of their sales and earnings from the Japanese market. Yet Japan's market remains a difficult market to crack. Japanese consumers have high expectations regarding product pricing, quality, packaging, and after-sales guarantees. Setting up and operating an office or manufacturing facility and hiring domestic labor continues to be costly. Obtaining the necessary licenses and permits and teaming up with the right domestic partners is a lengthy process that takes a series of personal contacts and negotiations. Developing products for the Japanese market and promoting them successfully requires a well-orchestrated, three-fold business strategy: 1) Adapt to the Japanese business practices, consumer preferences, and constraints and rules of competition; 2) Develop new products and new services that cater to the needs and imagination of the consumers of a dynamic market; and 3) Promote products and services aggressively through traditional and nontraditional marketing and distribution channels.

In addressing Japan's emerging New Economy and the opportunities and strategies for world businesses, this book has three objectives. The first objective is to review the rise and fall of the country's Old Economy and the emerging New Economy. The second objective is to point to the trends and opportunities of the Japanese market. The third objective is to outline a strategy that will help foreign companies compete efficiently and effectively in the Japanese market.

Covering a broad number of topics, this book is written for a diverse audience. International business executives will be interested in the comprehensive analysis of the opening of Japan's market and the trends and opportunities for world businesses. Graduate and undergraduate students of international management and marketing studying the evolution of Japan's markets and management systems will discover many valuable lessons in business strategy. And, of course, the general reader will be eager to find out the fate of the economy of the Rising Sun that blinded the world with its brightness in the 1980s.

CHAPTER 1

INTRODUCTION

It was a hot and humid Saturday afternoon at Shibuya Station, one of Tokyo's busiest districts. The streets were crowded with young people, some wearing American jeans, T-shirts, sneakers, and Swiss-made mechanical wristwatches, others dressed in European designer clothes. Most of them were heading for the dozens of western fashion boutiques, fast-food restaurants, Starbucks coffee shops, and western-style cafeterias. In one of those coffee shops, I met two Japanese students, who with an unconventional openness asked me which country I was from. In the lengthy chatting that followed, I was impressed with the strong interest of young Japanese in western culture, products, and lifestyles, and the admiration of foreign business executives running Japanese companies.

Interest in western products, lifestyle, and management is not confined to the coffee shops and boutiques of Shibuya Station and the Ginza district, nor are fashion and fads for young people only. It is spreading across Japan to all generations and all social groups, including the country's seniors. In the tiny streets of Japanese cities, foreign luxury cars are parked conspicuously. In department stores and fashion boutiques, under the sounds of western music, Japanese women are shopping for imported designer clothes, handbags, cosmetics, and jewelry, even in the face of the country's prolonged stagnation. In Japanese households, traditional *kimonos* and *Yucata* are being replaced by western dresses and suits, *tatami* mats by western style beds, and chopsticks by silverware.

The growing interest of Japanese consumers in foreign products and management systems is part of a broader trend: the transformation of the Japanese economy from a production, export-oriented economy to a consumption, import-oriented economy that offers enormous opportunities for world businesses. Japan's 127 million people with stable jobs, a high per capita income and savings crowded into a land area equal to that of California, and a growing appetite for western products make it the world's second single largest market after the US. Which company wouldn't be reaching for it?

The world's large, multinational corporations are already there. Coca-Cola, IBM, Motorola, Nestle, Digital Equipment, BMW, Pfizer, Glaxo

Holdings, Wal-Mart, Carrefour SA, Applied Materials—to mention but a few—are all thriving in the Japanese market. But what about the smaller corporations that lack the financial strength and marketing networks of larger corporations? How can these companies enter the Japanese market? What should they know about tariff and nontariff barriers? What should they know about Japan's New Economy? Where are the opportunities? What kind of business strategy should they follow? This book addresses all of these important questions and more.

For decades, Japan was a nation obsessed with economic growth, trade protectionism, and government regulation. In what has been frequently referred to as the "Old Economy," pre-1985 bubble economy, government bureaucrats adopted an activist policy that included government ownership of corporations, protection of certain industries from domestic and foreign competition, and guidance regarding future business opportunities. Companies invested heavily in capital equipment, paid little in dividends, and forged partnerships with labor unions, thereby promoting employment stability, worker participation, on-the-job training, joint consultation, flexible compensation, and decision by consensus. Workers demonstrated discipline and cooperation, worked long hours, and saved a large portion of their income.

In the beginning, Japan's obsession with growth, protectionism, and regulation yielded a number of desired results.* High economic growth allowed Japan's workers to enjoy stable employment, high income, and a reputation of teamwork and craftsmanship second to none, placing Japan next to developed nations.** Most notably, the country's management system and government policies served as examples for the emerging economies of Southeast Asia and as case studies in MBA programs around the world, while the country's bank giants commanded fear and admiration in the world financial community.

---

* For the period 1960–73, Japan's economy grew at a rate of 6.3 percent, compared to 2.5 and 4.8 percent corresponding US and OECD growth rates. For the period 1974–79, the country's economy grew at a slower rate of 3.6 percent, but again above the US and OECD growth averages of 2.6 and 2.9 percent. Japan's superior performance continued for the periods 1980–82, 1983–87, and 1990–92. In 1986, Japan registered the lowest discomfort index (unemployment plus inflation), 9.9 percent, compared to 15.8 percent for the US, 17 percent for France, and 21.2 percent for the UK.

** Japanese contributions caught up with and even exceeded those of the US. In 1990 alone, Japan contributed $5.6 billion to the Official Development Assistance (ODA), the second largest contribution after the US. In 1987, Japan contributed $5.7 billion to the World Bank and $8.1 billion to the International Development Association; $3.1 billion to the Asian Development Bank; $2.9 billion to the Asian Development Fund; and $4.2 billion to the International Monetary Fund; and made considerable contributions to the UN and various UN organizations. For the period 1988–92, Japan's transfer of $100 billion cumulative direct and indirect assistance to developing countries dwarfed the early postwar Marshall Plan for Europe.

Eventually, Japan's obsession with economic growth yielded an unintended consequence: economic dualism—a modern, open and competitive sector that included the automobile, consumer electronics, machine tool, and office equipment industries, but at the same time a backward, closed and uncompetitive sector that included utilities, distribution, finance, insurance, and construction. Economic dualism was further extended to the labor market that included two sectors: a core sector that enjoyed stable employment, rising wages, and union protection, insulated from market fluctuations, and a peripheral sector that enjoyed none of the above, functioning at the whim of market fluctuations.

Economic dualism fueled external and internal frictions. External frictions revolved around the country's export promotion policies and market barriers in the noncompetitive sector that kept foreign competitors off the Japanese market and created soaring trade surpluses. Internal frictions revolved around the high cost of living and the gap between production and consumption, as well as a poor infrastructure, which turned Japan into a rich country with poor consumers. Japan's economic model had delivered growth and jobs, but not prosperity.

Early on, external friction was mild and well contained. Japan's trade partners, especially the US, were willing to let Japan get away with her obsession of high economic growth and market protectionism in exchange for political and military benefits.★ In the 1980s, all this changed, however, and external frictions proliferated.★★ Beginning with the Carter Administration in 1980 and continuing with the Reagan Administration, the US demanded that Japan open its markets to foreign products and competition. In 1989 Japan, together with Brazil and India, was included in the list of unfair trade nations under the "Super 301" section of the Trade and Competitiveness Act of 1988. The Act initially called for negotiations to open the Japanese market to American supercomputers, telecommunications, and wood products, although it was only the precursor to the Structural Impediments Initiative (SII) that called for broader market access for American products.

★ Japan was an indispensable military and political ally in America's efforts to constrain the spread of communism in the Asian Pacific region.

★★ With the collapse of the Soviet Union, Japan was no longer an indispensable military ally. Besides, the US recession of the early 1980s and the aggressive acquisition of American assets by Japanese companies multiplied the voices calling for restraining Japan's overseas expansion.

Yielding to these calls, the Japanese government shifted its economic priorities from production and exports to consumption and imports. Following the 1985 Plaza Accord, the Bank of Japan launched an aggressive monetary easing to boost domestic demand. The Japanese government then launched a number of policies to open domestic markets to foreign business:

- It offered tax and credit incentives to domestic retailers for the importation of selected commodities and the establishment of foreign business in Japan.
- It lowered tariff rates for a number of manufacturing products.
- It simplified the government procurement system and made public construction projects accessible to foreign bidders.
- It lifted financial regulations, opening the financial sector to foreign banking, securities, and insurance.
- It simplified customs procedures, speeding up imports.
- It adjusted product standards to those of other industrial countries and reached new bilateral agreements in highly disputed sectors, such as semiconductors and pharmaceuticals.
- It revised corporate law to allow for class action lawsuits and antitrust enforcement.
- It lifted heavy tariffs and quotas on specific agricultural products like beef, and abandoned the complete ban on rice, opening this sacred market to foreign imports.
- It revised labor laws to allow for the hiring of temporary staffing.

Japan's early progress with removing trade barriers and bans on foreign investments was noticed in a 1990 US Congressional hearing:

Japan has made progress over the past decade in removing traditional trade barriers in an effort to open its market to foreign participation. The formidable array of formal trade barriers that Japan employed at the border in the 1950s and 1960s to protect its industrial sector— high tariffs, extensive quotas, and bans on foreign investment—have been mostly dismantled.[1]

Progress was also noticed in an American Chambers of Commerce in Japan survey, which found that more and more American entrepreneurs and business leaders have revised their views on the Japanese market, especially since the Plaza Accord in September 1985:

> The overall conclusion of the study is that the environment for trade and investment in Japan, though not as favorable as in the US or many major industrialized countries, has improved during the past five years. . . . Overall, 55 percent [of the survey respondents] indicated that the current climate had improved either somewhat or significantly since 1985, and only 5 percent sensed deterioration in the environment for foreign investment during that period. Looking ahead over the next few years, 63 percent expect to see either some or significant improvement in the climate for investment in their sectors, 34 percent anticipate no change, and only 3 percent predict deterioration.[2]

Eventually, Japanese government and business began assisting foreign companies in importing products or setting up business in Japan. In January 1994, the Japanese government assisted foreign construction and engineering companies in participating in future project bidding. In July 1993, Japan promised to improve access for medical, telecommunications, and insurance products. In January 1992, during President Bush's celebrated visit, Japan agreed to (1) raise purchases of US-manufactured auto parts by Japanese factories in the US from $7 billion in 1990 to $15 billion in 1994, and (2) raise imports of US-manufactured auto parts by Japanese auto makers in Japan from $2 billion to $4 billion over the same period. In 1991, Japan's Ministry of International Trade and Industry (MITI)—now the Ministry of Economy, Trade and Industry (METI)—and the US Department of Commerce developed the Japan Corporate Plan to assist American companies in either expanding existing operations or establishing new ones.

More recently, Japan's prolonged stagnation and substantial decline in equity prices provided world business an express track to the Japanese market: the acquisition of equity stakes in domestic companies, often their competitors. General Motors, for instance, took equity stakes in Isuzu Motors, Suzuki Motors, and Fuji Heavy Industries; Roche Group took a 50.1 stake to Chugai Pharmaceutical Co.; Wal-Mart a 6 percent stake in Seiyu; Ford took a 33 percent stake in Mazda; while China-based Shanghai Electric and Morningside took over Akiyama Machinery Manufacturing. Lower real estate prices made it easier for foreign companies to set up offices, warehouses, and factories in Japan.

Japan's progress in opening up her markets to foreign products is not even across all sectors. Some sectors, such as construction, retailing, financial, accounting, and legal services by and large remain inaccessible to foreign companies. Other sectors have yet to overcome the complexity of the country's distribution system. As the American Chambers of Commerce in Japan reported:

> Once products have cleared customs, they still must navigate Japan's convoluted and multilayered distribution system before they find their way to the customer. The bottlenecks in the distribution system, even in the best cases, add unnecessarily to the price. In the worst cases, such as film and flat glass, they essentially prevent meaningful market access.[3]

Though less binding, economic barriers, such as the high real estate/rent and the high cost of local labor, continue to limit the ability of smaller foreign companies to set up subsidiaries in Japan and compete effectively against their domestic counterparts. For some foreign companies, the problem with market access is not just a matter of barriers, but rather a matter of failure to adjust to the demands of Japanese consumers, business partners, labor, and most notably product quality, branding, and prompt decision making. For other companies, the problem with market access is an array of factors, ranging from shortage of qualified personnel, low market potential, and excessive production costs.* In the retailing and distribution sectors, foreign discount retailers like Wal-Mart face fierce competition from foreign and domestic counterparts.[4]

Japan's transformation from the Old to the New Economy was not a smooth and orderly process, but a rough roller-coaster ride. The sharp upturn and prolonged expansion in the 1980s, known as the Bubble Economy, was followed by a sharp downturn and a prolonged contraction in the 1990s, known as "the Burst of the Bubble," which dragged the country into a financial crisis and deflation lasting well into the early 2000s.** But as the bubbles burst away, Japan is emerging as a "normal," mature, economy,

---

* As of 2002, Japan's combined local and national corporate tax rate was standing at 48.34 percent, compared to 40.8 percent in the US and 31 percent in the UK.

** Between 1991 and 1998, a period of world recovery and robust expansion for the US economy, the Japanese economy slid into a contraction: The GDP growth dropped from 6.1 percent in 1988 to 3.8 percent by 1991, to negative territory by 1994; and after a 3.5 rise in 1996, growth dipped 1.1 percent in 1998. The Nikkei stock average dropped from close to 40,000 in 1989 to under 12,000 by early 2000. Official unemployment increased from 2.5 in 1991 to close to 5 percent by 2000; and Japanese banks accumulated over $300 billion in bad loans. Japan's share to the world GDP dropped from 15.2 percent in 1990 to 14.9 percent in 2000.

where people place consumption and leisure ahead of production and work. Japanese consumers are reaching for foreign products and services to better their lives—everything from less expensive chocolates from Nestle, discounted toys from Toys "R" Us, milk from Australia and New Zealand, luxury cars from Europe, and beef and citrus from American farmers, to banking and financial services from American banks and financial service companies.

In short, Japan is no longer what it used to be, a tightly protected and regulated economy that exports but doesn't import. Competition and deregulation have been transforming the country from an emerging to a mature society, from a production- to a consumption-oriented society. Japan's New Economy presents opportunities to world businesses prepared to adapt their products to the tastes of the Japanese consumers and to adhere to the Japanese business practices and rules of competition.

A number of books have already addressed Japan's transformation from the Old to the New Economy. In the *Transformation of the Japanese Economy* (1999), Sato, the editor, and a number of contributing authors discuss Japan's economic development and position in the global economy.[5] In the *Japanese Economy Reconsidered* (2000), Ito and Itoh discuss the growth and Burst of the Economic Bubble.[6] A number of other books, most a decade or more old, discuss the opening of Japan's markets and the opportunities and strategies for foreign business. In *Second to None: American Companies in Japan*, Robert Christopher provides a good discussion of the record of successful American companies in Japan, which can serve as raw models for newcomers.[7] In *Beating Japan*, Francis McInerney and Sean White alert American companies to the danger of Japanese expansion and provide valuable lessons in beating the Japanese on their own home turf.[8] In *Cracking the Japanese Market*, James Morgan and Jeffrey Morgan review the experience of Applied Materials in the Japanese market, and make inferences about the ways foreign companies can access the Japanese market.[9] In *Unlocking Japan's Markets*, Michael Czinkota and Jon Wonoff provide an evaluation of the progress made in opening the Japanese market and give their own suggestions for accessing the Japanese market.[10] In *Doing Business with the Japanese*, John AS Abecasis-Phillips discusses the peculiarities and specifics of the Japanese markets and provides valuable insights for dealing with Japanese consumers and businesses.[11]

Updating and expanding this literature, the remainder of this book takes a closer look at Japan's transformation from an Old to a New Economy and the opportunities and strategies for world businesses. Part I recounts the rise and fall of the country's Old Economy, the subsequent rise of economic dualism and government activism, the growing external and internal frictions, competition and deregulation, and corporate and industry restructuring. Part II looks at how the New Economy benefits world businesses, reveals the opening of domestic markets to foreign products and competition, examines the trends that shape current and future business opportunities, and documents the experience of a number of foreign companies that have been early movers to the Japanese market. Finally, Parts III and IV outline a business strategy to assist world businesses in competing efficiently and effectively in Japan's New Economy.

Specifically, Chapter 2 discusses one of the features of Japan's Old Economy—dualism. This period in Japan's economic history was marked by the coexistence of a modern, export-oriented sector that escaped government protectionism (for example, automobiles, consumer electronics, office equipment, and machine tools), to which Japan owes her reputation as an efficient and successful economy, and a backward, domestic-oriented sector that remained under government protectionism (including transportation, utilities, and distribution), to which Japan owes her reputation as an inefficient and unsuccessful economy, or a rich country with poor consumers. Dualism even applied to the labor markets that included two sectors: The noncontractual sector, where labor enjoyed lifetime employment, seniority wages, and union protection; and the contractual sector, where labor didn't enjoy any of the above. Economic dualism in commodity and labor markets nurtured institutions and attitudes that constrained the entry and expansion of world businesses in the Japanese market.

Chapter 3 discusses another feature of Japan's Old Economy, which was government activism, a set of policies that fostered cooperation between business and government, often termed Japan, Inc. These policies resulted in close cooperation between business and government in the importation of foreign technology, the imitation and development of western manufacturing facilities, and the coping with economic contractions; indicative planning, or the protection of domestic industry, meaning the setting of broad guidelines for the economy's future; export promotion; and the channeling of economic resources to emerging technologies. Economic activism constrained the entry of world businesses to the Japanese market by nurturing world-class competitors and local oligopolies.

Chapter 4 discusses the size, structure, and sources of Japan's soaring trade surpluses that were at the core of the country's frictions with American and European trade partners. The chapter's first section investigates whether

Japan's trade pattern was consistent with her development stage, i.e., whether it exported too much and imported too little, and concludes that Japan had an irregular import pattern attributed to tariff and nontariff barriers, an undervalued currency, and high savings. It was these factors that were at the root of the country's trade pattern—policies that turned Japan into a rich country of poor citizens—and placed it on a collision course with her trade partners and citizens, an issue addressed in the second section.

Chapter 5 discusses how the growing friction between Japan and her trade partners and citizens led to a shift in the country's economic priorities, specifically a reduction in working hours, expansion of domestic demand, a stronger yen, the lifting of tariff and nontariff trade barriers, and the deregulation of distribution, retailing, and financial sectors. The chapter further discusses how this shift in economic priorities started Japan's economy on a roller-coaster ride—the Economic Bubble and its Burst that pulled the banking system into a prolonged crisis and the Japanese economy into her worst post-war stagnation.

Chapter 6 discusses how Japan's business and political systems have been restructuring to deal with the new economic environment shaped by trade liberalization, deregulation, and the prolonged stagnation. Businesses have been revising their corporate objectives to become more stockholder rather than stakeholder oriented, emphasizing profits over sales growth and market shares, re-locating their manufacturing facilities to China and other low-cost Asian countries, and de-emphasizing the traditional institutions of lifetime employment, seniority wages, and enterprise unions. The country's political system has become more open, meaning that politicians rule and bureaucrats execute rather than the other way around.

Chapter 7 discusses how the lifting of trade protectionism has allowed foreign companies to crack the Japanese market by acquiring stakes in domestic companies, forging joint ventures with domestic competitors, and setting up wholly owned subsidiaries. The chapter further discusses the appeal of the Japanese market for world businesses: A large, highly integrated market, a basis for Asian trade and investment, a test ground for competition, and a world innovator.

Chapter 8 reviews in more detail the trends and opportunities of the Japanese market: A growing appetite for imports, smaller and graying households, a shift from goods to services and from quality to value, and the use of more credit and less cash. It also reveals the opportunities these trends create for world businesses in terms of a growing market for products geared toward single households and graying households.

Chapter 9 reviews the experience of foreign companies that have been early movers into the Japanese market, such as their modes of entry, industry presence, performance, and problems encountered in establishing and expanding their presence in the Japanese market. The chapter further includes four case studies—AFLAC, Pfizer, Digital Equipment, and Jardine Fleming—that have been considered successful in their industries in Japan.

Chapter 10 discusses the first part of my three-pronged adapt, develop, and promote (ADP) strategy: how foreign companies can adapt to the peculiarities and specificity of the Japanese consumer, business practices, and competition. The chapter emphasizes the importance of product quality, prompt delivery, and after-sales services for pleasing Japanese consumers. It also covers the role of long-term planning, long-term relations between trade partners, and rules of competition.

Chapter 11 discusses the second part of the strategy: the development of new products for the Japanese market. Particular emphasis is placed on the difference between the Japanese and American models of product development. The Japanese model is more market driven, with an emphasis on applied research and incremental improvements, on the early rather than later product stages, and on the integration of product development with manufacturing.

Chapter 12 discusses the third part of the strategy: how foreign companies can promote their products in the Japanese markets. The chapter explains how the product promotion schemes of Japanese corporations differ from those of western companies. It then further identifies creative ways for addressing the complexities of the Japanese distribution system.

Chapter 13 summarizes the discussion of the book, and looks into a number of problems that world businesses are expected to encounter in the future, including high start-up costs, labor shortages, market saturation, and increasing competition from the emerging economies of Southeast Asia and China. The book concludes with a discussion about learning to live in an ever-changing world.

Endnotes

1. Joint Congressional Committee, "The Japanese Market: How Open Is It?" 44.

2. The American Chambers of Commerce in Japan, *Trade and Investment in Japan: The Current Environment,* 1 and 22.

3. American Chambers of Commerce in Japan, *2001 U.S.-Japan Business White Paper,* 17.

4. "Pacific Aisles: Wal-Mart's Foray into Japan Spurs a Retail Upheaval," A1, A6.

5. JETRO, *The 9ᵗʰ Survey on Attitudes of Foreign-Affiliated Companies,* 9.

6. Ibid, 10.

7. Christopher, *Second to None: American Companies in Japan.*

8. McInerney and White, *Beating Japan.*

9. Morgan and Morgan, *Cracking the Japanese Market: Strategies for Success in the New Global Economy,* 10–15.

10. Czinkota and Woronoff, *Unlocking Japan's Markets: Seizing Marketing and Distribution Opportunities in Today's Japan,* 25–30.

11. Abecasis-Phillips, *Doing Business in Japan,* 50–52.

PART I

FROM THE OLD ECONOMY TO THE NEW

Japan's fading Old Economy was a market sanctuary created by institutions and policies that limited access of foreign products and businesses to Japanese consumers. One of the institutions that kept foreign products and businesses off the Japanese market was economic dualism, the coexistence of open, competitive sectors with closed, noncompetitive sectors. One of the policies that kept foreign products and business off the Japanese market was government activism, the close cooperation between business and government, known as Japan, Inc. Japan's Old Economy was further characterized by friction with trade partners and citizens over the problems such a sanctuary created for them.

Japan's emerging New Economy is no longer a sanctuary, but an open, competitive market created by a number of policies that expanded access of foreign products and businesses to Japanese consumers. One of these policies was the elimination of tariff and nontariff barriers. Another policy was the lifting of regulations that constrained the entry of both domestic and foreign competitors to a number of sectors of the Japanese economy. A third policy was a number of revisions in the country's corporate governance laws that shifted power from managers to stockholders, and made it easier for foreign companies to acquire equity in Japanese businesses.

Transition from the Old to the New Economy has taken the country on a roller-coaster ride. The sharp upturn of the late '80s, known as the Bubble Economy, was followed by a prolonged stagnation, known as the Bubble and its Burst. In the end, economic growth is coming closer to earth, and consumption and leisure are gaining ground against savings and work. Most notably, real estate prices are falling, making it easier for world businesses to expand their presence into the Japanese market.

CHAPTER 2

ECONOMIC DUALISM

- When GM, Chrysler, and Ford tried to enter the Japanese market in the 1980s, they faced a difficult challenge in trying to compete against the Hondas and the Toyotas that flexed a competitive muscle that was difficult to match on their own home turf.
- When Toys "R" Us tried to open its megastores in Japan's major cities in the early 1980s, it faced a formidable barrier: Japan's Large Department Store Law that constrained the opening of large stores.
- When American financier T. Boone Pickens assumed 25 percent of Koito manufacturing, the Japanese press portrayed him as a ruthless corporate raider, while a web of cross-equity holdings prevented him from assuming control of the management.

These stories of American automobile makers, retailers, and financiers highlight a number of impediments world businesses encountered when they tried to establish or expand their presence in Japan's Old Economy: formidable domestic competitors, government regulations, exclusive business relations, and local suspicions toward foreign investors and managers.

For decades, Japan was a dual economy consisting of both a modern, open and competitive sector that included the automobile, consumer electronics, machine tool, and office equipment industries, and a backward, closed and uncompetitive sector that included utilities, distribution, finance, insurance, and construction. Economic dualism was further extended to the labor market, encompassing two sectors—a core sector that enjoyed stable employment, rising wages, and union protection, insulated from market fluctuations, and a peripheral sector that enjoyed none of the above, and thus were subject to the whim of market fluctuations.

Economic dualism constrained the entry and expansion of world businesses in a number of ways. In the modern automobile sector, GM, Ford, Chrysler, and their European counterparts faced fierce competitors, such as Honda and Toyota. In the backward retail sector, American large retailers like Toys "R" Us and Costco faced formidable regulations, including the Large Department Store Law, as well as exclusive relations between Japanese retailers and wholesalers. In both sectors, world businesses faced high start-up costs and the reluctance of Japanese workers to work for foreign employers, especially mid-career professionals enjoying lifetime employment, seniority wages, and union protection. Economic dualism further constrained the presence of foreign business in another, more indirect way. It nurtured a culture of workaholism and thrift that limited both domestic and foreign consumption. Japanese people spent too much time seeding for the future rather than enjoying the harvest of the present.

A more detailed discussion of the country's dualism and its implications for world businesses, this chapter examines dualism in commodity markets, dualism in labor markets, and finally how dualism constrained foreign businesses' access to the Japanese market.

Dualism in Commodity Markets

Japan's Old Economy was divided into two sectors: (1) the low-productivity domestic sector, where market concentration and regulation limited market entry, rivalry, and competition; public utilities, construction, insurance, finance (especially banking), transportation, telecommunications, food, retailing, local manufacturing, agriculture, and fibers are examples of industries in this sector, and (2) the high-productivity export sector, where market concentration intensified rivalry and competition; consumer electronics, automobiles, machine tools, semiconductors, and chemicals are examples of industries in this sector. In 1990, for instance, productivity in the little-regulated machine tools industry was 35 percent above its US counterpart. By contrast, productivity in the highly regulated transport and communications industries was 70 percent below their US counterparts.[1]

The Domestic Sector: Limited Rivalry and Competition

The domestic sector was a closed, highly protected, and regulated sector. Tariffs, quotas, and product standards kept foreign competitors off the Japanese market. Zoning laws limited the entry of large supermarkets in the retailing industry, while *keiretsu* relations limited entry in the electronics sector. Cross-ownership limited the entry of foreign companies to the sector by acquiring domestic companies, while the government maintained its monopoly position in a number of industries. Tight financial regulations determined the allocation of household assets between securities holdings and bank deposits; the modes of corporate financing, and the scale and scope of the banking industry.[2]

Protectionism and regulation favored market concentration and control by *keiretsu* groups. In 1990, *keiretsu* groups controlled 5.0 percent of corporate employment, 16.2 percent of sales, and 13.3 percent of current income. Industrial conglomerates were bound together by cross-stock ownership and business deals. In 1989, about 40 percent of all publicly held stock was locked in cross-ownership holdings among corporations.[3] Specifically, 26.51 percent of Sumitomo stock was owned by other Sumitomo firms; 25.50 percent of Mitsui stock was owned by other Mitsui companies; and 25.60 of Mitsubishi stock was owned by other Mitsubishi firms.[4] Toyota, for instance, controlled 24.66 percent of Toyota Automatic Loom Works, 21.2 percent of Aichi Steel Works, and 48.3 percent of Kanto Autoworks.[5] In the beer industry, four companies controlled 100 percent of the Japanese domestic market.

Japanese conglomerates replicated the pyramid-like *han* fiefdom system of feudal Japan. At the top of the pyramid, in the place of the *daimyo* (feudal master) and his family, sat the parent company and its related companies. Below the parent companies were the primary subcontractors, the secondary subcontractors, etc. "*Keiretsu* are the ultimate force in Japanese industry. The manufacturing companies within them are controlled to some extent by the needs and policies of the group, just as each of the manufacturing industries has its own huge pyramid of subcontractors that functions as a group," explained Koniyasu Sakai in a 1990 *Harvard Business Review*.[6]

Japanese conglomerates were unique in two respects. First, they were far more ranging in several industries—including production, trade, and finance—than in other countries. Second, Japan's cartels were tolerated and even encouraged by government. Two government agencies, the famous MITI (Ministry of International Trade and Industry—now known as METI for Ministry of Economy, Trade and Industry and the FTC (Fair Trade Commission)—allowed and even encouraged the formation of cartels in certain industries and markets. Transportation and insurance cartels, rationalization cartels, anti-recession cartels, and export-import cartels were all cases of legal cartels.

In some industries, the presence of local conglomerates and oligopolies was reinforced by a host of government regulations. As of 1992, construction, financial services, electricity, gas, and mining were 100 percent regulated

Exhibit 2.1   Share of Regulated Industries in the Japanese Economy

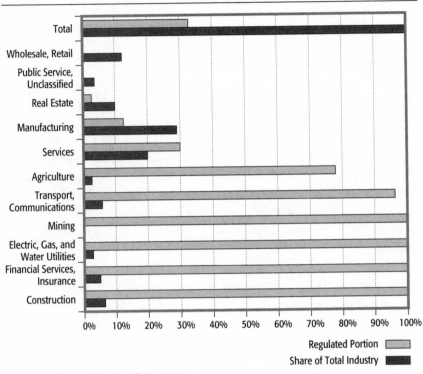

Source: Fair Trade Commission Compilation, 1994

(see Exhibit 2.1).[7] In other industries, like railroads and tobacco, government was the owner and monopolist.

In short, the domestic sector of Japan's economy was dominated by business conglomerates and *keiretsu* relations that limited entry of new competitors to the market and favored market concentration, creating oligopolies that kept the prices of the sector well above those of the competitive sector, an issue to be further addressed in Chapter 4.

The Export Sector: Intense Rivalry and Competition

Unlike the domestic sector, the export sector was an open, competitive sector. As of 1987, the air conditioning industry included 13 rivals, the audio equipment industry 25, the camera industry 15, the machine tool industry 112, the television set industry 15, the shipbuilding industry 33, and the semiconductor industry 34.[8] Rivals competed with each other in three ways: cost cutting, product quality, and new product development.

Following the two oil shocks and the yen shock, to give an example of cost-cutting practices, Japanese companies managed to curtail costs by putting more pressure on subcontractors and introducing microelectronics that save resources, enhance productivity, and improve product quality. One of the largest shipbuilding companies, the Mitsui Engineering and Ship-building Company, emphasized the development of new ships at competitive prices.

Product diversification also became important.[9] One of the world's largest camera companies, Canon, emphasized the development of new products, product quality, cost efficiency, and marketing networks. Sony Corporation also emphasized marketing, product quality, and the development of new products. Akio Morita, founder and long-time head of Sony, said, "For many years now we have put well over 6 percent of sales into research and development, and in some years over 10 percent. Our plan is to lead the public with new products rather than ask them what kind of products they want."[10]

Although rival export manufacturers competed with each other to meet Japanese consumers' demands in terms of quality, prices typically played a secondary role. In a survey of foreign companies in Japan, Douglas and Craig reported: "Price was neither a central nor a focal element in the strategy of any of the companies interviewed. All had moderate, comparison-based pricing strategies. While this might in part have been due to their lack of cost advantage over local competitors, it appeared also to reflect the characteristics of the market environment in Japan. Japanese consumers, in general, were considered to be extremely demanding in terms of product quality and service, and to exhibit little price sensitivity. This resulted in a premium pricing and conceptions that price competition was unlikely to be an effective strategy."[11] Lack of price sensitivity did not mean that companies could charge any price nor change prices frequently. Prices had to be reasonable and changed once or twice a year, normally at the beginning or the middle of the year.

Part of the credit for the success of the export sector should be assigned to thousands of small and medium enterprises (SMEs) that were subcontractors and indispensable associates of larger companies. In 1992, companies of 1 to 19 employees created 36.4 percent of employment, compared to 25.6 percent for their US counterparts and 25.9 percent for their German counterparts.[12] SMEs accounted for more than 99 percent of all Japanese enterprises, employing more than 79 percent of the work force. Their contribution to employment varies widely by sector, but is highest in small-scale, traditional industries.[13]

Small companies were often subcontractors to large enterprises, providing them with quality, low-cost components and special technologies. Close to 52 percent of large companies used subcontractors to cut costs, 40.1 percent to take advantage of special technologies.[14] Small companies further served as a recession buffer for the large enterprises, bearing the burden of recessions. In the Ota Ward alone, an area in Southern Tokyo, 7,000 small factories vanished between 1985 and 1995.[15]

In brief, Japan's Old Economy was a dual economy consisting of an open, competitive sector and a closed, noncompetitive sector. Both sectors were highly concentrated. In the closed, noncompetitive sector, market concentration led to cartels and conglomerates that had limited competition. In the competitive industries, market concentration led to intense rivalry and competition in the form of cost cutting, product differentiation, and new product development. The export sector was further benefited by the existence of thousands of medium and small enterprises that provided low-cost, intermediate products, and acted as recession buffers for the larger companies, as did dualism in labor markets.

Dualism in Labor Markets

Aside from self-employment, employment relations in Japan's Old Economy may be classified in two categories: (1) noncontractual employment based on an implicit understanding between labor and management, an informal contract regarding job security, labor remuneration, and matters of labor deployment, and (2) contractual employment based on an explicit understanding between labor and management, a formal contract that specifies the term of employment, labor remuneration, and the terms of labor deployment, if any. Both employment sectors have their own distinctive characteristics, but each depends on the other in various ways.

The Noncontractual Sector

Employment relations in the noncontractual sector are often identified by the four "features" of Japanese management: (1) lifetime employment, meaning a mutual labor-management commitment lasting until workers retire, (2) seniority wages, which was a labor remuneration system that emphasized tenure with the company as a major factor for wage increases and a significant factor for promotion, and (3) enterprise unionism, which was a form of worker organization by enterprise rather than by trade; and (4) an internal labor market and the application of measures, such as training, retraining, work reassignments, and labor transfers, that allowed firms to adjust labor input to varying economic conditions and to introduce new technology.

Lifetime employment

The term "lifetime employment" described an employment system whereby a worker started employment with a particular company that was expected to last until retirement. Though broadly known and highly praised, lifetime employment was, perhaps, the least understood Japanese institution and deserves several clarifications:

1. Lifetime employment was an agreement without contract, a mutual, implicit understanding between labor and management (*inshin-denshin*). Yet Japanese labor law required that companies apply every other method to adjust employment to changing market conditions—i.e., saving on raw materials and energy resources, laying off part-timers and temporary workers before laying off regular, lifetime employees.

2. Japanese workers did not always start and end their working careers with the same employer. Job shifting and job search occurred, and "voluntary" quits and early retirement sometimes terminated a "lifetime" employment commitment. Thus, "long-term employment," an institution existing in all industrial countries, may be a more appropriate term to describe employment in the noncontractual sector at this time.

3. Long-term employment applied to less than 50 percent of the Japanese labor force.

4. Because Japanese society expected women to quit work upon marriage, long-term employment was primarily confined to men.

5. While long-term employment (ten years or longer) extended throughout enterprises of all sizes, it prevailed only in large enterprises.

Cross-country comparisons of long-term employment are sensitive to the definition (number of years with the same company) and the reference period adopted, however. Long-term employment was more prevalent in the US in the 1960s, but the trend was reversed in the 1970s. Between 1966 and

1978, the proportion of employees with long-term employment (15 years and over) dropped from 22.2 percent to 19 percent in the US. Between 1962 and 1979, the proportion in Japan increased from 17.7 to 33.1 percent.[16]

As with any other long-term relationship, employers and employees searched thoroughly and thought carefully before they found one another and committed themselves. Prospective employees underwent a complex selection process that included two stages. The first stage, school selection, started with elementary education and continued with high school and university education. Students strove to enter and graduate from reputable institutions. The second stage, recruitment, took place upon graduation in the spring of every year, in what was called *teiki sayo,* when professors submitted their student recommendations to major corporations that had approached them for this purpose.

The origin of lifetime employment is controversial. Institutional economists, on the one hand, trace lifetime employment to the vestiges of feudalism, the religious influence of Confucianism, the Labor Mobilization Law enacted on the eve of the Second World War, and the egalitarian spirit of the Occupation (Labor Standards and Labor Security Acts). They claim that lifetime employment rewards and reinforces company loyalty, as well as job and income security in line with social justice. In fact, this view appears to have been supported by the majority of Japanese corporate executives. Lifetime employment further cultivated the spirit of egalitarianism broadly held in Japanese society. It was an alternative to social welfare, and provided for employment and income stability that tended to reduce business fluctuations.

Neoclassical economists, on the other hand, trace lifetime employment to the rational behavior of employers and employees under conditions of imperfect information and uncertainty. In one set of models emphasizing the asymmetric risk behavior of employers and employees over the business cycle, lifetime employment is a form of an employment insurance policy that firms underwrite to employees that guarantees employment in periods of business decline in exchange for wage restraints in periods of business expansion. In another set of models emphasizing labor transaction costs, lifetime employment minimizes labor turnover and the high transaction costs associated with it in the face of higher labor transaction costs. In a third set of models emphasizing company-specific human capital over general human capital, employers and employees have too much to lose in human capital in case of a separation. Therefore, the longer employees stay with the same company, the more they invest in human skills specific to that company, and the less likely they are to quit.

Under the lifetime employment system, workers were divided into numerous teams that made production decisions and coordinated and bore the responsibility for the production process. Through frequent training, job rotation, and interdepartmental transfers, workers acquired a good knowledge of the whole production process. From product development to production planning and operation, production on and off the shop floor was the outcome of team effort. Under these conditions, the team, not the individual, was credited with any success and debited for any failures. This means that the hard working members had good reasons to discipline the members working not so hard. Regular and after-hours meetings provided the forum for dealing with discipline problems without the need for management intervention. Besides, Japanese workers viewed their companies as an extension of their families, and, therefore, they considered it a pleasure and an obligation to pursue the welfare of the company, which in turn must support them in bad times.

In short, the counterpart of long-term employment existing in western societies, lifetime employment was not for life. It began upon high school or university graduation and ended upon retirement, and extended only to regular employees, as did the system of seniority wages.

Seniority wages

Seniority was an important factor in the labor compensation system of the Old Economy. In 1987, seniority accounted for 46 percent of wage increases, with ability accounting for the rest. Ability is reflected in rank; the higher the rank, the higher the wage. In 1989, for instance, branch managers were earning close to 700,000 yen monthly, more than double the earnings of the ordinary staff.[17]

In the conventional economic wisdom, the term "seniority wages" is used to describe the direct relationship between on-the-job experience and wage growth, a hypothesis well tested with data from several countries. When applied to the Japanese economy, the term has a slightly different meaning, however. First, company-specific experience exerted a higher impact on wage increments than general experience. Second, wages were primarily assigned to workers, not to jobs, which made it easier for companies to rotate workers from one job to another.

Institutional economists trace the origins of the seniority wage system back to the Occupation and even to feudalism. Seniority wage increases reward and reinforce worker loyalty to the company, promote equity pay across occupations, and allow workers to enjoy a rising living standard.[18]

Workers identify themselves with the company and promote the interests of the company, just as family members promote the interests of the family.

Neoclassicists argue that seniority wages are consistent with the rational behavior of employers and employees under certain constraints. In one set of models emphasizing labor transaction costs (recruitment and layoff costs), seniority wages discourage quitting and therefore minimize such costs. In another set of models emphasizing company-specific investments in human capital, seniority wages represent the labor share in the rents generated through joint labor-management investments in human capital. In a third set of models emphasizing the cost of shirking and supervision, the seniority wage system is a device that discourages shirking and therefore minimizes supervision costs.

Enterprise unions

The union system of the Old Economy was quite complex. Central unionization was quite weak and confined to annual wage negotiations. By contrast, company unionization or enterprise unionism was quite strong, especially among larger companies, and extended to a number of managerial issues that allowed unions to share decisions with management.

Enterprise unionism was a form of workers' organization where workers banded together within a firm, rather than across a craft or profession, as is the custom in the US. According to Shirai, enterprise unions displayed four general characteristics: (1) membership was limited to the regular employees of the company, i.e., employees who enjoy long-term employment; (2) membership included both blue-collar and white-collar workers; (3) while in office, union officials retained employee status, but they were paid by the union; and (4) a large proportion of enterprise unions, about 72 percent, were connected to corresponding national federations without loss of independence.[19]

The enterprise union performed a dual function: as a workers' representative and as a member of the enterprise team. As a workers' organization, the union bargained collectively in a manner similar to the way US unions bargain. Collective bargaining sessions were held several times a year: during the "spring offensive" to resolve wage matters, during the fall to resolve fringe benefits matters, and as needed for lump-sum allowances.

As a member of the enterprise team, the union was involved in joint consultations, a "firm relationship" of mutual trust and understanding, like co-determination arrangements in West Germany, Switzerland, and other European countries. The Japanese system, however, differed markedly from the system of co-determination in Western Europe. Co-determination in Western Europe is compulsory and mandated by law; Japanese co-determination was voluntary and, therefore, likely to be more efficient than that of Western Europe.

Japanese and Western scholars have offered a variety of explanations for the rise of enterprise unionism. Komatsu traces the origins of enterprise unionism to the emergence of industrial conglomerates and state enterprises in the 1920s.[20] Kawada argues that enterprise unionism is the result of the early postwar communist strife influenced by the World Federation of Trade Unions' declaration of "one single union in one plant."[21] Shimada argues that enterprise unions emerged after the splitting of the labor movement following a period of labor unrest in the late 1940s and the early 1950s. Specifically, after a long period of strikes in major enterprises, workers were divided into two groups: those adopting a radical strategy of confrontation and those adopting a conservative, pro-management strategy, with the latter ultimately dominating most enterprises.[22]

The three "sacred treasures" provide stability for noncontractual employment relations and reinforce loyalty, dedication, and harmony reflected in the low employee absentee ratio, short vacations, and short strikes. In 1990, the average Japanese worker was absent for three days and took nine days of paid vacation, while the average American worker was absent for seven days and took 19 days paid vacation, and the average German worker was absent for 12 days and took 29 days paid vacation. Strikes are frequent in Japan, but labor disputes are settled relatively quickly. In 1991, Japan lost about 2,000 days in labor disputes compared with 5,600 days lost in the US and about 4,800 lost in the UK.[23]

While broadly known and broadly praised, the three "sacred treasures" are only one tale of the labor-management relations in the noncontractual sector. The other tale is the internal labor market.

Internal labor market

Separated from the external market, employment relations in the noncontractual sector were conducive to the development of the internal market, a mechanism that adjusted labor compensation and input to varying business conditions.

Labor compensation in the noncontractual sector was fairly complex, and reflected the concept of corporate welfare. Like families, the company took care of the needs of its members. Remuneration consisted of basic wages, fringe benefits, bonuses, and overtime payments. Fringe benefits were extensive and included housing, dormitories for singles, and housing loans; medical and health care; living support (nurseries, shopping and canteen facilities); mutual-aid credit facilities; cultural, sports, and recreational facilities (libraries, gymnasiums, seaside and mountain lodges, ski resorts); and such "additional benefits" as employee shareholdings and supplementary labor compensation insurance.

While basic wages were set at relatively low levels, actual remuneration was augmented by sizable bonuses. According to the Japanese Labor Department, in the late 1980s worker bonuses, paid twice a year, amounted on average to 1.5 to 2 times monthly salaries. Bonuses rose with company size, from 1.5 times the monthly salary in companies with less than 100 employees to 2.5 times in companies with more than 500 employees. Bonuses were reduced or eliminated in times of recession. Therefore, even in bad years, firms could adjust the amount of bonuses and other allowances and thereby adapt to the firm's profit position while leaving the number of employees fairly unaltered. Overtime was extensive, accounting for 8 percent of the hours actually worked. But overtime premiums accounted for 25 percent of pay—half as much as in the US—contributing to the flexibility of labor compensation and employment adjustment in Japan.[24]

Labor compensation flexibility—meaning employment adjustments in the noncontractual sector—were aided by labor deployment, meaning labor hoarding, training and retraining, labor rotation, and labor transfers. For example, Toyota's collective bargaining agreement stated that "the philosophy inherent in labor-management relations in Japan is that the healthy growth of a company is essential in improving the living conditions of its employees."[25]

Labor hoarding is a practice that allows firms to stand up to the promise of long-term employment in the face of adverse economic conditions. Firms opt not to lay off workers but rather to keep them on the payroll, reducing the hours of work and emphasizing labor training and retraining. In a 1987 survey comparing labor practices in Japanese and US factories, Professor Higuchi found that 24.00 percent of workers in Japanese companies received training in the preceding twelve months compared to 13.48 percent of workers in American companies. In dollar terms, Japanese spending on training amounted to $550.70 per worker compared to $392.40 per worker spent by US counterparts.[26]

Training and retraining were enhanced by job rotation and labor transfers. Toyota, for example, rotated employees as frequently as once every three years. Canon set a three-department rotation as a prerequisite for promotion eligibility, and Honda had a plan of extensive job rotation. "An electrical engineer may go from circuit design to fabrication to assembly; a technician may work on a different machine or in a different division every few years; and all managers will rotate through all areas of business."[27] Under the Old Economy, a typical Japanese worker changed jobs five times by age 65, while his US counterpart changed jobs 11 times.[28] A typical steel worker in the US would have worked in about a dozen different jobs within the steel plant by retirement, whereas as a similar worker in Japan would have worked in about three dozen jobs.[29] Job rotation allowed workers to develop a better understanding of the entire work process, and to acquire the skills that would enable them to choose the task in which they could contribute the most to the company.[30] Job rotation further allowed companies to adjust their labor force to the changes in production needs brought about by new technology and international competition.

Labor transfers can be classified as regular and emergency. Regular labor transfers were another part of the Japanese training and promotion system. Before promotion, workers who held managerial positions were transferred to domestic or foreign subsidiaries. For instance, in 1986, Toyota transferred about 600 employees to foreign subsidiaries for a three-year period.

Unlike regular transfers that were considered promising to a worker's career, emergency transfers were considered as an alternative to layoffs. Transfers of this sort involved assignments to new jobs that were often less satisfying, inducing workers to quit. For instance, some steel companies transferred steel workers to a newly developed business of eel aquariums.[31] In addition, as some emergency transfers were from the automated divisions to the nonautomated ones, they resulted in productivity and wage gaps that prompted the opposition of unions: Personnel transfers should be confined to within the establishment, wage conditions should not deteriorate as a result of the labor transfer, and proper training should be given to employees.

In brief, employment relations in the noncontractual sector were fairly flexible. They were facilitated by the internal labor market, an in-firm mechanism that continuously adjusted labor input and compensation to business fluctuations. It should be emphasized, however, that the noncontractual sector and the internal market that lubricated its wheels made up only one segment of the labor force employed in Japanese enterprises. The rest were employed in the contractual sector.

The Contractual Sector

Employment relations in the contractual sector featured explicit contracts between labor and management, specifying the duration of employment, the amount and the terms of labor remuneration, and the ways, if any, by which labor could be deployed to perform different tasks.

The contractual sector included all workers who could not or would not find employment in the noncontractual sector. Unlike the noncontractual sector, where the typical worker followed a standard profile, contractual workers followed several profiles. It included young workers searching for the right noncontractual job, married females, and early retirees who worked in part-time, temporary, *arbaito* (occasional), and dispatch jobs. According to the Japanese Labor Department, in 1992, 94.5 percent of all part-time workers were women and 32.5 percent were more than 50 years old. Likewise, 66.3 percent of temporary day workers were more than 50 years old.[32]

Economists theorize contractual employment in various ways. Contractual employment is consistent with the conventional wisdom of general equilibrium under the conditions of perfect information and certainty, low transaction costs, and a homogeneous labor pool (for each job category). In this abstract setting, it is efficient for both employers and employees to form a short-term affiliation with one another, based purely on relative wage remuneration.

Unlike in the noncontractual sector, where adjustment came in the form of labor quality, adjustment in the contractual sector affected labor quantity. Firms could lay off workers and then appeal to the market to hire new ones. Workers could quit their jobs and search for new ones (inter-firm mobility).

Interaction Between Noncontractual and Contractual Sectors

Despite the significant differences, contractual and noncontractual employment should not be seen as two isolated sectors, but rather as integral parts of

Exhibit 2.2   Selective Characteristics of the Noncontractual and Contractual Sectors

Parameters	Noncontractual Sector	Contractual Sector
Employment Duration	Long-term	Short-term
Enterprise Union	Yes	No
Seniority Wages	Yes	No
Labor Deployment	Yes	No
Layoffs	No	Yes
Compensation	Flexible	Fixed

the Japanese Old Economy. Both employment sectors extended throughout all Japanese enterprises, with noncontractual employment prevailing in large enterprises and contractual employment prevailing in small enterprises. Any change in one sector affected the other. For instance, a hiring freeze or early retirement measures taken in the noncontractual sector released more workers into the contractual sector.

By tying one part of their labor force to the noncontractual sector and the internal labor market associated with it, and another portion to the contractual sector and the external market, Japanese firms maximized functional flexibility. While external labor markets allowed firms to appeal outside their own organization and adjust labor requirements (lay off or hire new labor), internal labor markets allowed firms to appeal to their own internal networks and adjust to new labor requirements through labor deployment measures. Thus, each mechanism was both rigid and flexible in its own way. The external mechanism was rigid in terms of occupational tasks and compensation but flexible with regard to the required size of the labor force; the internal market was rigid in terms of the size of the labor force but flexible in terms of labor deployment. And the coexistence of the two sectors within the same enterprise provided the firm with the mechanisms to adjust labor to market fluctuations (see Exhibit 2.2).

In short, the Old Economy's labor market included two sectors: the noncontractual sector and the contractual sector. Employment in the noncontractual sector was characterized by an implicit understanding between labor and management regarding employment duration, labor remuneration, and labor deployment. This implicit contract was overseen by an enterprise union.

How Dualism Constrained Entry of Foreign Businesses to the Japanese Market

Economic dualism constrained the entry and expansion of foreign business in the Japanese market in a number of ways:

1. The export-oriented sector nurtured world-class competitors—Toyota, Honda, Sony, Canon and the like—that were difficult for foreign companies to beat.

2. The high prices associated with the domestic-oriented sector nurtured a mentality of thrift and bias towards work over leisure, both constraining consumption spending, including spending on imports, an issue to be further addressed in Chapter 4.

3. Tariff and nontariff barriers priced many foreign agricultural companies off the agricultural sector. Tight regulations and exclusive vendor relations, as well as cross-ownership holdings, created an iron web that blocked the entry of foreign companies to the Japanese market. Cross-stock ownership, for instance, made foreign acquisitions difficult, if not impossible.

4. Suspicion over their ability to offer lifetime employment made it difficult for foreign companies to recruit and retain a qualified labor force. A 1991 American Chambers of Commerce in Japan survey reported: (1) 77 percent of foreign firms recruiting new college graduates achieved 50 percent or more of their target numbers but only 40 percent achieved at least target, (2) 33 percent of firms reported increasing success in recruiting new college graduates but 29 percent reported decreasing success, (3) only 12 percent of foreign firms reported that mid-career recruitment was becoming easier, while 54 percent said it was becoming more difficult.[33]

Because of the difficulties in recruiting local labor, foreign affiliates offered an attractive employment and compensation package: shorter work-week schedules, longer holidays, later retirement, and a wage premium over their Japanese counterparts. In 1986, for instance:

- 9.3 percent of workers in foreign affiliates worked 35.59 hours or less, while only 2.9 percent worked 48 hours or more. By contrast, only 1.1 percent of workers in domestic companies worked 35.59 hours or less and 35.9 percent worked 48 hour or more.

- Close to 65 percent of workers in foreign firms received a full five-day workweek holiday and only 1.1 percent received one weekly holiday; the corresponding figures for domestic companies were 6.2 percent and 47.9 percent.

- Close to 11 percent of workers in foreign companies retired at the age of 55 and 68.8 percent at 60; the corresponding figures for domestic companies were 23 percent and 53.9 percent.

- Foreign affiliates paid higher salaries for both new recruits and mid-career workers but lower bonuses and special pay, including term-end allowances. Starting salaries in foreign affiliates ranged between 150,000 and 156,000 yen for female and male university graduates, compared to 147,300 and 142,100 yen in domestic firms.[34]

To sum up, Japan's Old Economy was a dual economy, consisting of a modern, export-oriented sector that included consumer electronics, machine tools, and automobiles, and a backward, domestic-oriented sector that included distribution, finance, insurance, and utilities. Economic dualism was extended to the labor market, which included a noncontractual sector, where labor enjoyed lifetime employment, seniority wages, and union protection, and a contractual sector, where labor enjoyed none of the above. Employment in the contractual sector was described by an explicit contract regarding duration, labor remuneration, and labor deployment, if any. Both employment sectors sliced through Japanese enterprises of all sizes, with the ratio of noncontractual to contractual employment rising with enterprise size.

Dualism in commodity and resource markets constrained the entry and expansion of world businesses in the Japanese market, fueling external and internal frictions that unleashed social and political pressures, paving the way for the transition to the New Economy.

Endnotes

1. Economic Planning Agency Bureau, *A Modern-Day Open-Market, Free-Guild Policy: Deregulation and Economic Rejuvenation,* 6.

2. Hoshi, T. and Kashyap, A., *Corporate Financing and Governance in Japan,* 92.

3. Shinposha and Soran, *The Japan Economic Journal,* 26.

4. Shinposha, *The Japan Company Handbook*.

5. Ostrom, *Tokyo Business Today,* Table 3.

6. Sakai, "The Feudal World of Japanese Manufacturing," 5.

7. Compilation of Fair Trade Commission, "Regulations and Decisions," 1994.

8. Porter, M., *The Competitive Advantage of Nations,* 412.

9. Kono, *Strategy and Structure of the Japanese Corporation*.

10. Morita, *Made in Japan,* 79.

11. Douglas and Craig, 5.

12. OECD, *Industrial Policy in OECD Countries,* 1993, 125.

13. Hall, R., "The Importance of Lifetime Jobs in the US Economy," 716–24.

14. Oishi, Sh., "The Bakuhay System," 213–231.

15. Pollack, "Japan's Companies Moving Production Overseas," 12.

16. Hashimoto, "Bonus Payments," 1088; and Hashimoto and Raisin, "Employment Tenure," 726.

17. Mroczkowski and Hanaoka, "Continuity and Change in Japanese Management," 46.

18. Frank and Hutchins, "Wages, Seniority and Demand," 251–276.

19. Shirai, "A Theory of Enterprise Unionism," 118.

20. Komatsu, "Development of Enterprise Unionism," 12.

21. Kawada, "Workers and Their Organization," 25.

22. Shimada, "Japan's Capitalism: The Irony of Success," 23.

23. Bank of Japan, "Bank of Japan Comparative Statistics."

24. Mourdoukoutas, *Japan's Turn*.

25. Toyota Motor Company, *1992 Annual Report, Toyota City, Japan,* 17.

26. Higuchi, "A Comparative Study of Japanese Plants," 10.

27. Ouchi, *Theory Z,* 50.

28. Hashimoto and Raisin, "Employment Tenure," 725.

29. Koike, "Workers in Small Firms," 28.

30. Iwami, "What is 'Japanese Style' Management?" 32.

31. Mourdoukoutas and Roy, "Job Rotation and Public Policy," 58.

32. "Trends in Diversification of Employment Types," www.mhlw.go.jp/ english, 1/30/05.

33. American Chambers of Commerce in Japan, *Trade and Investment in Japan: The Current Environment,* 5.

34. Mourdoukoutas, "Economic Barriers for Foreign Affiliates in Japan," 58.

CHAPTER 3

GOVERNMENT ACTIVISM

- When IBM tried to expand into the Japanese computer hardware market in the early 1970s, it faced a consortium of six domestic competitors financed and guided by the Japanese government.

- When Motorola tried to expand its presence into the Japanese market in the late 1970s, it faced NTT's government monopoly of the local telecom market.

IBM's and Motorola's examples highlight yet another barrier world businesses faced when trying to enter the market of Japan's Old Economy: Japan's activist government cooperated closely with the private sector to beat the foreign competition, and in some cases, to create outright government monopolies that kept both foreign and domestic competitors off domestic markets.

As with many aspects of the Old Economy, government activism has received mixed reviews by western observers. For some, a proactive government was one of the major factors for the country's economic success. For others, Japan's government activism—known as Japan, Inc.—was an unfair competitive practice deployed against foreign trade partners, a coalition between business and government designed to conquer world markets. In either case, government activism was an important element of Japan's Old Economy, based on the prevailing premise at that time that government bureacrats were in a position to see the "Big Picture" better than corporate managers and to pursue certain national objectives better than individual companies. Even as recently as 2000, Porter, Takeuchi, and Sakakibara, in *Can Japan Compete?,* wrote:

> The underlying rationale for the Japanese government's active role in the economy is that it enjoys an overarching perspective no firm possibly could. The government model is premised on the beliefs that exports drive economic growth; that certain industries should be targeted and supported because they offer better prospects for growth, exports, and a rising standard of living; that Japan should conserve resources and avoid the wasteful and destructive aspects of competition;

and that industries need to be sheltered to allow them to gain the scale needed to compete internationally. Japan's rapid economic growth and competitiveness are widely credited to a set of policy initiatives that have grown out of this general framework.[1]

This message is even echoed in the 2002 Ministry of Economy, Trade and Industry (METI) industrial policy statement, where METI pledges to identify new technologies and new demands and channel resources to growing industries:

> [METI] will work to empower the people of Japan to challenge the future, boost Japan's industrial competitiveness, and maximize the potential of the Japanese socioeconomy. METI will advance forward-looking structural reforms. More specifically, by working to identify innovation and demand (consumption), METI will create new markets, industries and jobs, constantly introducing new measures to power forward the self-sustaining shift of human and capital resources to growth sectors with high productivity and strong social and consumer needs, as well as developing the necessary safety nets for SMEs, employment, etc.[2]

Government activism in the Old Economy ranged from measures to deal with externalities and uncertainties associated with a market system to measures that sped up market adjustment, and channelled resources to targeted industries. Even today, France, Great Britain, Germany, and the US provide tax incentives, grants, and subsidies to channel investments to targeted industries. What makes Japan's former industrial policy different from that of other countries, especially the US? The answer is in the configuration of the following seven factors, which will be addressed in greater detail in this chapter:

- Close cooperation between business and government
- Export promotion
- Indicative planning
- Decision by consensus
- Protection of domestic industry
- Consistency and continuity
- Technology policy

The importance of these seven factors differs from period to period. Close cooperation between business and government, for instance, was very strong in the early years of Japanese industrialization and the first two decades following the Second World War, but has weakened in the last twenty years, especially after the Plaza Accord and the banking crisis. Export promotion and protection of domestic industry was the obsession of the '50s, '60s, and early '80s.

What is most important to understand is that government activism, and most notably close cooperation between business and government in export promotion, created some sort of state-private conglomerate—Japan, Inc.—which competed aggressively against foreign competitors. American and European companies weren't competing against the Sonys, the Hondas, and the Toyotas so much as they were attempting to compete against Japan, Inc.

Close Cooperation Between Business and Government

After the Meiji Restoration, of the 1860s, Japanese business and government began to enjoy a close relationship with each other, a kind of political and economic partnership that allowed Japanese government to assume an active role in the allocation of economic resources. This "developmental state" relation between business and government was not formal—not defined by the constitution or by any other law—but was rather an informal network of personal contacts between politicians and their business clients. The former had the power to influence the business climate and the latter the money to influence political campaigns, as several scholars have noted:

> The relations that developed between the Meiji government and the private investors were not formal or official but, rather, personal and unofficial. They usually took the form of direct contacts between one or another of the oligarchy and an entrepreneur with access to him.[3]
>
> Each sector of the Japanese economy has a clientele relation to a ministry or agency of the government. The ministry by statute can wield various sticks and carrots in dealing with the economic sector, but it also holds a general implied administrative responsibility and authority that goes well beyond what is customary in the United States, though it may come close to French practice.[4]

The business/government cooperation was particularly important during the militaristic years, when the government closely cooperated with business groups in the importation of new technology, and in the initiation and development of western-style manufacturing for the iron, steel, and silk industries.

The government's active role in economic affairs continued after the Second World War. Japan's mighty METI (formerly MITI), along with the Economic Planning Agency and the Ministry of Finance, became a powerful triad that provided the vision, resources, and determination to navigate the Japanese economy through the waves of the energy shocks and the yen shock. In the '70s, for instance, the three agencies were instrumental in the transfer of resources from declining to expanding industries. Under the Temporary Act for the Specially Designated Industries, the three agencies provided incentives to persuade companies affected by the oil shock to reduce capacity and move on to new business. MITI also brought together corporations to develop technological applications and to deal with the two oil shocks and the yen shock.

This element of industrial policy—the creative destruction of industry—holds one of the secrets to Japan's success in dealing with structural changes. By contrast to European policy makers that favor preservation of declining industries, Japanese policy makers are ruthless in scrapping such industries and transferring resources to new ones. And unlike American policy makers that let individual corporations bear the entire cost of adjustment, Japanese policy makers manage to spread the cost of adjustment among stockholders, management, labor, and government, as was the case with export promotion.

Export Promotion

In the Old Economy, Japan was a country obsessed with exports. Exports were seen as a vehicle to gain foreign currency for the importation of natural resources, especially in times of sluggish domestic demand. MITI's early export promotion policies included: the foundation of the Japan External Trade Organization (JETRO); The Export Council and Trade Council Classified by Overseas Commodities; export finance (Export Advance Bill System, Foreign Exchange Fund Loan System, Export-Import Bank); Export Insurance System; Export Promotion Taxation Systems; Inspection Systems of Export Goods; improvement of the design of goods and the prevention of imitation; maintenance of the order of foreign trade by the Export and Import Trading Law; and export promotion policy on foreign currency (compensation trade, mutual letter of credit method, Thomas' letter of credit method, escrow letter of credit method, and the link system).[5]

MITI's export policy was not confined just to measures that accommodated exports. They extended to measures that strengthened export companies and improved their competitiveness. Promising industries and companies were assisted with learning to compete in world markets, such as the textiles and heavy metal industries in the early '50s; chemicals, shipbuilding, and consumer electronics in the '60s; and semiconductors, capital machinery, medical products, and telecommunications in the '70s and '80s.

MITI provided the vision that pointed to winning and losing products, industries, and technologies of the future, while the Ministry of Finance provided the financial incentives to persuade the parties to work together. MITI further assisted domestic companies in creating research consortia to compete efficiently and effectively against foreign invaders of the home market. In 1971, for instance, in an attempt to limit IBM's expansion into the Japanese market, MITI asked the six largest computer companies to form three research consortiums: NEC-Toshiba, Fujitsu-Hitachi, and Mitsubishi-Oki.

It should be noted that Japan is not the only country that promoted research consortiums for key industries. European nations have followed suit by promoting joint research in the aerospace, electronics, and computer industries. Even the US, which avoids the term "industrial policy," has pursued similar policies. In July 1992, with partial financing from the Pentagon, four of the nation's largest technology companies formed a research consortium to explore optical devices that transmit data by light. This trend intensified during the Clinton Administration with the appointment of pro-activist economists Laura Tyson as chair of the Council of Economic Advisors, Robert Reich as Labor Secretary, and Jeffrey Garten as Undersecretary for Commerce for International Trade. With such a pro-activist team in place, the Clinton Administration called for the cooperation with the private sector in building a new green car, developing better computer chips and a flat-panel display, expanding the information highway, and opening up new business opportunities abroad. As reported by David Sanger in *The Wall Street Journal*:

> After years of false starts, Washington is finally taking a solid crack at a sport long familiar to the Japanese and the Europeans: commercial diplomacy. Not since the days when the American Navy was sent to open up trading ports in Japan and China—a less subtle form of government advocacy for business—has the United States made such a concerted effort to win deals for American companies.[6]

The Commerce Department's "advocacy center" managed to win several deals for American companies: a $2.6 billion energy contract for General Electric in Indonesia; a $1.6 billion contract for McDonell and Douglas in China; a $1.4 billion contract for Raytheon in Brazil; a $65 million contract for General Railway Signal in Taiwan; and a $5.5 million contract for Teradyne in South Korea.[7]

Japan's industrial policy regarding R&D projects fell in between the two extremes. The government not only provided the funds but coordinated the joint research efforts. Yet Japanese government bureaucrats did not dictate choices to individual companies in the way that European bureaucrats do. They allowed them to decide how to allocate the research funds, which made the choice of which projects to pursue more efficient.

Indicative Planning

Indicative planning entailed a set of directions, not in the form of commands that firms had to comply with as in central planning, but in the form of signals and guidelines that firms were persuaded to follow in order to achieve certain policy objectives, as described by Michael Porter in *The Competitive Advantage of Nations:*

> Another unique dimension of Japanese policy, dating back many years, is the Japanese government's role in signaling. Through high-visibility government reports, joint industry, academic and government committees, highly publicized campaigns, cooperative research projects, and the like, MITI in particular has sought to nudge and influence innovation and changes in companies.[8]

Japan's government "signaling" was not confined to pointing business opportunities. It extended to securing cooperation among companies and smoothly running economic activities, as Kazuo noted in *Japan Echo:* "Unlike Western governments, which function as regulators of industry, the Japanese bureaucrats serve as a facilitator, an organization dedicated to securing cooperation in keeping economic objectives going smoothly."[9]

While all three government agencies were involved in indicative planning, industrial directions came primarily from MITI and the Economic Planning Agency in the form of a vision regarding economic prospects. The state of consumer and industrial demand, economic resources, international competition, and economic policy were projected for five years, nine years, and even for longer time horizons. Products and industries of strategic importance were identified and assisted to expand in MITI's direction. In the late '80s, MITI further assisted Japanese industries in adjusting to the two oil shocks and to the yen shock, and prepared Japanese companies for the coming globalization and labor shortages.

MITI formulated its vision by conducting surveys and hearings; disseminated its vision through outside lecturers, briefings, and subcommittee reports to the public; and implemented the vision through special legislation, industrial base strengthening, taxation, subsidies, and policy-based financing.

Despite the popular view of a divine and omnipotent MITI, which always succeeded in convincing the private sector of its vision and steered them accordingly, things have not always turned out satisfactorily. MITI's attempts to consolidate the two oil refineries, Idemitsukosan and Daikyo Sekiyu, failed. So did MITI's first attempts to assist the aluminum industry. Their efforts on behalf of the automobile and computer industries in the mid-'60s also failed, a blessing for both industries.[10]

Again, Japan was not the only country to channel resources to certain industries. Other industrial countries, such as France and Germany, have pursued similar forms of planning for selected industries. Even the US government provides a variety of information services regarding the future state of the domestic and international economy, and gives incentives to persuade companies to enter certain industries, including semiconductors, aerospace, and energy conservation. The Trade Act of 1988, for instance, set up the National Advisory Committee on Semiconductors to draft policies and directions to assist American semiconductor manufacturers in maintaining world leadership in this industry. Like the MITI, the US government has financed joint research and development projects with the private sector. But while the US government's role ends there, MITI's indicative planing was far more comprehensive, extending to the coordination of private research efforts. Ronald Dore, writing in *Flexible Rigidities,* observed:

> The role of the [Japanese] government has not been simply to finance research, but also, on occasion, to direct and coordinate the research effort of private industry. In the computer and machine tool fields, MITI took the lead in bringing the major firms together for joint research projects into basic technologies, which the separate firms have then individually taken over to bring to commercial viability of competition.[11]

MITI's involvement also included social consensus building, an important element in a country that emphasizes group behavior and harmony of interests.

Social Consensus

From factories to offices, from schools to the local community, *nemawashi,* or consensus building, is an important element of the Japanese way of doing business. The design of industrial policy under the Old Economy was no exception. For every major issue, academicians formulated the policy theory, the ruling party turned it into a proposal, a council investigated and drafted the issues, and the cabinet made the final resolution. During this process, all parties directly or indirectly affected by a proposed policy were consulted until a common ground was found or a broad consensus was reached. Though time consuming, this process made a difference when Japan's industrial policy was compared to that of other industrialized countries. The end result reflected not the concerns and wishes of special interests, but by and large, the interests of the society—or at least a good balance among various interested groups—and minimized the social friction associated with economic and technological change.

Industrial policy was designed with the active participation of industry, unions, academia, and the community. With frequent surveys and forecasts, MITI and the Economic Planning Agency cultivated a broad debate among business, academia, and the community at large on the problems and the prospects of the Japanese economy, building a consensus about the desirability and feasibility of various projects.

A good example of *nemawashi* was the handling of the adjustment in declining industries like steel, textiles, and shipbuilding in the '70s. The burden of adjustment was shared by all three parties concerned—corporations, labor, and government—rather than by one or two parties, as often happens in other industrialized countries. Ronald Dore explained:

> Whatever the source of trouble for the problem industries, however, the measures used to tackle their problems have been the same, and they have been rather more deliberate, more thorough-going and more closely planned with the whole industry than in most other industrial countries.[12]

> The close cooperative relations between government and business have a quality apt to be missing in countries where individualistic versions of "free enterprise" actually constitute an article of faith as well as rhetoric.[13]

Consensus was much easier during the early postwar years, in the catch-up stage, but became increasingly difficult in the '80s and '90s, as Robert Dekle noted in his 1994 article, "The Japanese Big Bang:"

> Today Japan leads the world in many industries, so picking industries for special treatment is much more hazardous for the Japanese government. That is, there is no longer a national consensus on what industries or companies are best for Japan's future.[14]

In short, in Japan's Old Economy, government bureaucrats were instrumental in building a social consensus on the economic policies pursued, as was the case with the domestic industry protection.

Protection of Domestic Industry

Protectionism in Japan's Old Economy underwent several stages. Back in the late '40s and early '50s, protectionism was in the classical form, the infant industry type. Imports of commodities and resources that would threaten Japan's infant industries were formally restricted. In the '60s and '70s, however, formal import barriers were replaced by informal bureaucratic procedures, delaying the pace or even blocking foreign competition until domestic companies could develop and flex sufficient competitive muscle. In the semiconductor and computer industries, for instance, MITI introduced stiff trade barriers for foreign companies, denying import permits and licenses and discouraging Japanese executives from working for foreign computer companies.[15]

While protectionism of the Japanese industry in the early postwar years was tolerated and even encouraged by the US, protectionism in the '60s, '70s, and '80s was aggressively criticized by the US. In the '80s, in particular, both President Reagan and President Bush took measures that forced Japan to lift many trade barriers and, in many cases, abandon completely projectionist policies, an issue to be further addressed in subsequent chapters.

Though protectionism is often synonymous with monopolistic practices that limit rivalry and competition, one must be careful when applying this generalization to Japan. Monopolistic practices did exist in one sector of the

Japanese economy—the domestic market. In the other sector that extended to the foreign market, however, rivalry and competition were extensive, as Michael Porter explained:

> While the *zaibatsu* structure concentrated economic power in prewar Japan, its breakup by the allies unleashed a level of competition that is unmatched in any nation. Virtually every significant industry in which Japan has achieved an international competitive advantage is populated by several and often a dozen or more competitors.[16]

In spite of protectionism, rivalry and competition were maintained in many industries, especially those that were successful in world markets. The number of competitors ranged from four in motorcycles and musical instruments to 25 in audio equipment and 112 in machine tools. Thus, unlike European industrial policies, which use protectionism to restrict competition, Japan's industrial policies used protectionism to strengthen competition, at least in some sectors, and to prepare companies for the world market.

As was the case with all the measures discussed before, protectionism of domestic industries and assistance with preparations for entry to world markets is not a unique measure applied by Japan alone. At one point or another, every country has taken similar measures to protect certain industries from foreign competition or to assist them in competing effectively in world markets. Japanese bureaucrats merely performed these policies with remarkable continuity and consistency.

Continuity and Consistency

In democratic societies where governments rise and fall at the whim of political tides, consistency and continuity of policy measures are rather tricky issues, especially in developing countries where governments change frequently. But as is the case in many East Asian societies, economic policy is designed and implemented not by politicians but by career bureaucrats, and that guarantees some degree of continuity and consistency, as Robert Dekle explained:

> One of the strengths of the East Asian government is that their economic policies are consistent over many years. Perceived changes in the mood do not bring practitioners in the latest economic fad to the government. Economic policies in East Asia are usually enacted by bureaucrats and others close to the seat of power.[17]

Allowing bureaucrats to formulate economic policy has certain drawbacks. First, a strong, independent bureaucracy takes the power of decision making away from the politicians and the people who elected them. Second, bureaucrats may lack the flexibility of politicians to deal with both domestic and international challenges. Japanese bureaucrats have, for instance, been unable to successfully elevate the domestic standards of living or to open Japan's market to domestic products and competition. They have also been unable to deal with the banking crisis, which to some extent they nurtured, an issue to be further addressed in a later chapter.

MITI's Technology Policy

Under the Old Economy, MITI was often credited with propelling Japan's technological advances. Although its policies have been already discussed in the previous sections, they deserve further attention.

Early on, MITI's technology policy was concentrated on applications of imported technology rather than on the development of original, breakthrough technologies. Reflecting this policy, Japan ran up an imbalance in the technological payments account. And although this imbalance has been narrowed, it was still standing at $70 million in 2001, a sharp contrast with the US's $13.8 billion surplus.[18]

Early on, MITI's efforts were directed toward the identification of key technologies, and on the formulation of visions on the ways these technologies could be assimilated by various industries. Once such technologies were identified, MITI followed up with regulation and financial incentives to designated companies to adapt those technologies. But MITI's efforts were not limited just to visions and financial incentives; they extended to the formation of research consortia, thereby spreading the risk and the benefits of ambitious projects.

The formation of research consortia and the spreading of risk was particularly important for small corporations that, in the 1980's, accounted for 25 percent of R&D spending, as compared to 6 percent in the US.[19] One of the most known examples of such consortia is that of the semiconductor industry in the mid-1970s for the development of VLSI chips. Other projects identified and supported by MITI include: the development of coal liquefaction and justification, solar power generation, and geothermal and hydrogen energy (1974); the development of energy conservation technology, such as magnetohydrodynamic power operators (1978); the development of fifth-generation computers (1982); and the development of automated systems for producing software.[20]

But unlike in many European countries, it was the private sector and the market rather than MITI that determined which technologies and industries would be promoted, and it was private rather than government funds that financed those technologies. In fact, in 1992, close to 73 percent of R&D spending in Japan was financed by private sources, compared to 50.7 percent in the US and 60.5 percent in Germany.[21] With R&D funds in Japan coming mostly from the private sector, they were perhaps better allocated than in the US and Germany at that time.

At any rate, Japan's efforts to import and develop applied technology were clearly succesful. According to a MITI's self-evaluation report, by 1992, most conventional Japanese industries manufactured products technologically equal or even superior to comparable products in other industrialized countries, and the technological level of Japanese products continued to improve.[22] Yet, as the same report points out, Japan lagged behind her industrial counterparts in basic, breakthrough technology. Reflecting this gap, between 1982 and 1992, Japanese scientists managed to win only one Nobel Prize, as compared to 40 won by their American counterparts.

Addressing this deficiency, MITI's technology policy for the 1990s shifted from applied technology to original, breakthrough technology: "A new stream of technological innovation suggests that it is not only necessary to develop new technology by building on existing ones, but also to initiate a creative technological innovation which will induce broad new technologies based on scientific inventions and discoveries, and apply the results to the resolution of global problems."[23] Reflecting this shift in focus, MITI's goals included strengthening basic and creative R&D, fostering centers of excellence, identifying seeds of new innovations, and promoting cooperative international technology efforts.[24]

In a 1993 MITI-sponsored conference on the twenty-first century, business executives, academics, and bureaucrats devised a strategy for the future of manufacturing. To foster basic research, MITI and the Japanese government adopted an open-door policy toward foreign students that began arriving in Japan in droves in the '80s. (The number of foreign students in Japan increased from a little below 10,000 in 1979 to more than 50,000 by 1990 and 117,302 by 2004.)[25]

How Government Activism Constrained the Entry of World Businesses into the Japanese Market

Government activism in Japan's Old Economy constrained the entry of world businesses in a number of ways. First, government protection of domestic industry made it difficult for foreign companies to obtain the necessary licenses and patents to estblish a presence in the Japanese market. Second, close cooperation between business and government nurtured local monopolies and oligopolies that kept certain sectors of the Japanese economy off limits for foreign business. Third, incentives to reduce capacity and develop new technologies while maintaining competition at the same time nurtured domestic competitors, making it hard for foreign companies to compete.

To sum up, in the high-growth years, Japan's industrial policy was based on seven principles: close cooperation between business and government, export promotion, indicative planning, decision by consensus, protection of domestic industry, continuity and consistency, and the promotion of new technologies. Industrial policy was instrumental in channeling private and government resources to certain technologies. However, Japan's industrial policy has been changing in the last fifteen years to address the side effects of the country's success: external and internal frictions.

Endnotes

1. Porter, M., Takeuchi, and Sakakibara, *Can Japan Compete?,* 18.

2. METI, *2002 Economic and Industrial Policy Forward-Looking Structural Reform Toward Self-Sustained Growth,* 20.

3. Johnson, *MITI and the Japanese Miracle,* 85.

4. Patrick and Rosovsky (eds.), *Asia's New Giant: How the Japanese Economy Works,* 487.

5. JETRO, "White Paper."

6. Sanger, "Japan's Bureaucracy: No Sign Its Losing Any Power," *A1.*

7. Ibid., 1.

8. Porter, M., *The Competitive Advantage of Nations,* 415.

9. Kazuo, "A Dose of Deregulation to Buoy Business," 25.

10. Flamm, "Making New Rules," 23.

11. Dore, *Flexible Rigidities,* 135.

12. Ibid., 142.

13. Ibid., 147.

14. Dekle, *The Japanese Big Bang,* 20.

15. Flamm, "Making New Rules," 24.

16. Porter, M., *The Competitive Advantage of Nations,* 424.

17. Dekle, *The Japanese Big Bang,* 20.

18. Bank of Japan, *Balance of Payment,* 12.

19. Hulten, *Productivity in Japan and the United States,* 11.

20. MITI, *Outline of Small and Medium Policies.*

21. OECD, *OECD Economic Observer,* 15.

22. Watanabe and Honda, "Inducing Power of Japanese Innovation," 56.

23. Ibid., 57.

24. Ibid., 58.

25. "No. of Foreign Students Tops 110,000," 1.

CHAPTER 4

ECONOMIC FRICTIONS

Under the Old Economy, Japan's economic dualism and government activism created external and internal imbalances that fueled friction with trade partners and citizens. External imbalances were manifested in the country's soaring trade surpluses, while internal imbalances were manifested in a growing gap between production and consumption, which turned Japan into a rich country with poor consumers.

In the beginning, external frictions were mild and well contained. Japan's trade partners, most notably the US, were willing to let Japan get away with her obsession of high economic growth and market protectionism for two reasons. First, Japan's corporations were still small, posing no major threat to American giants. Second, Japan was still an indispensable ally in America's efforts to curtail Soviet expansion in Asia. Thus, American governmental administrations were willing to forego economic for political and military benefits.

In the 1980s, all this changed, however, and external frictions proliferated. Early in the decade, the US recession multiplied the voices that demanded a reciprocal market access between the two countries, while the collapse of the Soviet Union in the late 80s made Japan less of an indispensable ally for the US. American politicians were no longer willing to give up economic for political benefits, and became anxious to see Japan's market opening to American products. Beginning with the Carter administration in the late 1970s and continuing with the Reagan administration, America demanded that Japan improve world business access to her markets through a number of macro- and microeconomic measures (Exhibit 4.1). Most notably, in 1989, Japan, together with Brazil and India, was included in the list of unfair trade nations under the "Super 301" section of the Trade and Competitiveness Act of 1988, which called on Japan to open her markets for supercomputers, telecommunications, and wood products.

A more detailed discussion of Japan's external and internal frictions follows in two sections. The first section discusses the size and sources of the country's trade deficits with the US and the EU, which fueled the country's external friction, while the second section discusses the gap between

49

Exhibit 4.1   Highlights of the US-Japan Trade Friction

Year	Administration	Issue
1978	Carter	Beef/citrus/exchange rates
1983	Reagan	Exchange rates
1985	Reagan	Market specific sector negotiations
1988	Reagan	Size of trade imbalance
1989	Bush	Market access
1994	Clinton	Results-Oriented policies
1998–2000	Clinton	Promotion of deregulation and competition

domestic production and consumption, which fueled the country's internal friction.

External Frictions: Trade Surplus with the US and EU

Japan's Old Economy was among the main beneficiaries of growth in international trade in the last quarter of the twentieth century, running surpluses with most of her trade partners. According to data from the Japanese Ministry of Finance, in 1992, Japan had a trade surplus of $145,816 billion and a current account surplus of $129,333.[1] High value-added products, such as computers, office and telecommunications equipment, TVs and VCRs, cameras, cars and trucks, and industrial equipment, made up most of Japan's trade surplus with her trade partners. Low value-added products, including food, beverages, cigarettes, and raw and energy materials, were some of the categories in which Japan ran and still runs a deficit with her trade partners. Exceptions to this trade pattern included high value-added imports from the US and Europe, such as aircraft, pharmaceuticals, and industrial equipment, as well as some US services. In 1992, Japan's surplus with the US in computers and telecommunications reached $22.3 billion. Surplus in cars and trucks reached $20.5 billion, and surplus in industrial equipment $9.0 billion, while vehicle parts counted for close to 15 percent of America's overall trade deficit with Japan, and vehicles counted for close to 35 percent.[2]

Perhaps more extreme than the Saudi Arabian trade deficits of the 70s, Japan's current account and trade surpluses under the Old Economy were unprecedented in postwar economic history. Current account surpluses rose from nearly $49 billion in 1985 to $87 billion in 1987, easing to $36 billion in 1990, then rising again to nearly $129 in 1992. Trade surpluses increased from $56 billion in 1985 to $96 billion in 1987, easing to below $63 billion in 1990, and climbing to $146 billion in 1992.[3]

The persistent rise in Japan's trade surpluses should be viewed with caution, however. Part of the increase can be attributed to the stronger yen rather than with a rise in the volume of Japanese exports. Japan's yen-adjusted trade balance has consistently declined since. A close look at the volume rather than the value of trade further confirms this trend. In 1992, for instance, Japanese exports to the US rose by 10 percent in dollar terms, but fell by 1.8 percent in volume. Likewise, exports to the EU fell by a whopping 14.2 percent in volume.[4]

As expected, Japan's ongoing trade surpluses irritated her trade partners. "Japan's trade surplus is threatening world trade," said US Treasury Secretary Lloyd Bentsen, quoted in a CNN interview in July of 1993.[5] Secretary Bentsen was a moderate voice in the Clinton administration, however. Others, including presidential advisor Laura Tyson and US trade representative Mickey Kantor, voiced concerns even more loudly, handing Japanese officials import lists and ultimatums. Adding to the US concerns, EU officials posted their own list of complaints against Japan, seeking formal inclusion to any future US-Japan negotiations.

Japan's trade surpluses and friction with her trade partners were neither new nor unique in world economic history. Great Britain's rise in the world economy in the third quarter of the nineteenth century was followed by trade surpluses and friction with her European trade partners and the US. Succeeding Great Britain, America's rise in the world economy in the last quarter of the nineteenth century was followed by trade surpluses. Persistent US trade surpluses fueled trade friction with European trade partners, which led to projectionist measures on both sides during the Great Depression. With the exception of the mid-1930s, America was running trade surpluses with the rest of the world until the late 60s!

Cutting into America's economic dominance, Japan's rise in the world economy in the 70s and 80s was followed by trade surpluses and friction with trade partners, especially the US, which affected both sides of the trade equation. On the export side, Japan was accused of dumping textiles, semiconductors, computer games, laptop computer screens, and consumer electronic products on the international market at below domestic prices and for industrial targeting, i.e., governmental promotion of certain products like automobiles, computers, and semiconductors. On the import side, Japan was accused of protecting domestic markets by erecting formal and informal barriers to keep out foreign products. Products such as beef, rice, citrus, lumber, and telecommunications satellites, as well as construction, insurance, and financial services were some of the sectors still under protection. Trade friction also rose with the EU, but less so. Yet, under intensive negotiations between Japan and the US, many tariff and nontariff barriers were removed and Japan's market began to open to the world.

What theoretical principles governed Japan's Old Economy trade? Is there anything unusual about the country's persistent trade surplus? Namely, did Japan's Old Economy export too much and import too little? To answer these questions, Japan's trade pattern and structure must be placed in perspective.

Trade Patterns: Theoretical Considerations

What determines trade flow across countries? At the "pure" theoretical level, three models claim to have an answer to this question: the Ricardian Model of Comparative Advantage, the Heckscher-Ohlin Model of Relative Endowments, and the Technology Gap Model.

1. *The Ricardian Model of Comparative Advantage:* Trade flows are based on relative labor costs, i.e., differences in relative labor productivity. Countries specialize in the production and export of commodities that have a comparative advantage in labor productivity. Simply put, to allocate labor efficiently, each country specializes and exports what she can do best, importing the rest from other countries. Assuming only one resource of production, the Comparative Advantage Model is useful in explaining short-term trade flows. What about long-term trade flows? They can be better explained with the Heckscher-Ohlin Model.

2. *The Heckscher-Ohlin Model* (H-O): Generalizing the Ricardian Model, the H-O Model suggests that the direction of international trade flows is based on the allocation of factor endowments across countries. Labor-rich countries are expected to export labor-intensive commodities, and capital-rich countries are expected to export capital-intensive commodities. But what about resources that are not endowed but developed, like technology?

3. *The Technology Gap Model:* Trade flows are determined by technological gaps across trade partners. Countries specialize in the production and

exports of products for which they have a comparative technological advantage and import products for which they have a comparative disadvantage.

Which model can explain Japan's trade patterns? All three are applicable, but each one applies to different periods. As labor was abundant in the 50s, Japan's exports of labor-intensive products (textiles, for example) in that period are consistent with the Ricardian Model. As labor became less abundant and capital more abundant in the 60s, Japan's shift to capital-intensive commodities is consistent with the Heckscher-Ohlin Model. As both labor and capital became less abundant in the 70s and 80s, Japan shifted into technology-intensive products. In particular, Japan specialized in exporting products produced in automated sectors—machine tools, semiconductors, consumer electronics, and telecommunications equipment—while importing aerospace, chemicals, and drug products from the US and Western Europe. This trade pattern is consistent with the Technology Gap Model.

Though pure trade theory is useful in pointing to the underlying microeconomic forces of international trade, it leaves many things as yet to be explained. Why, for instance, did Japan run persistent trade surpluses with the US and Western Europe, even in products for which the US and Europe had a strong presence in world markets? Were trade flows distorted by tariff and nontariff barriers and an undervalued currency? The answers to these questions require a closer examination of the country's trade structure and tariff and nontariff barriers.

Trade Structure

Exports

Did Japan's Old Economy export too much? Commonly used indicators of export structure such as exports per capita, the ratio of exports to GNP, export elasticity, and export concentration are inconclusive. Japan's per capita exports, for instance, were not unusually high. In 1992, Japan's per capita exports were $2,170, well above the corresponding US rate of $1,319, but below the $2,551 for the UK, $2,241 for Italy, and $3,016 for France. Japan's exports as a percent of GNP were higher than those of the US, but lower than those of other OECD countries. For the period 1970–92, Japanese export/GNP ratio ranged between 11.3 percent and 16.4 percent, while US export/GNP ratio ranged between 6.8 percent and 12.8 percent, the French between 15.5 percent and 24.1 percent, the German between 22.6 percent and 35.1 percent, and the British between 21.9 percent and 28.8 percent.[6]

Statistics indicate that Japan's exports were more sensitive to changes in world income and prices than those of her trade counterparts. According to estimates by the Japanese Ministry of Finance, between 1975 and 1978, Japan's export income (1.667) and price elasticity (1.494) were above those of the US and West Germany. This means that an increase in world income, or a decrease in world prices, had a stronger impact on Japanese exports than on the US and West German exports.[7]

Unlike most other countries with similar economic conditions, Japan's exports were concentrated in a few products.[8] In 1985, two three-digit export categories accounted for 25 percent of all exports, and six three-digit export categories accounted for 50 percent of all exports. The corresponding figures were three- and nine-digit export categories for the US, six- and eighteen for France, and three- and thirteen for the former West Germany.[9] What is even more disturbing is that export concentration advanced in the 1970s before leveling off in the late 1980s. From 1970 to 1983, the top 25 exporters' share rose by 10 percentage points, and the top 50 exporters' share rose by 13 percentage points.[10]

Some Japanese products were produced almost exclusively for export. About 87 percent of the production of 35 mm cameras and watches, for instance, was for export, as was about 54 percent of passenger cars.[11] This rather peculiar export pattern led many of Japan's critics to talk about industrial targeting, an orchestrated industrial policy of Japan's mighty MITI.[12] Several commodities were included in MITI's target list: automobiles and computers in the 60s, and consumer electronics, industrial machinery, and semiconductors in the 70s and 80s. Semiconductors, in particular, constituted the single most important case of industrial targeting, making it the objectionable case most often cited by the US in the Structural Impediments Initiative Talks.

Back in the mid-1960s, the computer industry attracted the attention of MITI, which unsuccessfully launched projects for the development of high-speed mainframe computers. In the mid-1970s, however, MITI promoted research consortiums in the semiconductor industry. During the period 1976–79, MITI's funding accounted for 40 percent of the semiconductor industry's funding.[13] MITI's efforts bore fruits this time. By 1980, Nippon Telephone and Telegraph had two programs for the development of VLSI, and MITI had completed its own, setting the stage for Japan's phenomenal success in the semiconductor industry.

Export concentration should not necessarily be interpreted as an unfair trade practice, however. Japan's success, for instance, in exporting automobiles to the US in the late 70s was the result of the energy crisis rather than the result of unfair trade practice on Japan's part. Moreover, although Japan's exports were concentrated in a few products, the matrix of these products has changed to respond to changes in international demand. Japan's flexible industrial system has facilitated such adjustment.

In conclusion, evidence on the Old Economy's export pattern appears to be inconclusive. On the one hand, Japanese per capita exports and exports as a percent of GNP were higher than those of the US, but below those of European countries. On the other hand, Japan's export elasticity is higher than those of the US and the former West Germany, and exports were concentrated on a few products. But even then, it is unclear whether such export "peculiarities" reflected an orchestrated policy or a legitimate competitive advantage.

Imports

Another key question is, Did Japan's Old Economy import too little? Five criteria—per capita imports, the ratio of imports to GNP, the ratio of manufactured imports to GNP, the size of import elasticity relative to GNP, and the level of intra-industry trade—provide an affirmative answer to this question.

In 1992, Japan's per capita imports of $1,535 were above the South Korean figure of $1,231 but well below those of the OECD countries. Japan's imports as a percent of GNP were higher only than those of the US, but lower than those of the OECD countries. Between 1970 and 1994, Japanese import/GNP ratio ranged from 8.7 percent to 15.8 percent. During the same period, the US import/GNP ratio ranged between 5.9 percent and 13.1 percent, and the UK import/GNP ratio ranged between 21.2 percent and 30.2 percent. Japan's ratio of manufacturing imports to GNP was 40 percent less than it should have been, given the country's level of economic development.[14] In 1994, for instance, auto part imports counted for only 2 percent of the parts used in Japan, compared to 32.5 percent in the US and 60 percent in the UK.[15]

Japan's imports were insensitive to domestic income and price changes. According to estimates by MITI, Japan's income and price import elasticity were 0.766 and 0.310 respectively, well below the corresponding elasticity for the US and the former West Germany.[16] This means that an increase in domestic income or a decrease in import prices had little impact on imports.

Based on these findings, especially the relatively low income elasticity, it is hard to understand why the American government pushed the Japanese government to stimulate spending.

According to a 1985 study by Carliner, Japan's intra-industry trade index was 0.26 in 1982, compared to 0.59 for the US, 0.77 for the United Kingdom, and 0.63 for the former West Germany. A 1990 MITI calculation indicated that Japan's intra-industry trade continued to remain low: 28 percent for all industry and 33 percent for manufacturing, compared to 55 and 60 percent for the US, 78 and 81 percent for the United Kingdom, and 65 and 69 percent for the former West Germany.[17] While it is quite normal for the US, a large country rich in natural resources, to import little from the rest of the world, is it normal for Japan? Saxonhouse, for instance, found that only 8 of the 62 industries imported too little.★[18]

In brief, Japan's persistent trade surpluses with most of her major trade partners in the Old Economy reflected a peculiar trade structure, especially on the import side. The US and the EU accused Japan of unfair trade practices, dumping undervalued currency, product targeting, and nontariff protectionism.

The Highlights of the US-Japanese Trade Friction

As the US was the country with the largest trade deficit with Japan, trade frictions between the two countries were frequent and intense at times, especially following the US economic stagnation in the 1980s. Specifically, the US objected to:

- The dumping of textile products and the overall size of the trade balance in the early '70s
- Protectionism for specific products, such as citrus fruits and beef
- The undervalued yen in the late '70s
- Restricted access to specific Japanese sectors, such as lumber and electric appliances
- Government construction projects for products like supercomputers
- Restricted access to telecommunication satellites, medical products, auto parts, insurance products, flat glass, and the undervalued yen in the '80s

---

★ This finding is further supported by a similar study by Burbone (1988).

For the most part, trade friction was defused through trade negotiations rather than retaliation. The American and Japanese governments held bilateral trade talks on all major issues: on textiles and the overall trade balance during the Nixon administration; on beef, citrus, and the exchange rates during the Carter administration; on the exchange rate and market specific sector negotiations and on the size and structure of the trade imbalance, especially in products and industries for which America has a strong presence (Market-Oriented Sector-Selective, or MOSS, negotiating process) during the Reagan administration; on market access (Structural Impediment Initiative) during the Bush administration; and Results-Oriented negotiations during the Clinton administration.

The US-Japan trade friction reached its peak in the 80s, when economic stagnation and persisting trade deficits for goods for which the US had a strong international presence—for example, supercomputers, telecommunication satellites, medical equipment, pharmaceuticals, forestry products, electronics, and financial products—prompted the US Congress to pressure the Reagan and Bush administrations for concrete action against Japan.

In November 1983, the Reagan administration began talks with Japan regarding the opening of Japan's capital markets and the appreciation of the yen, an effort that led to the Plaza Accord of September 1985. Parallel to these efforts, early in 1985, the two sides opened talks on another front, the Market-Oriented Sector-Selective negotiations. The talks covered four specific areas of trade friction: electronics, medical equipment, telecommunications, and pharmaceuticals. One year later, in 1986, the two sides agreed to establish the Structural Economic Dialogue, a preface to the Structural Impediments Initiative (SII), which addressed trade issues for specific products on a regular basis (every six months). In 1988, the US Congress enacted the Omnibus Trade and Competitiveness Act that called for retaliation against unfair trade partners. On May 25, 1989, President Bush, applying the Omnibus Trade and Competitiveness Act, listed Japan, along with India and Brazil, as unfair trade partners and ordered an investigation of her trade practices on the imports of selective American products.

As expected, such unilateral actions prompted criticism on Japan's part. Japan's Minister of Foreign Affairs was quoted as saying, "Unilateralism, together with the tendency toward bilateralism, sectorism, and managed trade, jeopardizes the multilateral trade system and damages the Uruguay Round trade negotiations."[19] Fortunately, once again, reason and dialogue forestalled trade retaliation. The two countries agreed to revive the Structural Economic Dialogue, turning it into what is known as the Structural Impediments Initiative, a set of concrete steps for removing impediments to trade between the two countries, such as the imbalance between consumption and savings in the two countries and Japan's informal trade barriers for selective American products. In light of the progress in those bilateral talks in which the two countries pledged to continue communications on the implementation of SII resolutions, President Bush announced in April 1989 that he was taking Japan off the list of priority countries under the "Super 301" provision.

Under the shadow of "Super 301," negotiations continued under the Clinton and Hosokawa administrations. But when talks between the US and Japan broke off in February 1994, the US threatened to impose sanctions against a selected list of products under the "Super 301" provision. Six months later, however, talks were resumed, and Japan agreed to measures that opened up markets for insurance and financial products, medical products, and government procurement. In mid-1995, talks continued on the three most disputed areas of the auto industry: access to dealerships, replacement parts, and original equipment.

With a few exceptions, trade negotiations were mainly positive. During the Carter talks, Japan agreed to stimulate her economy, expand American imports, and impose voluntary quotas on car exports to the US. During the Reagan talks, Japan agreed to a stronger yen, to stop the dumping of computer chips in the US market, and to expand market access for American beef and citrus fruits. Under the Bush administration talks, Japan agreed to open her markets to American construction and engineering companies, telecommunication satellite companies, and wood product companies. During the Clinton administration, Japan agreed to open her rice, insurance, finance, medical technology, flat glass, and telecommunications markets (see Exhibit 4.2). In the December 1996 agreement, for instance, the Japanese government agreed to open its life and nonlife insurance market to foreign competition. In 2000, Japan's major telecom company, NTT, agreed to cut by 50% the fees it charges to foreign telecom companies.

While many US-Japan trade issues have been resolved by negotiations, the persistence of the Japanese trade surplus dictates a deeper search into the roots of this surplus, an issue to be addressed after the discussion of the highlights of EU-Japan friction.

Exhibit 4.2   Highlights of Structural Impediments and Results-Oriented Initiatives

Goals for	Improving US-Japan Economic Relations
Japan	Spend $2.8 trillion on infrastructure for the next decade
	Spend $180 billion in community development
	Implement 24-hour import clearance procedures
	Improve pricing mechanism
	Improve market access for specific products and sectors, such as satellites, semiconductors, lumber, construction, etc.
	Introduce new financial products
	Improve distribution system/restrict the power of *keiretsu* system
	Step up anti-trust enforcement
	Review land policy
	Open rice, insurance, finance, telecommunications, auto parts, flat glass, and medical technology markets
US	Raise domestic savings/reduce government deficit
	Improve educational system/labor training system
	Enact the Cooperative Production Act
	Hold joint US-Japan symposium on Japanese resource development
	Address issues of corporate behavior/corporate law
	Emphasize research and development

The Highlights of the Japan-Europe Friction

As was the case with the US, Japan's successful entry into European Union markets and the persisting trade imbalances that followed created friction between Japan and the European Union, mostly in the same areas as those between Japan and the US: access to Japan's distribution system; access to the financial and insurance sectors; access to medical technology and telecommunication sectors; licensing, product standards, and a certification system; and government procurement. Trade problems, requests, and proposals between Japan and the EU have been highlighted in several documents published by the EU Commission and by member governments (see Exhibit 4.3).

Although the US was able to establish an ongoing, formal negotiation framework with Japan, EU members did not.

Negotiations took place between the Japanese MITI and the EU 113 committee, or between MITI and the individual EU nation members. The

Exhibit 4.3   Highlights of the EU-Japan Trade Friction

"The Safeguard Clause" (1971)

Toshio Mission (1976); Simplification of commodity inspection procedures (1978)

EU-Parliament: EC-Japan Declaration (July 1991); Moorhouse Resolution (December 1991)

113 Committee; Follow-up of MITI's Europe-Japan cooperation package (May 1993)

EU-Commission Council: "A consistent and global approach" (annex) (May 1992); List of obstacles (September 1993); "Market Access to Japan–State of plan" (November 1993, updated in January and again in July 1994); Lists on deregulation priorities (April 1994);

Commercial Counselors: Big Ticket issues (December 1991, updated April 1993); List of obstacles (December 1991, updated April 1993); List of priorities (Spring 1993); non-exhaustive list of products proposed for public procurement (April 1993).

---

lack of a formal negotiation forum between EU and Japan placed Europe in a disadvantaged position compared to the US. In any deal cut between Japan and the US, Europeans were relegated to picking up the leftovers.

Recognizing this problem, the EU asked Japan to establish a permanent negotiating forum or to be included in future negotiations between Japan and the US. Responding to these requests, in 1994, Japan:[20]

- Agreed to dialogue with the European Commission on the implementation of the measures taken in light of the US-Japan framework talks in a comparable manner and using the same information as the consultations with the US.

- Agreed that whenever the Japanese government invited representatives of foreign (including US) business interests for consultations regarding government procurement, it would extend the invitation to business interests of any foreign country on an equal basis.

- Welcomed contracts already taking place between the European semiconductor industry and Japanese users.

- Noted with satisfaction the participation of a representative of European business interests in the specialized subcommittees on semiconductors.

Though Japan's response did not completely meet all of the EU's requests, it gave the EU a better avenue for monitoring US-Japan negotiations and sharing the benefits of any market opening agreements.

In short, Japan's trade friction with the EU has been less intense and less explicit than with the US. The EU has chosen to take advantage of any

progress made in US-Japan negotiations rather than to set up its own negotiating team.

Sources of Japan's Trade Surplus with the US

The sources of the Japanese trade surplus were many and changed over time,
including the attention focused on the high savings and productivity rates,
the undervalued yen, and tariff and nontariff barriers.

Savings and Productivity Differentials

In the early stages of economic growth in any country, hard work and high
savings are the vehicles for coping with day-to-day necessities and reaching
for higher standards of living. In the later stages of economic growth, a
strong preference for leisure and consumption typically gradually replace the
proclivity for hard work and high savings. America's growth experience is a
good case in point. When America was at the early growth stage at the turn
of the century, Americans worked long hours and saved a great deal, but as
America reached the later stage of growth, both working hours and savings
declined substantially and they are far below those of Japan, which is a
growth stage behind in its development. And as macroeconomic accounting
suggests, those consumption and savings imbalances can become the source
of trade imbalances. Excess commodities and funds from countries with low
consumption and high savings flow to countries with high consumption and
low savings, causing a trade imbalance in favor of the high-savings country.

In what is known as the "twin deficits" hypothesis, economists claim that
the US-Japan trade deficit reflected the difference between the two countries in attitudes about savings and consumption. The rising private and
public consumption and the explosive government deficits in the US fueled
higher inflation and interest rates. Higher interest rates, in turn, attracted
Japanese savings and strengthened the dollar against the yen, thereby penal-
izing US exports and favoring imports, which led to a trade deficit.[21]
According to data published in *International Financial Statistics* and IMF's
Direction of Trade Statistics between 1989 and 1992, US current and trade
account deficits increased by an average annual rate of $33 and $85 billion,
respectively, while, Japan's current and trade account surpluses increased at a
rate of $95 and $118 billion. Meanwhile, the bilateral US-Japan trade deficit
increased at a rate of $41 billion.[22]

Japan's Old Economy had the highest savings rate among the OECD countries. In 1988, Japan's savings accounted for 9.3 percent of GNP compared to Canada's 6.9 percent, France's 3.1 percent, and America's 3.2 percent. As the domestic private investment and government deficit were not sufficient to absorb the full amount of savings, a net flow found its way to countries with low savings, such as the US. In other words, Japanese savings financed the appetite of other countries, including the US, for Japanese products. In 1988, for instance, Japan's private investment (5.3 percent) and government deficit (−0.8 percent) were insufficient to absorb domestic savings (9.3 percent), with the surplus funds (3.6 percent) flowing to countries with low savings. The same year, US private investment (2.6 percent) and government deficit (−3.3 percent) far exceeded domestic savings (3.2 percent), with the shortage of funds (−2.8 percent) coming from countries with surpluses, like Japan.[23]

High savings contributed to Japan's trade surplus through another channel: they provided low-cost financing for investments in capital equipment. Between 1980 and 1988, for instance, Japan's gross capital formation rose by 69.5 percent compared to a meager figure of 27.3 percent for the US and 20 percent for the EU. In turn, high investment growth contributed to Japanese productivity, international competitiveness, and trade surplus.[24] The country's labor productivity rose by 9.4 percent before 1973, 3.3 percent between 1973 and 1979, and 3.1 between 1979 and 1989. The corresponding rates for the US were 2.2 percent, 0.3 percent, and 0.9 percent, respectively. Higher productivity gave Japanese companies a leading edge in curtailing labor cost. Between 1976 and 1986, for instance, Japan's labor cost rose by 1.9 percent, compared to 3.4 percent in Germany, 6.4 percent in the US, and 8.4 in the UK. In 1995, Japan's labor cost rose by 1 percent, compared to 1.3 percent for Germany, 1.2 percent for the US, and 0.7 for the UK.[25]

In short, differences in consumption/savings and work/leisure attitudes—indicative of the difference between a mature and an emerging industrial society—are the root causes of the US-Japan trade imbalance. High savings in Japan financed America's appetite for Japanese products, as did the weak yen.

The Undervalued Yen

Any trade disequilibrium cannot be maintained for too long under flexible exchanges rates. Up to 1985, Japan maintained an undervalued currency, i.e., an exchange rate below a level sufficient to eliminate the trade surplus. In 1985, the Japanese currency stood at 250 yen to a dollar, but at the Plaza Accord (September 1985), Japan acceded to the demands of other industrialized countries to let the yen/dollar exchange rate reflect the trade balance between the two countries. Indeed, since then, the yen has appreciated dramatically, trading at 132 yen to a dollar in 1992, below 100 in 1994, and around 105 in early 2005. Yet, in spite of the substantial yen appreciation, between 1985 and 1994, Japan's trade surplus continued to grow, a disturbing factor for the politicians who orchestrated the Plaza Accord.[26]

While politicians looked at Japan's import and export structure for unfair trade practices, economists looked at the direct and indirect effects of the yen appreciation and the time lags between price and quantity adjustments. In 1989, Noland claims that the yen appreciation between 1985 and 1987 was expected to reduce the Japanese trade surplus by 35 percent from its mid-1987 level, or by about two percentage points of GNP by 1990.[27] In another 1989 study, Hickok found that the rise of Japan's trade surplus between 1985 and 1988 could be attributed to four factors: (1) the commodity structure of Japan's imports and exports, (2) profit-cutting measures of Japan's export industries, (3) the statistical effect on the accounting of the trade balance, and (4) the savings from the lower oil prices.[28]

Tariff and Nontariff Barriers

Every country has tariff and nontariff barriers that, at times, can cause trade imbalances. In spite of progress in international trade negotiations, did Japan have more tariff and nontariff barriers than other industrialized countries? The answer is affirmative for the '70s and early '80s, but things began to change as of the late '80s. Under the intense negotiations described earlier, both tariff and nontariff barriers lifted and Japan's market opened to foreign products and competition, an issue to be further addressed in the next chapter.

In short, Japan's Old Economy was characterized by soaring trade surpluses fueled by a peculiar trade structure, especially on the import side, which formed the basis for the friction with her trade partners. Such a peculiar trade structure can be attributed to the country's high savings and productivity *vis-à-vis* her trade partners, an undervalued currency, and tariff and nontariff barriers that turned Japan into a rich country with poor consumers.

Internal Friction and the Paradox of Success: Rich Country, Poor Consumers

If prosperity is the ultimate goal of every economy, did Japan's Old Economy deliver it? By some standards, the answer was yes. High growth rates, stable employment, and rising incomes placed Japanese consumers on a par with or even ahead of their industrial counterparts. By other standards, the answer was no. Small houses, tiny apartments, long working hours, a high cost of living, and a poor infrastructure put Japanese consumers behind their industrial counterparts. But why was the cost of living so high in Japan? Why was Japan's infrastructure lagging behind that of her industrial counterparts? Why did the Japanese economy fail to deliver consumer prosperity?

Because the cost of living, the state of the infrastructure, and the prosperity of a society depend on several factors, these are difficult questions to answer. One plausible answer could be found in the scarcity of land and natural resources, especially when Japan is compared to countries rich in land and natural resources, like the US. Another answer could be found in the policies of the postwar era. In most western societies, policy makers are concerned with consumer prosperity. But not in Japan, where production comes before consumption, work before leisure, and corporation before family. "Grow or perish"—that's how the Yoshida Doctrine defined Japan's economic strategy in the postwar era. Indeed, all three economic plans from 1958 to 1970 explicitly stated maximum growth as the most important goal. The Income Doubling Plan of 1959, for instance, called for high savings and investments as the vehicles to achieving rapid technological innovations and high growth, as did the 1958–62 plan.

Companies, workers, and government all joined forces to achieve this objective. Companies invested heavily in capital equipment and paid little in dividends. Throughout the '60s and '70s, gross domestic investment accounted for 30–40 percent of the GDP, compared to 13–18 percent in the US.[29] In 1990, Japanese companies had a layout ratio (the proportion of earnings paid out as dividends) of 30 percent, compared to 54 percent of US companies and 66 percent of British companies.[30] At the same time, companies formed a partnership with labor that promoted worker participation, training, joint consultation, flexible compensation, and decision by consensus. On their part, workers demonstrated discipline and cooperation, worked long hours, and saved a great deal. In the mid-1980s, Japanese workers worked 15–20 percent more than their American counterparts and

25–30 percent more than their Western European counterparts. In 1993, Japan's savings accounted for 14 percent of disposable income, compared to Canada's 9.7 percent, France's 12.6 percent, and the US's 4.9 percent.[31] Joining efforts, the government provided for regulation and protectionism that favored certain relations between manufacturers and distributors, provided for economic visions, offered low interest financing, established research consortia, and reinforced protection of domestic industry from foreign competition.

By the early '80s, the objectives of the Yoshida Doctrine had been achieved and even exceeded, and Japan had grown and flourished. For the periods 1956–1960 and 1958–1962, Japan's economy grew at 8.8 and 9.7 percent, well above the corresponding 4.9 and 6.5 percent target levels. In the period 1960–73, Japan's economy grew at 6.3 percent, while the US economy grew at 2.5 percent and the OECD countries as a group by 4.9 percent. This growth hovered at 4–5 percent between 1973 and 1991, and was followed by the slowdown of 1993–94.[32]

High GDP growth rates accompanied by low inflation and unemployment allowed Japanese consumers to enjoy a rapid growth in their real income. For the period 1950–1990, real incomes rose from $1230 (in 1990 prices) to $23,970 (a 7.7 percent average annual growth rate), well ahead of the 1.9 percent growth of the US and 1.0 percent of Great Britain.[33] Robust economic growth, low unemployment, and a high per-capita GDP placed Japan next to developed nations. Japan's management system and government policies served as examples for the emerging economies of Southeast Asia and case studies in MBA programs around the world.

But as Japanese people paused for a moment to count their blessings, they become disenchanted with what they came to realize. Their economy had delivered growth and jobs, but not prosperity. As of 1991, the size of the average Japanese residence was 881 sq. ft., compared to 1,645 sq. ft. for the US. Only 3 percent of Japanese homes had central heating and 45.4 percent flush toilets,[34] whereas, the corresponding figures for the US were 85 percent and 99.8 percent, respectively. Japan's poor housing conditions, long working hours, and high cost of living placed her closer to less developed rather than to most developed nations, as Robert E. Cole reported in the *California Management Review* in 1992:

Total working hours are recognized internationally as long. In the eyes of many observers, these differences symbolize the failure of workers to share Japan's success. After all, we associate long working hours with poorly developed economies, and short working hours with advanced industrial nations. Japan seems to be an anomaly in this regard.[35]

Excessive government regulation and protectionism created a sanctuary for domestic competitors, turning Japan into one of the most expensive places to live. In 1993, a pound of rice was selling for $2.71 per pound in Tokyo, compared to $.89 in Manhattan; an apartment was selling for $715.67 per sq. ft. in Tokyo, compared to $309.00 in Manhattan; and a Sony Walkman sold for $209.92 in Tokyo, compared to $39.99 in the US.[36]

In addition to small houses and the high cost of living, Japanese people were also faced with a poor infrastructure, lagging behind those of other industrialized countries. Kazuo wrote, "In areas ranging from roads to sewer systems to airports, Japan is said to be so far behind its counterparts in the West as not to deserve the label of an advanced developed country."[37] In 1990, the average urban Japanese enjoyed 2.2 square meters of park space, compared to 19.2 for the average American living in New York, 30.4 for the average Englishman, and 37.4 for the average German.[38]

With commodity prices so high, Japanese people developed a strong preference for work over leisure and savings over consumption. As Eamonn Fingleton put it: "One of the least understood aspects of twentieth-century economics is that a determined government can make people save by the simple expedient of suppressing their consumption."[39] In fact, it was this kind of culture that fueled commodity and capital exports and caused unprecedented trade surpluses and friction.

As more and more Japanese consumers traveled abroad and saw how their western counterparts lived, they became disenchanted with their own standards of living and were inspired to change the situation. Robert E. Cole observed in 1992:

> International comparisons of living standards are a regular theme in the media, and more and more Japanese are traveling abroad. As a consequence, the difficult living circumstances experienced by the Japanese, relative to citizens of other advanced nations, is quite visible to the average person.[40]

But Japanese consumers were not the only ones eager to change Japan's economic situation. Japan's trade partners, who had grown impatient with persistent trade surpluses and difficulties in accessing the domestic economy, were also eager to elicit change. Clyde Prestowitz, writing in the *Washington Post* in 1994, stated:

> [Japan] must also recognize that the present structure of US-Japan economic relations puts US firms at a disadvantage and imposes burdens on the US economy and on the US citizens. The United States cannot accept this indefinitely and will need to respond to prevent harm of its citizens.[41]

In short, long working hours and low standards of living nurtured a consumer mentality that favored savings over spending and work over leisure, the root of Japan's import pattern and friction with her trade partners. Negotiations in the '70s and early '80s focused on the weak yen and the restriction of certain imports from Japan, such as automobiles, consumer electronics, and semiconductors. Negotiations in the late '80s and early '90s, in what has become known as the Structural Impediments Initiative, focused on exports of western products to Japan. In particular, the US, the EU, and many third world countries pressured Japan into making her market more accessible to foreign products by lifting structural barriers and paving the way for deregulation and competition in the New Economy.

Endnotes

1. Statistics Bureau, *Statistical Handbook.*

2. Ibid.

3. Ibid.

4. Kanrei, "Japan's Trade Surplus: Look at the Quantum Figures."

5. "Remarks by Micky Kantor," 17.

6. The World Bank, *World Tables.*

7. MITI, *White Papers,* 1988, 131.

8. Lincoln, E., *Japan's Unequal Trade.*

9. MITI, *White Papers,* 1988, 131.

10. Doi, "Aggregate Export Concentration in Japan."

11. Lincoln, E., *Japan's Unequal Trade,* 33.

12. Johnson, *Japan: Who Governs,* 25.

13. Flamm, "Making New Rules."

14. Lawrence, "Imports in Japan's Closed Markets or Minds?"

15. Pollack, "Japan Cites U.S. Demands In Collapse of Auto Talks."

16. MITI, *White Papers,* 1988, 131.

17. Carliner, "Patterns in Japanese and American Trade," 6.

18. Saxonhouse, "Japanese Trade Structure," 22.

19. Minister of Foreign Affairs, *Diplomatic Bluebook,* 15.

20. European Union, Brussels. European Commission, *Note for the Attention of the Members of the 113 Committee* (DEPUTIES).

21. Golub, *Is Trade Between the United States and Japan Off Balance?,* 56.

22. International Finanacial Statistics (1989–1992), CMF Direction of Trade Statistics (1984–1992).

23. Maki, "Personal Savings Rate," 3.

24. Golub, *Is Trade Between the United States and Japan Off Balance?,* 57.

25. *OECD Economic Outlook;* OECD Paris, various issues.

26. Mourdoukoutas, *Japan's Turn.*

27. Nolland, M., "Japanese Trade Elasticities and the J-Curve," The Review of Economics and Statistics, Vol. 71, pp. 175–179.

28. Japanese Trade Balance Adjustment to Yen Appreciation.

29. *OECD Economic Outlook,* various issues.

30. Morita, "A Critical Moment for Japanese Management."

31. OECD, *OECD Economic Outlook,* 130.

32. MITI, *White Papers,* various issues.

33. OECD in Figures, various issues.

34. Mourdoukoutas, *Adapt, Develop, Promote: How to compete in the Japanese Market.*

35. Cole, R., "Work and Leisure in Japan."

36. Reid, "Lifestyles of the Rich and Funless," 8.

37. Kazuo, "A Dose of Deregulation to Buoy Business."

38. JETRO, *Meeting the Challenge,* 9.

39. Fingleton, *Blindsided,* 192.

40. Cole, R., "Work and Leisure in Japan."

41. Prestowitz, "Getting Japan to Say Yes."

CHAPTER 5

DEREGULATION AND COMPETITION

The most important task is to increase the purchasing power of consumers by adopting a policy aimed at bringing about lower prices. Cutting prices as much as possible would increase the purchasing power of consumers, accelerate the distribution of goods, support firm economic growth, and subsequently help reduce the trade imbalance by boosting imports.

My contention is that we cannot expect traditional medicine to cure the current illness of Japan's slumping economy and lowering external surplus. Admittedly a dose of public investment will generate some new demand. But the record shows that even repeated doses of such stimulus have failed to revive the economy, and the reason is to be found in the nature of the Japanese economic system.[1]

Change has always been difficult and costly in every society. Sometimes, change comes slowly, a step at a time. At other times, change comes abruptly, in leaps and bounds. In either case, change stems from pressures from within or without the system that bury the old system like a tidal wave, replacing it with a new one.

In Japan's case, the transformation from the Old to the New Economy came from both external and internal pressures, the twin frictions that prompted many prominent Japanese businessmen and western scholars, such as those quoted above and below, to question Japan's early economic policies and to call for a shift in economic priorities:

Japan must cast off its growth-first obsession, shifting its attention from the sellers to the buyers. Pricing systems and other business practices must be reformed to provide consumer satisfaction in an era of multi-dimensional values.[2]

Starting with the Nagasone government and intensifying under the Hosokawa government in 1982, economic policy priorities have shifted away from production into consumption, and many import barriers and regulations of domestic industry have been lifted. Like previous developed countries, Japan is being transformed from an emerging, developing economy growing against her trade partners and citizens to a "normal," mature economy growing with her trade partners and citizens.

The shift from a producer- to a consumer-oriented economy has been a lengthy and painful process that has taken the Japanese economy on a roller-coaster ride known as the Bubble and its Burst. The sharp upturn and prolonged expansion in the 1980s was followed by a sharp down turn and prolonged contraction in the 1990s, which pulled the country into a financial crisis and deflation that lasted well into the early 2000s.

Addressing Japan's transition from the Old to the New Economy, this chapter is divided into three sections. The first section discusses Japan's shifting of priorities, the second section describes the growth of the Bubble Economy and its subsequent Burst, and the third section reveals how Japanese governments have coped with the lingering banking crisis.

Shifting Economic Priorities

Shifting economic priorities and promoting completion are two difficult tasks in every society, especially in Japan where bureaucrats and *keiretsu* groups commanded enormous powers over economic policy.[3] Yet, in response to growing consumer dissatisfaction and mounting foreign pressure, Japanese governments revised their economic priorities, trying to become a "normal society."[4] Goals, such as "contributing to the international community and promoting internal reforms" and "improving the quality of Japanese life," jumped ahead of economic growth on the priority list of MITI visions for the 1990s:[5]

> Over the medium to long term, we must put in place economic structures that are primarily based on domestic consumption and ensure that domestic social capital is provided to create a rich, vibrant society and economy in anticipation of the onset of an aging society.[6]

Starting in the late 1980s, Japanese governments took a number of measures to put in place economic structures that promoted domestic consumption: working hours were reduced, domestic demand was expanded, the yen began appreciating in value, tariffs were slashed, and domestic markets were opened to competition.

Reduction in Working Hours

In Japan's Old Economy, people worked long hours, on average 15–20 percent more than their industrial counterparts, and that did not include "offing time," or the time workers spent in the company in after-hour meetings without getting paid, as explained in this JETRO report: "In most sectors, career-track employees, particularly in administrative, creative, and high-tech positions, are unlikely to record all, if any, overtime hours. Although in many cases they may have two or three hours of paid overtime allotted by the company per day, these categories of employee generally are expected to work beyond these allotted hours at no extra pay."[7]

In Japan's New Economy, people do not work as much as they once did. Working hours have fallen from 2,100 in 1988 to 1,750 in 2002, closer to those of her industrial counterparts, particularly the US. Saturday working hours dropped from 4.59 hours in 1996 to 4.19 in 2002, while Sunday working hours dropped from 2.24 hours to 2.19 hours.

Expansion of Domestic Demand

Following the 1985 Plaza Accord, Japan launched an expansionary monetary and fiscal policy. Between 1985 and 1989, the Bank of Japan cut the official discount rate five times, from 5.5 to 2.5 percent. In the meantime, the Japanese government boosted domestic spending several times, especially spending on infrastructure. In February 1994, for instance, Hosokawa's coalition launched a stimulus package of $140 billion. But even before the Hosokawa government, domestic demand was expanding at respectable rates. Between 1985 and 1990, domestic demand expanded at 3.7 percent in 1985, 6.8 percent in 1988, and 4.6 in 1990. During the period of 1993–1999, the Japanese government launched seven stimulus packages, ranging from 6.2 percent of GDP (September 1993) to 23.9 percent of GDP (November 1998).[8] And while Japan boosted domestic spending, the yen gained in value against the dollar, making imports less expensive to Japanese consumers.

A Stronger Yen

In early 2005, the Japanese currency was trading at 105 yen to the dollar! That's hard to believe, given that ten years earlier, the Japanese currency was trading at 150 yen to the dollar, and that 20 years earlier it was trading at 300 yen to the dollar. But the persistence of Japan's trade surplus and the expansion of domestic demand finally took their toll on the Japanese currency, which had a pervasive effect on the Japanese economy. On the one side, as export prices rose, the export sector found it more difficult to compete in world markets. On the other side, as import prices declined, the domestic sector found it more difficult to fend off foreign competitors. Under these pressures, government deregulation and business restructuring were accelerated. With the rise in export prices, for instance, Japanese companies were compelled to cut costs and to allocate production overseas, an issue to be further addressed in the next chapter.

In short, after years of seeding and growth, harvest time had arrived in Japan in the late 1980s. Consumption and leisure began to replace savings and work. Stabilization policies had to be supplemented by structural measures that promoted competition by eliminating the long-standing protectionism and regulation that limit domestic and foreign competition and fueled external and internal imbalances.

Promotion of Competition

As is the case with everything else in Japanese life, the promotion of competition has been a lengthy and slow process. It includes measures to remove protectionism and to deregulate the noncompetitive sector.

Lifting Protectionism

Whether the country is Japan, South Korea, China, Germany, or the US, identifying and comparing tariff and quota barriers with other countries is fairly easy. Nontariff barriers, such as product standards and certification systems, distribution networks, and government regulation and government procurement, however, are more difficult to identify and compare. After all, every market has its own peculiarities and specificity as determined by economic and noneconomic barriers.

A developing country in the '50s and '60s, Japan had high tariff and nontariff barriers to protect her infant and inefficient industries. Different product standards and certification systems for electric products and extensive government regulation of the retail, transportation, and financial industries formed a formidable web that kept foreign products out of these markets. But as Japan joined the developed countries in the '70s and '80s, and many of her infant industries grew up and even exceeded their western peers, many tariff and nontariff barriers were lifted.

For instance, Japan eliminated tariffs for most of the industrial products for which she enjoyed a competitive advantage over her trade counterparts.

She also adjusted some product standards and certification systems to those of other industrial countries, and simplified customs clearance procedures. Yet Japan maintains tariffs and quotas for food and beverage products, textiles, chemical products, and machinery products, as well as regulation for retailing, construction, and financial services. According to some estimates from the Institute for International Economics in Washington, nontariff barriers doubled the cost of many imported products to Japanese consumers. In 1989, for instance, trade barriers cost Japanese consumers 10–15 trillion yen, which translates to between 2.6 percent and 3.8 percent.[9]

Lifting Tariffs

In an attempt to protect inefficient industries, Japan's tariffs and quotas were quite high in the '50s and '60s, well above its industrial trade partners. But as many of those industries became efficient by the '70s and '80s, tariffs were slashed across the board to levels below those of her major trade partners. With the exception of some agricultural products and alcoholic beverages, Japan's tariffs have been in line with those of the US and the European Union. In 2000, for instance, Japan's average tariff was slightly above 5 percent, while those of the US and EU were slightly below 5 percent (see Exhibit 5.1).[10]

Exhibit 5.1   Average Tariff Rates for Selected Countries

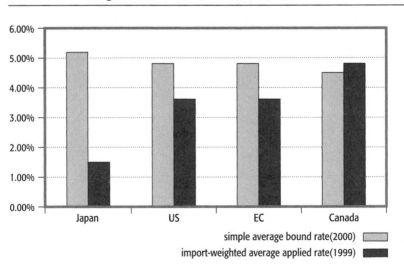

simple average bound rate(2000)
import-weighted average applied rate(1999)

Lifting Nontariff Trade Barriers (NTB)

Less visible and harder to identify and monitor, nontariff trade barriers are often far more formidable to international trade than tariffs. Nontariff trade barriers, such as customs procedures, product standards and certification, government procurement and subsidies, and a backward distribution system, have been blamed for slowing or even limiting access to Japan's market. From electrical appliances to transportation, nutrition, and pharmaceuticals, Japan had its own strict product standards and certification system. Concerns over natural disasters, limited space, an obsession for quality, and the protection of special interests are some of the factors that could explain Japan's adoption of such standards. Yet these standards limited foreign competition, yielding much higher prices for Japanese consumers.

According to an IMF (International Monetary Fund) report, the proportion of Japan's imports protected by NTBs in 1986 was about 43 percent, compared to 45 percent for the US and 54.1 percent for the EU.[11] Japan's progress in lifting product standards as a trade barrier at this point was confirmed in a survey by McKinney that found that 11.8 percent of the respondents thought that product standards had remained the same in 1986, as compared to 12.5 percent in 1979, and 18.1 said that changing product standards was frequently the case in 1986, as compared to 23.9 in 1979.[12]

As of August 2002, the Japanese government implemented a host of measures to bring product specification in line with those of her major trade partners. The Electrical Appliances and Material Control Law, for instance, simplified certification for foreign appliances and electric products. The Measurement Law simplified the procedure for the importation of measurement devices.

Lifting Barriers in Other Sectors

Progress was even made in such highly protected sectors as agricultural products, insurance products, automobiles, and automobile parts. In 1987, under pressure from Japan's two main beef exporters (Australia and the US), Japan reached an agreement that provided for a two-stage liberalization of beef imports. In the first stage, from 1988 to 1990, import quotas were raised from 274,000 metric tons to 394,000 metric tons, maintaining a 25 percent tariff. In the second stage, from 1991 to 1998, quotas were raised from 472,000 metric tons to 680,832 metric tons and tariffs were raised to 50 percent. Additionally, in 1993, under a severe rice shortage and pressure from the US, Japan opened her market to that highly protected product.[13]

In 1988, Japan made concessions in another disputed, yet lucrative, area for foreign firms: insurance products. Between 1988 and 1989, 49 companies received approval to sell cultural artifacts fire insurance, 22 companies received approval for savings installment plans, and many more received clearance for various types of accident and indemnity insurance policies. In 1995, Japan acceded to the US demand to monitor the progress made on new insurance policies underwritten on a year-to-year basis.

Between 1992 and 2001, progress was made in another disputed area, automobiles and automobile parts. During President's Bush trip to Japan in 1992, Japanese automobile companies promised to raise imports to specified targets: Toyota promised to import 5,000 GM cars and $5.28 billion worth of auto parts; Nissan promised to import 3,000 Ford cars and $3.7 billion worth of auto parts; and Honda promised to buy 1200 Chrysler and $4.94 billion worth of auto parts. The Japanese kept their promises. In 1994, imports of Ford cars reached 14,321 (180.2 percent over the previous year), imports of Chrysler reached 13,601 (+138.7 percent), and General Motors 8,696 (+2.0 percent).[14] Yet ten years later, in 1994, foreign-brand car imports remained at 20,823 units.

Deregulation

As discussed in Chapter 2, Japan's Old Economy consisted of a modern, export-oriented sector and a backward, domestically oriented sector. While the modern sector was open to domestic and foreign competitors, the backward sector was not. A host of government regulations, such as licensing and product standards and certification systems, kept industries in this sector sheltered from competition. Some industries, such as railroads, telecommunications, and tobacco, were still governmentally owned monopolies that cost Japanese consumers dearly. To elevate the Japanese standard of living to those of other industrialized countries, the government lifted many of those regulations in answer to the call of such Japanese economists as Ozawa, in the *Blue Print for a New Japan:*

> The excessive number of anachronistic regulations constrains the lives of people on every front. . . . Meaningless regulations tie up our lives in issues related to transport, finance, distribution and land use. They distort our lives. To build a truly liberal society, and to make our lives more pleasant, we must immediately commence deregulation.[15]

Nothing happens immediately in the Japanese society, however. Japan is ruled by career bureaucrats rather than elected politicians. And bureaucrats have too much power to relinquish and too much vanity to adopt foreign institutions. This was particularly true under the political environment of weak coalition governments of the mid-1990s, when the sagging economy and financial markets made things even worse. The precipitous decline in the Tokyo stock market, for instance, made it difficult for the government to pursue its privatization plan that started in the late '80s.[16] But let us review some of the measures taken so far, and the ways they have impacted the economy.

Distribution System/Retailing

Though an advanced, developed country in many respects, Japan's distribution system was still backward and outdated into the 1990s. Layers of wholesalers and a large number of small retailers formed a wedge between consumers and producers that kept prices high and sales low. Because of this, Japan's distribution system was the focus of the Structural Impediments Initiative. Japan's trade partners, especially the US, claimed that *keiretsu* relations and large numbers of small retail stores formed a formidable barrier between foreign products and Japanese consumers in two several ways.

Not only did *keiretsu* groups push local stores to discriminate against foreign products, they exercised market control by promoting consumer loyalty to domestic product brands. Such loyalty was not limited to inter-group purchases; it extended to individual purchases. Industrial companies that belonged to the Mitsubishi group, for instance, gave their banking, insurance, real estate, and trade business to other Mitsubishi subsidiaries or affiliates, as explained in this 1990 US Congressional report:

> Mitsubishi companies pay their wages through Mitsubishi Bank, rent their head offices from Mitsubishi Real Estate, and their storage space from Mitsubishi Warehouse. By choice, they use air-conditioning units made by Mitsubishi Electric, machinery made by Mitsubishi Heavy Industries, trucks made by Mitsubishi Motor and fuel supplied by Mitsubishi Oil. Their factories are insured by Tokyo Marine and Fire, the group insurance company, and their forget-the-year parties are supplied by Kirin, the group brewer.[17]

By maintaining monopoly power, the distribution system was in a position to profit from any yen appreciation rather than passing the savings on to consumers. In fact, between 1985 and 1990 import prices fell by 40 percent, but domestic prices fell by only 5 percent. A substantial decline in the import price of bicycles, leather shoes, and VCRs failed to stimulate the import volume of these products.[18]

Between the looming recession and deregulation, promising developments were soon underway in Japan's distribution system. First, as more independent retail stores opened, the power of the *keiretsu* system began to erode. In fact, in 1990, the share of the big six groups' current income dropped to 13.3 percent, and their share in the work force dropped to 4 percent, compared to the corresponding shares of 16.92 percent and 4 percent in 1985. But the biggest blow to the distribution system came from the recession, which pushed more and more consumers toward discount stores, mail orders, and many other nontraditional distribution systems.[19]

Second, under pressure from the US, the Japanese government revised its retail store laws, and practically abolished them by 2001. In 1978, a new law allowed the establishment of 300 square meter stores. In 1990, MITI introduced an 18-month time limit for the social approval of large-store applications. In May 1994, MITI exempted supermarkets of less than 1,200 square yards from the bureaucratic licensing process required of larger stores. In 1998, the Large-Scale Retail Store Law was repealed, and the Large-Scale Retail Store Location Law was enacted in 2000. Recently, discount supermarket chains, such as Daiei, began streamlining their operations and introduced state-of-the-art logistic systems to bring value to consumers.[20]

Financial System

For many developed countries, the era in which the government owned savings institutions and set interest rates on deposit is long gone, even forgotten, as is the era of regulated commissions for brokers. Yet, for Japan, this era only recently came to an end. In fact, it was not until the second part of the 1980s that the Japanese government lifted many restrictions on deposits and allowed the introduction of new financial products. And as of the early 2000s, the Japanese government still controlled the Post Office, which competes with banks for deposits.

In the meantime, the Japanese government took a number of measures to create an open, fair, and global financial system, comparable with those of New York and London:[21]

- March 1985: Money market certificates became available

- April 1985: Yen bankers' acceptance market inaugurated; decision made to allow foreign banks to enter trust banking business

- October 1985: Interest rates on large deposits liberalized; bond futures markets established
- June 1986: Foreign banks authorized to issue European bonds
- December 1986: Tokyo offshore market opened
- November 1987: Domestic commercial paper market opened
- October 1988: Ceiling on foreign banks and securities companies' share as underwriters of government bonds raised
- January 1989: New prime rates for short-term loans reflecting market rates introduced
- June 1989: Small-unit money market certificates introduced; Tokyo financial futures exchange opened
- June 1992: Revision of laws regulating financial system approved
- June 1993: Interest rates on time deposits fully liberalized
- October 1994: Interest rates on demand deposits liberalized
- November 1996: Fixed commissions on securities deregulated
- December 1996: New Insurance Business Law that allows bilateral market entry between life and nonlife insurance companies enacted
- June 1997: Financial Supervisory Agency established
- April 1998: The "Japanese Big Bang"—the boundaries between different financial service institutions lowered
- October–May 1999: Banks and other financial companies allowed to issue bonds; insurance companies allowed to enter banking business
- March 1999: Tax on securities transactions abolished; brokerage commissions and on-line transactions deregulated; 401(k)-style pension plans introduced
- October 2000: Banks allowed to sell insurance
- March 2001: Disclosure system improved; competition across different segments of the financial service industry promoted

Deregulation allowed banks and credit unions to expand their lending activities to high-risk activities: art collections, construction loans to *yakuza* (organized crime members), and the financing of real estate purchases at home and abroad. This banking deregulation, along with the easy monetary policy of the mid- to late-1980s, resulted in an unprecedented banking crisis that has been a major cause and symptom of the prolonged stagnation, as well as a source of intense political controversy.

Government Procurement

Government procurement is a complex business all over the world, especially in Japan, where *keiretsu* groups kept foreign bidders off government contracts. But things began changing in the early '90s. In June 1993, during the G-7 Tokyo meeting, Japan agreed to harmonize her bidding system with that of the US. In June 1991, Japanese trade negotiators agreed to simplify the government procurement system and double the number of public work projects accessible to foreign construction and engineering corporations, from 17 to 34. In the early 2000s, the Japanese government adopted a number of voluntary procurement procedures to improve foreign business access that goes beyond WTO requirements: clarification of government procurement procedures; expanded use of general tenders; improved qualifying procedures; and improved distribution of government procurement information. One of the provisions of these measures, for instance, is the lowering of the standard minimum procurement amount from 130,000 SDRs to 100,000 SDRs. Another provision makes procurement for contracts exceeding 800,000 SDRs more transparent.[22]

Other Sectors

As Japan transitioned to its New Economy, progress with deregulation spread in several other sectors as well:

- Telecommunications: the breakup of NTT in 1999; the privatization of KDD; the liberalization of interconnections, which introduced competition; and the lifting of restrictions on foreign ownership (June 1997).
- Government inspections: in July 1995, the government eliminated the certified garage bill.
- Taxis: in 1993, the government allowed taxi companies to lower their fares.
- Petroleum: in April 1996, the government abolished an import law that limited oil imports to refineries.
- Breweries: in 1994, MOF lowered the minimum capacity requirements from 2000 to 60 kiloliters.[23]

In short, Japan took a number of measures to deregulate its economy, putting it in line with those of other developed countries, most notably the US.

Deregulation Bears the Desired Results

In the telecommunications sector, deregulation prompted the entry of 6,600 companies since 1985 and a wave of foreign acquisitions and joint partnerships, including a 97.7 percent of IDC stake by British C&W and a partnership between NTT and AT&T. For the period 1990–1996, telephone rates dropped by 16.1 percent, while telephone charges in the Osaka area dropped from 400 yen to 90 yen. In the financial service industries, deregulation accelerated the introduction of holding companies, foreign acquisitions of Japanese financial companies, foreign insurers, and discount brokers. (The 1996 New Insurance Business Law, for instance, allowed foreign insurance companies like American Home Direct and AFLAC to sell insurance policies by mail.) The 1997 lifting of restrictions on bank business hours allowed the branches of foreign banks, such as Citibank, to offer 24-hour services. The 1999 deregulation of electronic transactions on brokerage commissions for commodities futures transactions prompted the entry of 36 new companies in the securities industries, including American discount broker Charles Schwab Co. Ltd in a joint venture with Tokyo Amrine and Fire Insurance Co., Ltd. In the transportation sector, the number of double-track routes increased from 6 to 37, while the triple-track routes increased from 6 to 25.[24]

In the retailing industry, deregulation led to a proliferation of large store openings around the country. Deregulation gradually eliminated the layers of wholesalers, bringing retail outlets closer to the factory walls; increased the number of suburban retailers due to lowered rent; and changed the Japanese consumer mentality toward convenience stores, concepts stores, and discount stores. According to the METI's *1999 Census of Commerce,* the total number of large retail stores increased from 14,632 in 1989 to 21,892 by 1997, while their sales increased from 32,813 billion yen to 48,278 billion yen.[25] Deregulation also prompted the entry of foreign-affiliated distributors, including Virgin Megastores and Toys "R" Us (see Exhibit 5.2).[26] Deregulation has further lowered the country's cost of living of the Japanese people, bringing it closer to those of other industrial countries. In 2000, for instance, Tokyo's overall cost of living was in par with that of Geneva, London, and New York and a little higher than Berlin and Paris (see Exhibit 5.3).[27]

In brief, in the late '80s and '90s, yielding to domestic and foreign pressures, Japanese governments launched a host of sweeping measures to change

Exhibit 5.2   Selected Foreign-Affiliated Distributors That Entered the Japanese Market in the 1990s

Year	Company	Country	Industry
1990	Virgin Megastores Japan Ltd.	UK	AMV Soft
1991	Toys "R" Us-Japan Ltd.	US	Toys
1993	Burger King Japan	US	Fast Food
	Nike Japan	US	Sporting Goods
1994	Esprit Japan	Hong Kong	Ladies' Apparel
1995	GAP Japan	US	Casual Apparel
1996	Starbucks Japan	US	Coffee Shops
1998	Office Depot	US	Office Products
1999	Boots MC Company Ltd.	UK	Cosmetics

Source: *The Changing Service Industries of Japan,* JETRO, Tokyo, Japan, 2001.

Exhibit 5.3   Cost of Living in Tokyo Compared to Other Major Cities Worldwide by Item (2000)

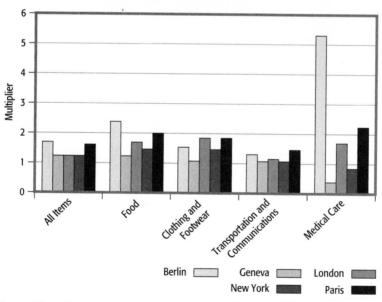

Source: Cabinet Office

economic priorities and open domestic markets to foreign competition. Working hours were reduced, domestic demand expanded, the yen appreciated, and progress was made in removing protectionism and regulation. The precipitous rise of the yen, the monetary easing, the massive fiscal stimulus, and the promotion of competition transformed Japan from a production, export-oriented economy to a consumption, import-oriented economy, and from an emerging to a mature, capitalist economy. The transformation, however, took the country on a roller-coaster ride, as described in the next section.

The Blow and the Burst of the Bubble

Japan's Bubble and her Burst can be traced back to the attempts to open up her economy and to elevate standards of living in 1985 after the Plaza Accord. Pressured by her trade partners to stimulate domestic demand and imports, the Bank of Japan and the Japanese governments launched expansionary fiscal and monetary policies and accelerated financial deregulation, taking the economy on a wild ride. Easy money flowed to everything, from real estate, to golf courses, to art collections, boosting prices into the stratosphere.

Eventually, the reversal of demand policies and deregulation burst the Bubble, crushing asset prices, which had a pervasive impact on both the export and the domestic sectors, especially on banking and housing and loan associations. The export sector suddenly had to confront the skyrocketing yen that eroded Japan's competitiveness in world markets. Meanwhile, the domestic sector had to confront the rising tides of imports and the price destruction associated with it. Banks and savings and loans, in particular, faced the eroding asset values and the rise of nonperforming loans, leading to a crisis that dwarfed that of the US in the 1980s. In addition, the Japanese economy of the 1990s was encumbered with an aging population and labor shortages.

In the beginning, between 1985 and 1989, the monetary and fiscal stimulus blew a tremendous economic bubble. It fueled robust economic growth, a soaring yen, and whopping gains in the stock and the real estate markets. The GDP grew from just below 6 percent in 1986 to over 6 percent by 1988. The yen appreciated from 220 yen to the dollar to 140 yen to the dollar. As reflected in the benchmark Nikkei Index, stock prices climbed by 160 percent, from around 14,000 in 1985 to close to 40,000 by 1989. Land prices in the Tokyo area more than doubled, and wages climbed by 30 percent, three times ahead of the rate of inflation. In the 1990s, Japan had the third lowest growth among OECD countries, close to that of Switzerland and the Czech Republic. The country's economy shifted from a state of 3 percent inflation in 1990 to a zero inflation by 1998 and to −1 deflation for the period 1998–2002.[28]

Rising stock and land prices elicited euphoria among Japanese corporate executives and bankers. With equity positions in other companies and land holdings in the Tokyo area, corporate executives found it easier to borrow from banks and to expand their ambitious domestic and overseas expansion plans. As is the case in major corporations, Japanese banks had both equity and land positions, and the rising land and stock prices strengthened their financial positions, allowing them to stretch their lending.

But with real estate prices skyrocketing, these policies lowered rather than elevated the standard of living. Japanese people found it more difficult than before to afford to buy a house, and businesses found it difficult to pay the higher rents and wages. To make matters worse, the appreciating yen and the labor shortages further eroded their competitive position and squeezed corporate profits.

To deal with this situation, the Bank of Japan reversed its policies, tightening up the money supply. Between 1989 and 1990, the Bank of Japan raised the official discount rate five times, from 2.5 to 6 percent. Japan's broad money supply dipped from 10 percent in November 1990 to below 1 percent in 1992, before bouncing back to around 3 percent in 1994. Meanwhile, the yen continued to appreciate, approaching the 100 yen per dollar mark by 1994 and the 80 yen per dollar mark by 1995.[29] Simultaneously, the government tightened up bank restrictions regarding land and housing financing and sped up deregulation of the domestic sector.

Stock and land prices began to come down to earth, profits dropped, and bankruptcies mushroomed. By 1994, the Nikkei average was back to around 15,000, and land prices had dropped by 30 percent. The drop in the land and stock prices haunted banks. In fact, every time the Nikkei stock average dropped, it undermined the banks' balance sheets. Japan's economy slid into the worst stagnation and recession in the postwar period. The GDP dropped from 6.1 percent in 1988 to 5 percent by 1991 and to negative territory by 1994. With the economy falling into a recession, unemployment increased from 2.5 in 1991 to 3 percent by 1994, and more than 5 percent by 2002.[30]

To fight the recession, Japanese policy makers reversed their policies once again, in the mid 1990s and early 2000s, launching a massive fiscal stimulus plan and cutting interest rates aggressively. Though the fiscal stimulus prevented the economy from sliding further into recession, the monetary policy had little impact on reviving private construction and consumer spending. The reason for this was the failure of the wounded banking system to accommodate monetary policy, what was known as "credit crunch." As was the case with the US in the late 1980s, the easy monetary policy translated into more speculation rather than a pick-up in the economy, an issue that the Japanese government has been to slow to address.

Coping with the Banking Crisis

The prolonged banking crisis is both a cause and a symptom of the prolonged stagnation of the Japanese economy in the first half of the 1990s. According to some estimates (actual numbers are difficult to pinpoint due to minimal disclosure requirements), Japan's banks and savings and loans associations have accumulated close to $400 even $500 billion of nonperforming assets, a figure that dwarfs that of the US banking crisis in the 1980s. Further, they have been slow in disposing of them. But how could Japan, a country run by the notorious regulators of METI and the Ministry of Finance, let her banking system slide into such mess? How are those regulators trying to deal with the problem?

Japan's banking crisis can be traced back to the two oil shocks in the mid 1970s and the early 1980s when crude oil skyrocketed. A slowing economy and soaring government and trade deficits with the oil-exporting countries shifted banks' functions from that of lenders to the domestic, private sector to that of buyers of domestic and foreign government securities. This shift in banking activities accelerated in the 1980s with deregulation, the expansion of Japanese companies abroad, and the easy monetary policy that the Bank of Japan adopted following the Plaza Accord in 1985.

But as the art market declined along with real estate prices, Japanese banks found themselves with repossessed paintings and real estate properties that could fetch only a fraction of the amount the banks had lent to the owners. The yen appreciation and the collapse of the Tokyo market undermined the banks' domestic and international equity holdings. As banks tried to survive on interest rate income, they became more and more reckless with lending, which led to the accumulation of additional nonperforming assets.[31] In 2001, at least half of the 21 major Japanese banks reported losses due to the write-offs of bad loans, with many of the remaining following suit soon after.[32] But why did Japan's regulators fail to avert this scenario?

The close ties with the institutions they are supposed to supervise have prevented Japanese regulators from pursuing prompt and diligent action. In some cases, like Daiwa's subsidiary in the US, the Japanese regulators even persuaded bank officials to conceal the losses from the US regulators! In what is known as *amakundori,* descent from heaven, former bureaucrats with the Ministry of Finance and the Bank of Japan end up getting jobs with the institutions they used to regulate. But even before they get there, even when they discharge their normal duties as regulators, they frequently socialize with bank executives, accepting generous gifts.

As more and more bureaucrats are at the center of financial scandals, their reputation is seriously damaged, a mixed blessing for the banking crisis and the Japanese society in general. In the short term, a weak bureaucracy has aggravated the banking crisis and prolonged the economic stagnation. In the long term, it presents a unique opportunity for Japan's political system to place bureaucracy under its control, as is the case in most modern, democratic societies.

In early 2002, the Japanese government began taking a number of measures to end the banking crisis: better disclosure of bad loans; expanded deposit insurance; the promotion of mergers between healthy and unhealthy institutions, such as Mitsui Trust and Chuo Trust, Sumitomo Bank and Nippon Trust, and Mitsubishi Trust and Bank of Tokyo; and the promotion of proper market transactions.[33] On their part, larger banks, such as Fuji Bank, Hokkaido Takushoku Bank, and Tokai Bank, have taken steps to write off nonperforming assets.[34]

Eventually, as was the case in the US in the 1980s, the taxpayers will end up bearing the cost of the massive cleanup.[35] The question is, which politicians will display the courage and determination to address and deal with the issue? In the meantime, the Japanese corporations have had to make their own adjustments to deal with the impact of the Burst of the Bubble.

To sum up, under both domestic and international pressures, Japanese governments began shifting their economic priorities from production to consumption by reducing working hours, stimulating domestic demand by removing trade barriers, and deregulating domestic industries. Slowly, Japan is being transformed from an emerging to a mature economy, and her business and political systems are restructuring accordingly.

Endnotes

1. Kazuo, "A Dose of Deregulation to Buoy Business," 23.

2. Tajima, "Catering to the Needs of a Diversifying Market."

3. Sanger, "Japan's Bureaucracy."

4. Ozawa, *Blueprint for a New Japan,* 196.

5. "MITI's Vision for the 1990s (cover story)."

6. Ryutaro, "Directions for the Future of the Japanese Economy."

7. JETRO, *Meeting the Challenge,* 44.

8. IMF, *Japan, Economic and Policy Developments.*

9. Holloway, "Soul of Inefficiency," 26.

10. OECD, *The Sources of Growth in OECD Countries.*

11. International Monetary Fund, *World Economic Outlook.*

12. McKinney, "Degree of Access," 54.

13. Ozawa, *Blueprint for a New Japan,* 12.

14. Toga, "94 Auto Imports Raced to Record High."

15. Ozawa, *Blueprint for a New Japan,* 198.

16. Sapsford, "Tokyo Hits a Wall with Economic Plans," A1.

17. US Congress Joint Committee, *Hearings on The Japanese Market—How Open is It?,* 48.

18. Japanese Ministry of Finance, "Export and Import Statistics."

19. Thornton, *Japan's Struggle to Restructure,* 36.

20. JETRO, *TRADESCOPE.*

21. Arayama and Mourdoukoutas, *The Rise and Fall of Abacus Banking in Japan and China,* Chapter 2.

22. JETRO, "White Paper."

23. Ibid.

24. MOFA, "Japan's Approach to Deregulation."

25. METI, *1994 Census of Commerce,* 20.

26. JETRO, "Japanese Money Report."

27. Prime Minister's Cabinet Office, *Index of Business.*

28. Arayama and Mourdoukoutas, Chapter 2.

29. OECD, "1994 Economic Survey."

30. Mourdoukoutas, *The Rise and Fall of Abacus Banking in Japan and China,* 75.

31. Ibid.

32. Sapsford, "Japan's Bureaucrats Balk at Curbing," A6.

33. Ibid.

34. Sapsford, "Tokyo Hits a Wall with Economic Plans," A1.

35. Reed, "The Banking Scandal Could Hamstring Hashimoto," 65.

CHAPTER 6

BUSINESS AND POLITICAL RESTRUCTURING

- In the late 1990s, Nissan was a typical Japanese company: a large conglomerate with equity positions in a number of different businesses, cozy relations with suppliers, low operating margins (OM), low rates of return on invested capital (ROIC), and a large debt. The company was further losing sales and market shares to its American, European, and other Japanese counterparts. By the early 2000s, Nissan was no longer a typical Japanese company, but a typical multinational company focused on its core business, operating margins, rates of return on equity, and on debt retirement. Sales, market shares, OMs, and ROICs have risen, while debt has declined. What made such a dramatic difference? An alliance with Renault and a western manager, Carlos Ghosn, paved the way for the company's radical restructuring, including the slashing of excess labor and capacity, the selling of non-core businesses, and the use of funds to retire debt and to build up the core business—the development, manufacturing, and selling of automobiles.[1]

- In 1999, Sony announced a sweeping restructuring plan, promising to slash its labor force by 10 percent, and to reduce the number of its worldwide factories from 70 to 55.[2]

Nissan's and Sony's cases exemplify an ongoing trend among Japanese companies to restructure and modernize their operations by blending traditional Japanese management practices like Total Quality Control and Cross-Functional Teams with western corporate governance structures to compete efficiently and effectively in the post-Bubble economy. Some of the many steps these Japanese industrial conglomerates have taken include:

- Scaling back their operations, modeling themselves after smaller, profitable outfits. Hitachi, Fujitsu, and NEC, for instance, have modeled themselves after Canon. Guth, in *Survival of the Slimmest in Japan,* 2003, explained, "The goal for the companies—such as Hitachi Ltd., Fujitsu Ltd., NEC Corp.—is to become more like smaller neighbor Canon Inc., which has become one of Japan's most profitable companies, thanks to an early restructuring and a focus on a few key growth areas."[3] Sanyo has modeled its business after GE, developing profit centers by business segments. "The consumer electronics maker has recently transformed itself from an industry best known for its low prices to a technology powerhouse focused on businesses where it has leadership in global markets," wrote Michyo Nakamoto in the *Financial Times*.[4]

- Closing down and liquidating unprofitable operations. Mitsui, for instance, liquidated 200 subsidiaries to return to profitability. Cosmetics maker Shiseido slashed inventories, narrowed its product portfolio, and closed down inefficient factories.[5]

- Relocating their manufacturing operations offshore discontinuing their traditional ties with subcontractors and associates, and even laying off workers—measures that threatened the traditional pillars of the Japanese labor relations: lifetime employment, seniority wages, and enterprise unionism.[*]

- Adopting new business models, decentralizing their operations, setting up multiple headquarters, and introducing IT systems that improve operational effectiveness and new product development. Retailer Seiyu, for instance, has teamed up with Wal-Mart to introduce the deep discount concept in Japan. "Many Seiyu stores have yet to get a makeover. The flagship store has introduced Wal-Mart's price rollbacks, discounts that run for an extended time, but it has yet to carry out Wal-Mart's most basic concept: everyday low prices. The idea does away with the necessity for constant advertising and weekly discounts to woo buyers."[6] Seiyu has further introduced Wal-Mart's logistics, enabling Seiyu stores to cut its full-time workforce and replace it with part-timers. "And Wal-Mart is bringing its technological know-how to Japan, introducing a computerized system to track inventory and purchases, which will boost efficiency and trim costs at Seiyu. Within two years, all the stores will have the electronic system. The technology has already enabled Seiyu stores to reduce the number of full-time workers and replace them with part-timers."[7]

As traditional management practices weaken and fade away, Japanese companies have been adopting new business models. Sony Corporation has

---

[*] Sony and Mitsubishi have cut their worldwide labor forces by 10 percent, while Nissan by 14 percent.

reorganized its operation by product group rather than product region, creating a network organization that consists of two levels: a Global Hub that is at the core of the network, and five product-group units at the periphery of the network. The Global Hub's function is to strategically integrate the company's resources and explore alternative uses for them. To strengthen cooperation among units and flexibility in dealing with changing market conditions, Sony has created a Management Platform that allows the different units to cooperate on matters of common concern. In addition, Sony Corporation has appointed two non-Japanese to its board and divided its headquarters between Tokyo (hardware business) and Los Angeles (software business).

To provide additional examples, Matsushita Electric Industrial Co. is decentralizing its operation, turning divisions into separate entities cooperating and competing with each other at the same time.[8] TDK Corporation is moving toward a network of four separate regional headquarters to handle all its major products.[9] Chipmakers like Toshiba and Fujitsu are forming strategic alliances for the development of systems chips, while Hitachi and Mitsubishi Electric are integrating their operations in the development of next-generation of microprocessors.[10]

Norihiko Shirouzu, reporting in *The Wall Street Journal,* provided another example of new business trends:

> To solidify their partnership relations and fend off competition, M&A (mergers and acquisitions) have replaced *keiretsu* relations. Diamond Lease Co.'s (an affiliate of the Bank of Tokyo-Mitsubishi Ltd.) acquisition of Ryoshin Leasing Corporation, a unit of the Mitsubishi Trading Company, is a case in point. The merger will allow the new companies to achieve the scale and efficiency to fend off competition by foreign companies like GE Capital Corporation and AIG. Hino Motors Ltd., an affiliate of Toyota Motor Corp., has absorbed its 40 percent owned stake of its affiliate Hino Motor Sales, Ltd., while Isuzu Motors Ltd. has acquired its real estate unit, Isuzu Real Estate Co.[11]

Japanese companies have been further adopting IT systems, such as Computer Aided Design (CAD), Electronic Data Interchange (EDI), the Internet and Intranets.[12] IT, for instance, is used to buy materials, but this does not mean that IT systems have severed the traditional ties between manufacturers and their suppliers. In personal interviews with Mr. Jagawa, executive vice president of Toyota Motor Corporation, and Mr. Okabe, CEO of Denso Corporation, they observed respectively:

> IT (information technology), is an effective means of buying raw materials, such as iron and aluminum, because they must conform to prescribed quality standards. But as for components or parts manufactured by suppliers, I think that IT can never be an effective means of buying them. We can never judge the quality of such components or parts based on information provided by IT.
>
> If we consider buying components or parts from new suppliers, we always go to the suppliers' factory to check the production management, in addition to the quality of the components or parts. We never decide to buy components or parts based on the information that IT provides.

Thus, IT is regarded as a tool for making voluntary arrangements between firms supplying strategic components, rather than as a tool for reaching low-cost suppliers or a tool for making spot market contracts. As Mr. Kato, CEO of Sony Minokamo Corporation put it to me:

> We have used IT for forming close relations with suppliers, which improves the quality of the strategic components we buy. As IT provides us with only a little information about the quality of components, we do not use it for researching new suppliers.

Restructuring is not confined to industrial conglomerates and individual companies. It extends to politics and policies of Japanese society. Japan's ruling political party has split into two political camps: the progressive camp that seeks to move forward with the New Economy, and the conservative camp that seeks to regress to the Old Economy. Gradually, policy-making authority is shifting from bureaucracy to elected officials.

The four sections of this chapter provide a more detailed discussion of the business and political restructuring of the post-Bubble Japan. The first section takes a closer look at the changes in the corporate governance and objectives of Japanese corporations. The second section reviews the "hollowing out" of Japanese business. The third section discusses the fate of traditional business practices, while the fourth section discusses the country's political restructuring.

Changing Corporate Objectives

In the Old Economy, corporate governance favored management and labor at the expense of stockholders. Management focused more on long-term objectives, such as sales growth and market shares, that served its own interests and the interests of enterprise union members, while overlooking short-term objectives, such as quarter-to-quarter profits and dividends that served the interests of stockholders. Institutional investors passively followed management, rarely participating in stockholder meetings and voting only on such important matters as election of directors, management compensation, and share repurchase. Management softened external shocks with savings in energy and raw materials, labor compensation cuts, labor deployment, and new product development rather than layoffs. Banks provided low-cost financing, while foreign loan demand made it up for the slack of domestic demand.

In the New Economy, corporate governance favors stockholders over management and labor. Companies have shifted their focus from sales and market share growth to profits and dividend growth. A 1993 JETRO report stated:

> Urgent measures are now in progress across the board in the manufacturing sector. Focus has turned sharply away from market share at all costs and towards making a profit, with the aim of survival and maintenance of at least a basic business health. Corporate departments increasingly are being held responsible for cost cutting and contributing to profitability. Restructuring is under way to streamline operations.[13]

Some companies have pursued stock repurchasing plans to boost shareholder value. Sony Corp., for instance, has initiated a 650 billion yen stock repurchasing plan, Hitachi 300 billion yen, and Nomura Holdings Inc. 221 billion yen.[14] A 2003 Nihon Keizai Shimbun survey found that 314 out of 1,838 surveyed companies planned to raise their dividend payout, close to 50 percent higher than a year earlier. Dividend hikes were particularly popular in the automobile sector, where more than 50 percent of the surveyed companies planned a dividend hike.[15]

Companies have been further slashing the size of corporate boards. Marubeni Corporation and Mazda Motor Co., for instance, slashed their board size by one-third.[16] At the same time, institutional investors have become more active in electing and monitoring corporate boards. According to the Pension Fund Association, in 2002, pension funds voted in a total of 970 motions—138 concerning election of directors; six concerning director remuneration; 124 concerning election of auditors; 161 concerning distribution of profits; 133 concerning bonuses to retiring directors; and 95 concerning the repurchasing of shares.[17]

The shift from a pro-management–labor organization to a pro-stockholder organization was fueled by a number of factors shaping Japan's New Economy. First, the Japanese government adopted a number of amendments to commercial and corporate governance laws, most notably a law that went into effect in April 2003, giving stockholders the power to control management. Specifically, the law:

- Makes corporate auditing mandatory.
- Increases the number of external auditors.
- Makes it easier for stockholders to file class action lawsuits.
- Requires that large corporations appoint additional in-house independent auditors.
- Lowers the size of shareholding needed to access company records to 3 percent from 10 percent.
- Lifts restrictions on the size of bonds issued by large companies.

Second, the loosening up of *keiretsu* relations and the uproar over "American-style" hostile takeovers, eliminated inefficient and ineffective management, enhancing shareholder value. Jason Singer, writing for *The Wall Street Journal,* reported:

> The uproar signals the arrival in Japan of American-style capitalism and the loud voice it gives to shareholders. As in the US in the 1980s when hostile takeovers and corporate raiders thrived, a lot of executives are decrying the development as a destabilizing force, fearing it puts too much power in the hands of financiers, looking for a short-term pay-day. On the other hand, as in the US, it could spur companies to be more efficient and accountable.[18]

Third, strategic alliances between Japanese corporations with American and European companies have multiplied—Mazda with Ford, Nissan with Renault, and Mitsubishi Motors with DaimlerChrysler, to name but a few. In some cases, these alliances have taken the form of equity stakes. General

Motors, for instance, took equity stakes in Isuzu Motors, Suzuki Motors, and Fuji Heavy Industries; Roche Group took a 50.1 stake in Chugai Pharmaceutical Co.; and Wal-Mart took a 6 percent stake in Seiyu. In his book *Globalization and Growth: Case Studies in National Economic Strategies,* Richard H. K. Vietor stated:

> More and more American firms operate inside the castle, with or without Japanese partners, employing large numbers of Japanese workers, who are increasingly participating directly in the Japanese policy process. American firms thus can become part of the domestic *niatsu* (inside pressure) process for change.[19]

Several of these alliances have resulted in a new synthesis, or "cross-fertilization," of cultures that turns problems into opportunities, as is the case with the Nissan-Renault alliance, reported by *Strategic Direction* magazine:

> In the case of the Nissan-Renault alliance, the cultural differences were a source of strength and cross-fertilization rather than problems. The Nissan management understood the severity of the difficulties they faced and saw the arrival of Renault as an opportunity. The revival plan had very strong, clear objectives and left no room for worrying about cultural conflicts. Instead, the emphasis was on seeing the different approaches that each company could bring to the joint objectives.[20]

Fourth, the swapping of debt financing in favor of equity financing gave stockholders a louder voice in management than creditors.*

In some cases, the shift from a pro-stakeholder organization to a pro-stockholder organization has already produced the right results. Corporate profitability (current ratio) has increased from 3.3 percent in 1999 to 4.6 percent in 2003. Excess capacity has declined from around 20 percent in 1994 to around 9 percent in 2004.[21] To give some specific examples, Honda's operating revenue has increased from 6,000 billion yen in 1999 to 10,000 billion in 2003. Toyota's operating margin increased from roughly 3 percent in 1993 to 8 percent in 2003, while its net income increased from roughly 10 billion yen in 1999 to 22 billion yen by 2003.[22]

In short, as Japan shifted from the Old to the New Economy, its corporations became more stockholder- rather stakeholder-oriented, emphasizing

---

* Interest-bearing debt has fallen from close to 200 trillion yen in 1999 to 175 by 2003.

profits over sales and making it easier for stockholders to monitor management performance.

Hollowing Out

"Hollowing out" refers to the offshore relocation of traditional manufacturing operations, a strategy that mature, industrialized countries often apply to cope with the strengthening of their currency. Great Britain and the US experienced this process, and certainly Japan couldn't escape it. The precipitous rise in the yen made it difficult for Japanese companies, especially consumer electronics companies, to compete effectively in world markets without shifting production to overseas plants in the US, EU, and especially Asia, as noted in a number of international business periodicals:

> In the past two years, Japanese consumer electronics makers have all but given up production of audio equipment in Japan. Production of ordinary color television sets, once a symbol of Japan's export juggernaut, will be shifted completely to other Asian countries within a few years. The number of people employed by Japanese companies overseas is soaring. And after four years of recession-induced decline, corporate Japan's direct investment overseas rose 5.5 percent in fiscal 1993 to $36 billion, due to the shift to offshore production.[23]

> Already, almost 70 percent of the color televisions made by Japanese companies are made overseas. For VCRs, the figure is about 30 percent. There are even a few Japanese companies, like Uniden, the cordless telephone maker, that do all their manufacturing outside Japan.[24]

Every industry that makes less sophisticated, low value-added products has been shifting production to Southeast Asian and China, transforming them into backyard assembly factories. An April 2001 JETRO survey entitled *Competitiveness of Chinese Products in the Japanese Market* found that close to 58 percent of Japanese companies imported products from China. Of these companies, 60.2 percent imported finished products, 29.6 percent semi-finished products, and 35 percent parts and materials. Additionally, 37.6 percent owned a plant in China, and 42.2 percent had plans to shift production to China.[25]

Increasingly, products made in Japanese transplants in Asia reach western markets. A confirmation of this trend is the reduction in Japan's surplus with the US and an increase in China's and Southeast Asia's surpluses with the US, plus the decline of China's surplus with Japan. In 2003, for instance,

China's trade surplus with the US soared by 20 percent, while its surplus with Japan dropped by 24 percent.[26]

The rush to Southeast Asia is not universal, however. Industries that make highly sophisticated, high value-added products like flat-panel displays and lithography equipment stay home, as noted in *The New York Times:*

> Much of the assembly of low value-added consumer products, like television sets, has already moved out of Japan. Much of what is left of Japan's exports are high-value components and machinery and products in which the Japanese face little competition, like flat-panel display for computer screens, some types of lithography equipment for making computer chips, and laser-printer mechanisms.[27]

Some Japanese corporations have devised a variety of strategies to counter hollowing out, such as the development of new products, the pioneering of another field, the changing of product lines, and the expansion in the domestic market. One survey of 219 responding manufacturers found that 42.7 percent of materials and processing industries applied product development as a strategy to deal with hollowing out.[28] This strategy continues in the early 2000s. Canon, for instance, makes its conventional digital cameras in China, but retains its endoscopes in Japan. Canon and Sony have also been shifting the manufacturing of their conventional, modular-type products to China, while retaining manufacturing of integral architecture products in Japan.[29]

As Southeast Asian countries and China begin to develop their own technologies and catch up with Japanese manufacturing, Japanese companies must re-evaluate their strategies. Japanese managers, who have found comfort in the thought that manufacturing is everything, must either come up with novel products and processes or shift to services, reaching outside the company and the country for new talents to develop the new products, processes, or services. Managers must develop a whole new corporate culture, a global rather than a Japanese culture. But can Japan afford to develop a whole new management culture without undermining, or even abandoning, the institutions that gave them flexibility and strength in the first place?

An End to Traditional Business Practices?

Business practices and business models have their place in history, meaning that they work in some historical instances, but not in all. And this seems to be the case with the three sacred treasures of the Japanese management system: lifetime employment, seniority wages, and enterprise unions. They worked well in the high-growth environment of the Old Economy of the 1950s and 1960s, but not in the prolonged stagnation of the 1990s, as explained by Ono, in a 2001 *Wall Street Journal* article.

> Young people are no longer offered lifetime employment. Instead of battling for scarce full-time positions, many young people are drifting from one part-time job to another in today's only growth industries: flipping burgers, delivering pizzas, selling soda in convenience stores. The media have dubbed these serial part-timers "freeters"—a Japanese neologism combining the English word "free" and "arbeiter," the German word for worker. It means anyone who chooses to make a living by juggling part-time work.[30]

The lifetime employment system has become less popular among the country's corporations. According to a survey conducted by the Prime Minister's Office, the percentage of companies abandoning the lifetime employment system increased from 36.4 percent in 1990 to 45.3 percent in 1999. This trend is more evident among smaller companies of 30–99 employees (see Exhibit 6.1). Over the same period, the share of female part-time workers to the country's overall employment increased from 33.2 percent to 39 percent, well above the corresponding OECD figures of 23.6 and 24 percent respectively (see Exhibit 6.2).

Exhibit 6.1   Declining Share of Companies with Lifetime Employment

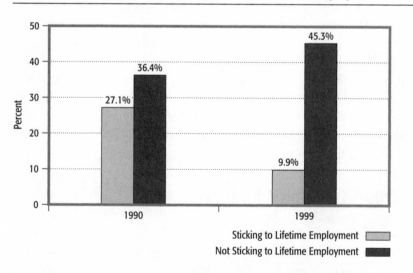

Exhibit 6.2   Rising Share of Part-time Female Workers in Japan

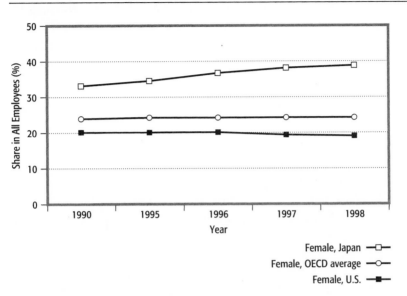

Source: *OECD Employment Outlook*, OECD, Paris, 1999

Do these statistics mean an end to lifetime employment? British sociologist Ronald Dore argues that Japanese companies will find it difficult to abandon such a popular institution. Instead, he expects companies to find ways to expand the employment opportunities for people who lack the skills and the ability to adjust to the demands of new technology.[31]

Compounding the problem of economic stagnation, the aging labor force and growing business complexity have made the seniority-based system both expensive and incompatible with the demands of the workplace, as explained by Sebastian Moffett in *The Wall Street Journal*.

Many companies, meanwhile, are being sapped by the effects of corporate traditions such as Japan's seniority-based wage system, where pay rises according to age. The average age at electronics behemoth Matsushita Electric Industrial rose to 41 in 2002 from 31 in 1980. The aging trend imposes a swelling wage burden, straining companies' bottom lines.[32]

Some companies have shifted from a seniority-based system to a merit-based system, as reported in *Focus Japan* magazine and in JETRO studies:

In the past, new workers were given on-the-job training and re-assigned every few years to give them broad experience.

Many of Japan's large companies are introducing a form of performance-based salary system, or *nenpo-seido,* at least on a trial basis. The new systems vary according to company, but they usually include a base salary (which may need to be negotiated by the individual employee periodically), and usually apply only to manager-level employees.[33]

According to a survey conducted by the Prime Minister's Office, the percentage of companies favoring merit over seniority increased from 37.8 percent in 1993 to 49.5 percent in 1999; while the percentage of employees favoring merit increased from 52.4 in 1978 to 63 percent in 1995. This trend is more evident among younger workers (see Exhibit 6.3).[34]

Some companies have been adopting even more revolutionary labor remuneration policies. Following the revision of the Commercial Code in 1997, 983 (30 percent of all listed) companies have introduced stock option packages.[35] In 2002, 983 or about 30 percent of Japanese firms offered stock option packages.[36] Does the gain in popularity of the merit system mean an end to the seniority-based system?

TDK President Ken Aoshima believes in the emergence of a mixed merit-seniority system to address the employment needs of less qualified workers, the handicapped and the elderly:

Sometimes in some business magazines or newspapers there are articles about corporations with very drastic merit-based compensation

Exhibit 6.3   Share of Companies Offering Merit System

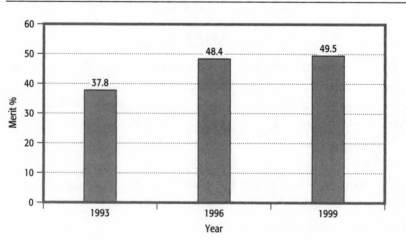

Source: Prime Minister's Office

systems that succeeded. But if you look at them from the other side, it is because the system was an exception that could become an article, not a case that could become a general feature of all corporations. If compensation is purely merit-based, then there would not be many older people or handicapped people working. This could be possible as an exception, but not all companies can do this. We live in a society with senior people who need to work. I think there should be some social or business system to guarantee this social aspect.[37]

The layoff of lifetime employees, the crafting of fictitious positions, and the hollowing out phenomenon have undermined the third tenet of the traditional Japanese labor market—enterprise unions—making them obsolete and irrelevant. In a personal interview with me, one Japanese worker reported:

> The Japanese people no longer think that unions are capable of solving the major problems in Japanese business today. Union activities are focused only on small, domestic problems, not on the far-reaching problem of overseas competition.

In brief, Japan's transformation from an emerging to a mature, capitalist economy, and the business restructuring that accompanied it, have shaken up traditional institutions but not completely eliminated them, as is the case with the country's political system.

Political Restructuring

The Burst of the Bubble has taken its toll on Japan's political system, creating mutations and permutations in the ruling LDP party, giving rise to coalition governments. In the early 1990s, for instance, rivalry among LDP factions led to a rift between conservatives and reformers, which in turn led to the 1993 creation of the Japan Renewal Party by 44 LDP members.

The splitting of the LDP party and the elections that followed in July 1993 put an end to one-party rule, opening up a period of sweeping change under coalition governments led by Hosokawa, Hata, Murayama, and Hashimoto. The splitting of the LDP further allowed the passage of electoral reforms that put an end to the policy that allowed four or five members to be elected by a single constituency, creating a whole new Japanese political system. As Neville de Silva reported in *Hong Kong Standard,* in 1996, "Japan's political culture has changed. The days of the old faction leaders, controlling politicians and powerful and rich political patrons buying votes seem to be dying, although it is far from dead."[38]

Far from dead, indeed! In July 1996, the LDP refused to support measures that would limit the powers of the legendary Ministry of Finance and clean up the banking mess. Instead, it proceeded with public works projects that boosted the bottom line of the construction industry, but failed to stimulate the ailing economy. In December of the same year, the newly formed LDP government failed to proceed with aggressive measures that would have limited the influence of the powerful Ministry of Finance on the Bank of Japan.[39] And the drafting of the 1997 government budget reincarnated the *zoku giin* the "tribes of the Diet"—members who pursued the old agenda of special interests rather than the modern agenda calling for deregulation and the weakening of bureaucracy.[40]

In the 1996 elections, the low voter turnout and the regaining of ground by LDP reflected both the disenchantment and the confusion of the Japanese people with the political system and the parties that represented it. The election result further reflected the clash between the old Japan, where politicians reigned and special interests ruled, and the modern Japan, where politicians reign and people rule.

The clash between the old and the new Japan continued with the 2001 elections, which led to the popular Koizumi government. Koizumi, for instance, departed from traditional Keynesian stimulus policies by adopting pro-growth monetarist policies, creating new institutions, privatizing governmentally owned companies, cutting taxes, limiting the power of special interests, and creating a smaller, more efficient government. It reduced the number of government ministries and agencies from 24 to 14 (see Exhibit 6.4).

MITI's failure to provide for industrial direction in the 1970s; the strengthening of corporations; pressure from trade partners after the first oil shock; the political and financial scandals that shook the Nagasone, Takeshita, and Kaifu governments; and the failure of the Ministry of Finance to avert the banking crisis all weakened the earlier cozy relations between the two parties. With the weakening of the business/government ties, MITI's powers drifted away, and by the mid-1990s, industrial policy gradually transformed from active to passive, in line with policies of other industrialized countries, as these Japanese economists explained:

> MITI was once one of the most powerful institutions in Kasumigaseki—Japan's Whitehall—orchestrating the country's

Exhibit 6.4   The Koizumi Agenda

Creation of New Institutions	Council on Economic and Fiscal Policy; create enterprise zones.
Administrative Reform	Consolidate the management and coordination agency with the Ministry of Home Affairs and the Ministry of Posts and Telecommunications; consolidate the Ministry of Transportation with the Ministry of Construction, the Hokkaido Development Agency, and the National Land Agency; consolidate the Prime Minister's Office, the Okinawa Development Agency, and the Economic Development Agency into the Cabinet Office; consolidate the Financial Reconstruction Commission and the Financial Supervisory Agency with the Ministry of Finance; consolidate the Science and Technology Agency with the Ministry of Education.
Stabilization	Cut public-works allocation in 2002 budget by 10 percent; introduce government subsidized programs.
Privatization/Deregulation	Privatize Narita and Haneda airports, Japan Highway Public Corp., Japan Oil Corp., The Urban Development Corp., the Housing and Loan Corp., and the postal services; introduce employee-pension scheme.
Banking Reforms	Require banks to write off nonperforming loans over three years.
Tax Policy	Cut taxes for business and stock investors; create tax incentives for equity investing.
Local Subsidies	Cut subsidies to local governments for infrastructure projects (an attempt to limit the power of construction company interests).
Social Welfare	Strengthen welfare and insurance, making people feel more secure; launch Medical Services Efficiency Program.

industrial policy in close cooperation with the business sector. However, now that Japan has achieved economic success and the role of industrial policy in economic development has diminished, the ministry has been marginalized among even clannish bureaucrats.[41]

In comparison to the high-growth era, the government, by which I mean the ministry or agency that was responsible for policy, became much more passive. In other words, during the high-growth period, the government was on the one hand seeking to bring about rapid growth through industrialization and a strengthening of international competitiveness, while on the other hand it was preparing for the transition to an open economy required by Japan's status under GATT and the goal of membership in the OECD. Positive activist policies were central. After the oil crisis, however, negative and passive policies became central.[42]

Passiveness weakened the ties between government and business to the extent that the two sides could no longer deal effectively with crises. In 1992, efforts by the Bank of Japan and the Ministry of Finance to convince brokerage firms to step into the market to support equity prices failed again, and the Nikkei average could not find a bottom heading to the 16,000 mark. Even worse, the same institutions failed to avert the banking crisis that caused the prolonged stagnation of the Japanese economy during that period.

To sum up, striving to survive and adjust to the new competitive and technological regime, Japanese companies took sweeping restructuring measures, including relocating production facilities overseas, shifting their priorities away from sales and market shares to profits, and reconsidering their stance towards the traditional institutions of lifetime employment. Restructuring was not confined to Japanese corporations; it extended into political institutions that modernized in line with other countries, opening the Japanese economy to world business. The decision making soon shifted from bureaucrats to elected politicians.

Endnotes

1. Tischler, "Carlos Ghosn Shifts the Once-Troubled Automaker into Profit Overdrive," 80.

2. SONY, "Sony to Reveal Restructuring Plan."

3. Guth, "Survival of the Slimmest in Japan," B5.

4. Nakamoto, "Manufacturing: The Japanese Art of Performance," 12.

5. Shiseido, *Company Annual Report.*

6. Kageyama, "Quietly, Wal-Mart's in Japan," 2.

7. Ibid., 3.

8. Matsushita Electric Industrial Company, *2002 Annual Corporate Report.*

9. Ibid.

10. Naito, "Chipmakers Seek Synergy in Union."

11. Shirouzu, "Japan Firms Tighten Ties to Affiliates," A19.

12. Makido, Kimura, and Mourdoukoutas, "IT and Competitive Advantage," 307–311.

13. JETRO, 22.

14. Ono, "Buy-back Plan Lifts Hitachi, Backfires on Sony," 12.

15. "Profits Net Shareholders Dividends," 4.

16. Marubeni Corporation, Corporate Annual Report; Mazda Motor Co., Corporate Annual Report.

17. Pension Fund Association, "The Behavior of Domestic Investors," 10.

18. Singer, "Hostile Treatment: With '80s Tactics, U.S. Fund Shakes Japan's Cozy Capitalism."

19. Ibid., 16.

20. Anonymous, "The Turnaround at Nissan Motors," 25.

21. OECD, *Economic Outlook,* 25.

22. Toyota, *2003 Annual Report.*

23. Hirose, "Hollowing Out: Can New Growth Replace Japan's Pruned Industries?"

24. Pollack, "Japan's Companies Moving Production Overseas."

25. JETRO, *White Paper on International Trade 2001.*

26. Moffett and Dvorak, "Asian Fusion: As Japan Recovers, an Unlikely Source Gets Credit: China," A1, A12.

27. "Shellshocked by the Yen, Japanese Companies Still Find Ways to Cope."

28. *Look Japan,* 7.

29. Takahiro, "A Twenty-first Century Strategy for Japanese Manufacturing."

30. Ono, "Buy-back Plan Lifts Hitachi, Backfires on Sony," A1 and A10.

31. Dore, "Japan in Recession," 6.

32. Moffett, "Going Gray: For Ailing Japan, Longevity Begins to Take Its Toll," A12.

33. JETRO, *Japanese Market Report.*

34. Prime Minister's Office, *White Paper on National Lifestyle,* 2000.

35. Hiroy, "Re-examining Corporate Governance in Japan," 1.

36. Ibid.

37. Ibid.

38. De Silva, "Hashimoto Faces Mammoth Task," 11.

39. Sapsford, "Japan's Bureaucrats Balk at Curbing Clout," A7.

40. Neff, "Why Hashimoto Has to Hang Tough."

41. Terazono, "Success Has Whittled Away MITI's Powers."

42. Komiya, Okuno, and Suzumura, *Industrial Policy of Japan,* 95.

PART II

HOW JAPAN'S NEW ECONOMY BENEFITS
WORLD BUSINESSES

While still in the "clay" stage, Japan's New Economy provides a "window of opportunity" for world businesses that understand the appeal of its markets and are prepared to ride a number of emerging trends: an appetite for imported products, smaller and graying households, the transition from a goods to a service economy, and the growing willingness of Japanese consumers to charge rather than pay in cash for purchases. Some companies—AFLAC Japan, Pfizer, and Jardine Flemming, for example—have already been cashing in on these trends and enjoying robust sales and profits.

CHAPTER 7

JAPAN'S MARKET OPENS TO WORLD BUSINESSES

As has been the case in other countries, foreign trade liberalization, deregulation and privatization, business and political restructuring, and prolonged stagnation have performed their magic in Japan. They have placed consumers rather than producers in the driver's seat, opening up the country's markets to foreign products and competition. Trade liberalization, for instance, has leveled off the playing field for foreign products destined for the Japanese market, bringing Japanese prices and consumption standards closer to those of the US and other western countries. Deregulation has eased entry barriers into domestically oriented industries, including distribution, retailing, telecommunications, and finance. In distribution, deregulation has cut off several layers of wholesalers, shortening the distance between producers and consumers. In retailing, deregulation has allowed large foreign retailers, such as Carrefour, Wal-Mart, and Costco, to bring their deep-discount model to consumers. Business restructuring has paved the way for foreign companies to speed up their entry into the Japanese market through acquisitions of domestic companies. The decline of traditional institutions—most notably lifetime employment—has made it easier and less expensive for foreign companies to recruit qualified domestic labor. The prolonged stagnation and industry deregulation and privatization have lowered rents and infrastructure-related costs, such as electricity and telecommunications rates.*

Japan's transformation from a producer into a consumer economy has made it a popular destination among foreign companies attracted by its high quality resources and R&D infrastructure. According to the 8th JETRO survey on the "Attitudes of Foreign Companies Toward Direct Investment in Japan," foreign companies ranked Japan as the most popular Asian destination in terms of ease of securing professional/high quality resources (40.5 percent), IT environment (37 percent), and support collaboration for universities/research institutions (33.6 percent).[1] Almost every major

---

* According to the March 2003 JETRO 8th survey on attitudes of foreign companies toward direct investment in Japan, 58.3 percent of foreign-affiliated companies noticed a significant improvement in start-up costs, while 53.2 percent noticed an improvement in infrastructure related costs.

western technology company, from IBM to Applied Materials, Corning, and Pfizer, have been setting up research centers to tap into the country's scientists and R&D infrastructure, and most of them are setting up Asian headquarters. Japan is also a popular destination among foreign companies attracted by the size of its domestic market, its geographic position, and reputation as a shrewd competitor.

Japan's popularity among world businesses is reflected in their rush to enter the Japanese market. In June 1989, following the slashing of import duties on foreign-made chocolates from 20 percent to 10 percent, Nestle expanded operations into the Japanese market. In June 1991, Toys "R" Us signed an agreement with Nintendo to allow the US retailer to sell Nintendo products in its newly established stores in Japan, a move that undermines Nintendo's ties with domestic distributors. Borden, America's dairy product giant, signed an agreement with Morinaga Milk Products Company to market milk from Australia and New Zealand in Japan. In July 1991, Compaq Computer announced the establishment of a Japanese subsidiary; IBM formed a consortium to take up Japan's giant NEC; and ALCOA signed an agreement with Kobe Steel for the joint production of aluminum cans in Japan. In 1993, Nike established its wholly owned Japanese subsidiary, and two years later Gap followed suit. In April 1999, Costco opened its first store in Hisayama, Fukuoka Prefecture. For the period 1993–2000, foreign direct investment increased from 1,072 cases in 1993 to 1,842 in 2000, while out-in mergers increased from 38 cases to 151.[2]

Providing a more detailed discussion of the opening of Japan's market, this chapter is divided into two sections. The first section is a discussion of the progress world businesses have made in cracking Japan's market—the rise of Japan's imports, the acquisition of equity stakes in domestic companies, the rise of market shares, and the challenge to domestic leaders in certain industries. The second section is a discussion of the strategic appeal of this market for world businesses: namely, a large, highly integrated market, a basis for Asian trade and investment, a test ground for competition, and a world innovator.

World Businesses Crack Japan's Markets

World businesses have made significant progress in entering the country's markets. In the five years that followed the Plaza Accord in 1985, imports increased by 50 percent, more than three times the rate of the overall national

Exhibit 7.1   Real GDP, Imports, and Exports (1986–2001)

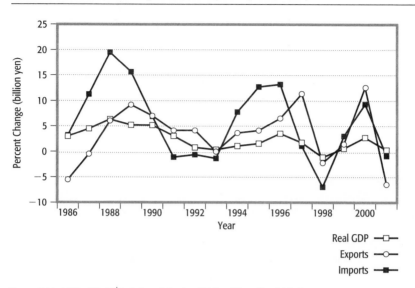

Source: Cabinet Office "The 2ⁿᵈ Preliminary Estimates of National Expenditure" Jul.–Sep. 2002

spending. Imports continued to grow rapidly (faster than GDP) in the mid 1990s, but followed an erratic pattern in the late 1990s and early 2000s, as deflation took its toll on the Japanese consumer (see Exhibit 7.1).[3]

Foreign direct investment to Japan increased from 23 billion yen in 1993 to 1451 billion yen in 1999, tapering off to 797 billion yen by 2002 (see Exhibit 7.2).[4] The number of new foreign affiliates established in Japan rose by 9.7 percent in the 1950s, 19.0 percent in the 1960s, 25.8 percent in the 1970s, 38.4 percent in the 1980s, 550.4 percent in 1994–1997 period, and 52.7 percent in 2002.[5]

The progress world businesses have made in entering Japan's markets in the 1980s is further documented by a number of surveys. The March 1989 "23rd Annual Survey of Foreign-Affiliated Companies in Japan" MITI survey found that close to 200 companies entered the Japanese market in the 1980s, compared to 133 in the 1970s and 98 in the 1960s.[6] An American Chambers of Commerce in Japan (ACCJ) survey found that in the 1985–1990 period: (1) 85 percent of foreign manufacturing companies in Japan increased their trade with Japan, (2) 80 percent of service companies increased their billings, and 41 percent more than doubled their billings, (3) 37 percent of the companies achieved their high priority targets set for

Exhibit 7.2   FDI Inflows 1993–2002

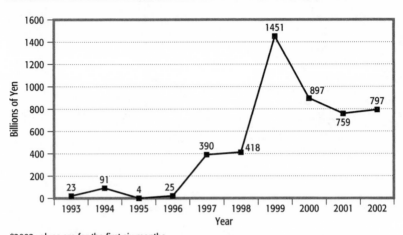

*2002 values are for the first six months

Source: Foreign Direct Investment (Ministry of Finance), Balance of Payments Monthly,
November 2002 (Bank of Japan)

their operations in Japan, and (4) 63 percent of the respondents expected the climate for trade and investment to continue to improve over the next five years.[7]

Entry of world businesses into Japan's market accelerated in the late 1990s and the early 2000s, as depressed equity prices and corporate bankruptcies provided foreign companies an express lane for reaching the Japanese market: the purchase of equity stakes in domestic companies. A 2002 ACCJ white paper reported:

> Over the past five years, continued economic stagnation and financial deregulation have altered the economic landscape, making larger-scale acquisitions by foreign companies feasible for the first time. Many have seized this opportunity. As a consequence, American firms in some sectors are increasingly opting for "inside-the-scale" approaches to doing business that require a deeper understanding of Japan's regulatory structure and business practices.[8]

General Motors, for instance, took equity stakes in Isuzu Motors, Suzuki Motors, and Fuji Heavy Industries; Roche Group took a 50.1 stake to Chugai Pharmaceutical Co.; Ford took a 33 percent stake in Mazda; while China-based Shanghai Electric and Morningside took over Akiyama

Exhibit 7.3   Selective Foreign Stakes in Japanese Companies as of 2002

Foreign Company	Stake (%)	Japanese Company or Industry
Merrill Lynch & Co.	100	Chemicals
Shanghai Electric and Morningside	100	Metals
New LTCB Partners	100	Chemicals
Ranbaxy Laboratories Ltd.	10	Nihon Pharmaceuticals
General Motors	49 20 20	Isuzu Suzuki Fuji Heavy Industries
Ford Motor Company	33	Mazda Motor Corp.
Renault SA	–	Nissan Motor
Roche Group	50.1	Chugai Pharmaceutical Co. Ltd.
Wal-Mart	6	Seiyu
AT&T and British Telecom	30	Japan Telecom
Virgin Entertainment Group	50	Virgin Megastores Japan
Adecco SA Group	100	Career Staff Co.
Cable and Wireless	98	Food
Schering	100	Mitsui Pharmaceuticals
Akzo Nobel	100	Kanebo Pharmaceuticals
Hermes Japan	10	Seibu Department Stores

Machinery Manufacturing (see Exhibit 7.3). Declining real estate prices have further attracted foreign restaurants, such as T.G.I. Friday's and Pizza Express, as well as retailers such as Wal-Mart, Carrefour (UK), Costco (US), Hermes (France), IKEA (Sweden), and Gap. At the same time, the decline of the traditional Japanese business institution of lifetime employment and rising unemployment allowed foreign companies to recruit a qualified labor force.

In some sectors, foreign affiliates and their domestic partners have assumed substantial market shares, even challenging legendary domestic market leaders. In the financial sector, for instance, American companies are challenging Nomura Securities, as reported by Singer in "Under Siege," in *The Wall Street Journal,* 2002:

> As corporate Japan goes through tough wrenching change, Nomura's decades-long dominance is facing an unprecedented threat. Japan's economic slide is increasingly forcing companies to merge, sell assets to foreigners and raise money from new markets. And the decline of

Exhibit 7.4   Foreign Company Market Shares in Selective Japanese Industries in 2000

Industry	Company	Market Share (%)
Unix Servers	Sun Microsystems	25
	HP	25
	IBM	13
Personal Computers	IBM	10
	Apple	6
Ice Cream	Häagen-Dazs	10
Instant Coffee	Nestle	65
	Ajimoto General Foods	24
Shampoo	P&G	12
	Bristol-Meyers Squibb	3
Sports Shoes	Nike	17
	Reebok	4
Pacemakers	Medtronic	30
Home Care	Baxter International	90

old-style conglomerate ties has lessened the role of Japanese banks in advising on corporate restructuring. That gives foreign banks an unprecedented entrée to Japanese CEOs.[9]

In 2001, American-based Goldman Sachs occupied the first place among merger-and-acquisition advisors (34.2 percent of the market), while Morgan Stanley occupied the third position (27.8) percent of the market.[10] In the Unix servers sector, Sun Microsystems and H&P hold 25 percent of the local market, while IBM holds 13 percent. In the instant coffee market, Nestle holds a 65 percent local market share, while Adjimoto General Foods holds 24 percent (see Exhibit 7.4).[11]

In other sectors, foreign acquisitions have turned around ailing Japanese companies. In the automobile industry, for instance, the infusion of foreign technology and business models has turned around Nissan and Mazda. Todd Zaun, writing for *The Wall Street Journal,* explained:

New models might finally give Mazda Motor Corp. the chance to complete its U-turn. Mazda, one-third owned by Ford Motor Co., is just one of a handful of Japanese car makers now being restructured under the guidance of foreign shareholders. But the Mazda turnaround has been slow, especially compared with Nissan Motor Co., which has recovered from near death to record profitability in less than three years under executives dispatched by its largest shareholder Renault SA.[12]

Expansion to the Japanese market has been rewarding for foreign affiliates and their parent companies. For the period 1991–96, return on equity of foreign affiliates was 11 percent, almost three times higher than that of their domestic counterparts, an issue to be further addressed in subsequent chapters.[13]

In short, as is evidenced by the growth of imports and investments, world businesses have begun to crack Japan's market. In some cases, they have been acquiring stakes in domestic companies, gaining a substantial market share. In other cases, they have been revitalizing ailing domestic companies.

The Appeal of the Japanese Market

Japan is a strategic market for world businesses for four reasons: (1) its large size and high degree of integration among her domestic markets, (2) its geographical and economic position in the Asian-Pacific region, (3) its reputation as the world's toughest competitor, and (4) its technological infrastructure and innovation capabilities.

A Large, Highly Integrated Market

Japan is a large, single-race, single-culture, well integrated economy. As of 2003, Japan's population of 127 million was about 45 percent of that of the US, while its GDP accounted for 15 percent of the world GDP and about two-thirds of that of the US. For the period 1960–73, the Japanese economy grew at a rate of 6.3 percent, compared to 2.5 percent in the US and 4.8 percent among OECD countries. For the period 1974–79, Japan's economy grew at a slower rate of 3.6 percent, but again above the US and OECD growth rates of 2.6 and 2.9 percent, respectively. Economic growth accelerated in the 1980s, during the Bubble years, but stalled in the 1990s and the early 2000s when the bubble burst.[14]

Brisk economic growth rates translate to a high disposable income that remained around 400,000 yen monthly (see Exhibit 7.5).[15] Japan is among the world's largest market for consumer products, especially luxury items. Louis Vuitton, for instance, draws one-third of its revenues from the Japanese

Exhibit 7.5   Household Disposable Income and Expenditures 1984–2000

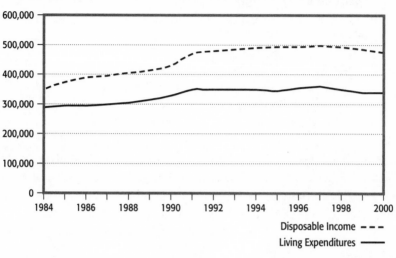

Disposable Income − − −
Living Expenditures ——

Source: Annual Report on Family Income and Expenditures

market. Japan is also a large market for sophisticated materials, components, and software, and a trendsetter in the electronics industries, churning out VCRs, digital cameras, and videos, an issue to be further addressed in subsequent chapters.

A Basis for Asian-Pacific Trade and Investment

Japan is an attractive location for Asian headquarters for world businesses for three reasons. First, its geographic proximity and frequent air connections to major Asian destinations make it easy to reach. As of 2003, 83 direct flights departed Japan for China, 91 for South Korea, and 103 to Southeast Asia. Tokyo is only a two-hour flight from Seoul, three hours from Beijing, almost three hours from Taipei and the Philippines, and about five hours from Bangkok. Second, its close cultural and economic ties with the region keep Japan well connected. Japanese companies have developed close ties with the region, manufacturing everything from air conditioners to television sets and electronic equipment. The number of Japan's Asian affiliates increased from 2,862 in 1990 to 6,919 in 2000. Japan's combined share of imports and exports accounted for 18.3 percent of East Asian trade.[16] Third, Japan has a reputation as a trendsetter for the rest of Asia, especially for the teenage market that takes its queue from Tokyo's Shibuya Station. "Shibuya, capital of

Exhibit 7.6   Revenue Growth in Japan and Asia Pacific (Percent of Xilinx Revenues)

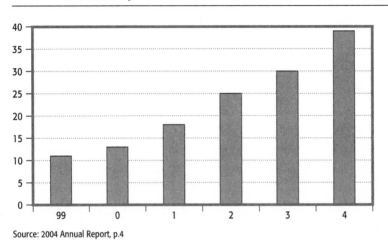

Source: 2004 Annual Report, p.4

Japan's teenage girls, is where fashion and consumer trends are born before spreading to the far reaches of the Japanese archipelago and to Taipei, Taiwan; Seoul, South Korea; and Shanghai, China," reported Norimitsu Onishi in the *Houston Chronicle*.[17]

A number of foreign companies, including Bodum Group, P&G, Applied Materials, Teradyne Corporation, and Starbucks have made Japan a basis for expanding their presence to Asia, while Xilinx, Inc. derives 39 percent of its revenue from Japan and the Asia Pacific, up from 11 percent in 1999 (see Exhibit 7.6).[18]

A Test Ground for Competition

The Japanese market is the toughest market in the world. New concepts and products are developed and tested much faster than in the US and Europe and are often introduced to other countries. In *The Wall Street Journal,* Singer and Fackler stated:

> Concepts can be concocted and tried at a much faster pace than in the US or Europe. And products that take off here often can be exported to the US, like Starbucks' green tea Frappuccino, which was devised in Japan and Taiwan and may be sold in the States.[19]

Japanese consumers have a reputation for quality and detail, and products that pass the test of the Japanese consumer survive everywhere. In an article for *Business 2.0,* Andy Raskin noted: "Japan is the most demanding market in the world. Japanese consumers look for quality in the tiniest details. Products that survive there have a better chance of succeeding in new markets."[20] And in his book, *The Competitive Advantage of Nations,* Michael Porter noted: "Rivalry is intense in every industry from air conditioning to videocassette recorders—112 rivals in machine tools; nine in automobiles; 25 in audio equipment; 16 in personal computers. Rivalry makes Japan an arena for international competition."[21] Companies that succeed in Japan have a better chance of succeeding everywhere in the world, and are in a better position to defend their home market from Japanese competitors, as explained by M. Czinkota, and J. Woronoff in *Unlocking Japan's Markets: Seizing Marketing and Distribution Opportunities in Today's Japan:*

> Japanese companies are among the world's most inventive and aggressive. They are consistently coming up with new products or improvements on old ones. And they export them with vengeance. A foreign company that does not pay adequate attention will know what those products are, and be able to come up with equivalent or superior ones, only when it is too late. That is, after the Japanese have entered the company's domestic market and are eating away at sales. With an establishment in Japan, it is possible to know what the competition is doing much earlier, to prepare for it back home, and possibly to react first on the Japanese market.[22]

To defend their own home market from Japanese companies, foreign companies must therefore take an offensive strategy, which Raskin calls "bulletproofing" their products, meaning learning how to compete in the Japanese market. P&G, for instance, "bulletproofed" its diapers and detergent products against competitors like Kao by adapting its products to the demands of Japanese consumers. The company's continuous efforts to fend off challenges by domestic competitors like Kao allowed it to defend its own home turf. Corning has maintained its lead as a glass material supplier by setting up R&D facilities in Japan and developing products for its domestic markets. Kodak tried—unsuccessfully—to "bulletproof" its products by expanding its presence in Japan's market. Its product couldn't penetrate Japan's distribution system.

A World Innovator

Japan has grown from a world imitator, a copycat of western technology, to a world innovator, churning out original, breakthrough products and

Exhibit 7.7   A Sample of Foreign Corporations with R&D in Japan

Company	Type of R&D
Pfizer	Antibiotics
Corning	Active Matrix Liquid Crystal Display Technologies
Applied Materials	Semiconductor Equipment
P&G	Consumer Products
Teradyne	Semiconductor Equipment
IBM	Computer Hardware
DuPont	Chemicals

processes that have conquered world markets. Robust private and government R&D spending and a well-educated population have contributed to this transformation. According to the Organization for Economic Cooperation and Development (OECD), 93 percent of the Japanese population ages 24–34 have a high school education, compared to 70 percent of the group average. In the same age group, the rate of four-year college graduates is 23 percent, the fourth largest in the OECD group. Japan also spends heavily on R&D. Even during the stagnation years, R&D rose steadily every year, reaching 16,289 billion yen in 2000.[23]

Many of the world's largest companies, including Digital Equipment Corporation, Corning Inc., Glaxo Holdings, Syntex Corporation, Proctor and Gamble, DuPont, Applied Materials, Teradyne, and Hewlett Packard have research facilities in Japan (see Exhibit 7.7). Corning Technology Center (CTC) focuses on R&D on display technologies, photonics, and special materials. The Corning Web site reports: "Scientists at CTC have developed world-class analytical techniques that allow them to simulate how Corning's products will act during a customer's process, and solve potential problems that customers may face. With its convenient location in Japan, CTC can also provide on-site technical support and training to Corning's Asia Pacific-based customers."[24] Others, such as IBM, Apple Computer, and AT&T, have set up joint ventures with their Japanese counterparts for the development of new products. A number of P&G products, for instance, were first introduced in Japan before launched in other Asian markets and the US, including their SK-II premium skin-care line. L'Oreal first introduced its Shu Uemura product in Japan before bringing it to Asian and western markets.

To sum up, Japan is a popular destination for world businesses. A large and growing economy, Japan offers a huge consumption and industrial market for foreign products. Japan's location in the world's fastest growing region provides foreign companies with a basis for investment and trade in Asia. A tough competitor and a world innovator make Japan an indispensable market for world competition, especially in the service sector, and most notably the "gray yen" industries, an issue to be further addressed in the next chapter.

Endnotes

1. JETRO, "8th Survey on Attitudes of Foreign Companies Towards Direct Investment in Japan."

2. Japanese Ministry of Finance, "Foreign Direct Investment in Japan."

3. Cabinet Office, "The Second Preliminary Estimates of National Expenditure," July–September 2002.

4. Japanese Ministry of Finance, "Foreign Direct Investment in Japan."

5. METI, "35th Survey."

6. JETRO, *The Challenge of the Japanese Market.*

7. American Chambers of Commerce in Japan, *Trade and Investment in Japan.*

8. The American Chamber of Commerce in Japan, *2001 US-Japan Business White Paper.*

9. Singer, "Goldman Again Tops List of M&A Advisors in Japan," A1.

10. Singer, "Under Siege," A11.

11. NESTLE, *2002 Annual Report.*

12. Zaun, "Shifting Gears: Mazda Nears Turnaround," A11.

13. JETRO, *White Paper on International Trade.*

14. METI, *White Paper.*

15. Ministry of International Affairs and Communications, *Annual Report on Family Income.*

16. METI, *White Paper.*

17. Onishi, "Japan Discovers Dark Side of Consumerism," 33.

18. Xillinx, *Annual Report,* 2004, Y.

19. Singer and Fackler, "In Japan, Adding Beer, Wine to Late List," B1.

20. Raskin, "How to Bulletproof Your Product (Hint: Take to Japan)," 54.

21. Porter, M., *The Competitive Advantage of Nations*.

22. Czinkota and Woronoff, *Unlocking Japan's Markets: Seizing Marketing and Distribution Opportunities in Today's Japan,* 2.

23. METI, *White Paper,* 2002.

24. Corning, www.corning.co.jp/en/, 5/4/2004.

CHAPTER 8

TRENDS AND OPPORTUNITIES IN JAPAN'S MARKET

- In the crowded streets of Shibuya and Harajuku, McDonald's hamburgers and french fries are replacing the traditional rice and *sushi* (raw fish meals), while Starbucks coffee is replacing green tea.
- In the tiny streets of Nagoya and Osaka, high performance cars from Germany are replacing the locally made Toyotas and Hondas.
- In the windows of Ginza department stores, designer clothes from France and Italy are catching the eye of young shoppers, who pay with plastic rather than cash.
- In small Tokyo apartments, rattan furniture from Indonesia, carpets from Pakistan, and handmade lace and embroidery from China are replacing the traditional Japanese decor.

In what could be called the "Second Meiji Restoration," Japan is being transformed from a closed, conformist society into an open, liberal society. Its consumers have become better informed and more individualistic, creating opportunities for marketers, as Paula Lyon Andruss noted in *Marketing News*:

> From better informed shoppers to a newfound desire for individuality, the Japanese consumer market is undergoing a transformation, and marketers must be aware of the changes before launching any kind of advertising initiative in the Land of Rising Sun.[1]

Breaking with long-standing tradition, Japanese consumers are looking for products that help them find their identity and assert their individuality, as Karl Moore and Mark Smith explained:

> Individuals are looking for help in "knowing who they are." Consequently, brands that are successful in Japan today help express the individual's sense of identity and self-expression, as are brands that see the Japanese and the market they represent as unique.[2]

Some Japanese consumers assert their identity and individuality with imported brand name products from Louis Vuitton, Chanel, Rolex, Coach,

123

and Prada. Others assert their individuality by eating out in fast-food and western-style family restaurants, while a third group travels to popular overseas destinations like Paris, New York, Hawaii, and the Fiji Islands.

Other trends are popping up as well. Plastic has become the currency of the land, especially among younger consumers. And Japanese households are growing smaller and older. Japanese couples are getting married later, having fewer children and living longer.

These considerations highlight the trends and opportunities of Japan's New Economy that benefit world businesses: a growing taste for imported products, smaller and graying households, a shift from goods to services, and a growing use of credit over cash. This chapter addresses these topics in greater detail by examining both the emerging consumer trends and the opportunities created by them.

Trends

As foreign products become less expensive and readily available, Japanese households are following the footsteps of their western counterparts. The households are becoming smaller, and the consumers getting older. People are spending more on services. They want longer shopping hours with better value, and they want to purchase on credit, not with cash.

A Growing Appetite for Imported Products

Japanese consumers are gradually shifting their preferences away from domestic products to foreign products. In a survey conducted by MITI in 1988, 46.5 percent of Japanese consumers indicated that they had "a taste for imported foods, if they are satisfactory, even at higher prices," compared to 4.9 percent five years earlier. Likewise 40.8 percent of Japanese consumers had developed a taste for imported apparel, as compared to 17.4 percent in 1983, and 59.9 percent had developed a taste for imported personal goods, as compared to 11.9 percent five years earlier.[3]

For the period 1995–2000, Japan's import volume increased by 23.7 percent, which reflected another shift in the country's trade structure. The country's import elasticity with respect to the GDP rose from .98 for the period 1970–1990, to 1.32 for the period 1973–2000.[4] Japan is now the world's largest market for luxury items, such as fashion accessories.

As Japan's economy becomes more open, a new breed of consumers is emerging. *Seikatsusha,* as these consumers are called, are anxious to break away from the tradition of group conformity and shape their own destiny. As M. Fujiwara reported in the *Journal of International Trade and Industry*:

> Japan's new breed of consumers, *seikatsusha*, are no longer happy to just keep up with the others in their society. They are anxious to make active efforts to change their lives, shape their lives, through consumption that suits their own tastes based on their individual values.[5]

The growing of *seikatsusha* consumers underlines the shift away from mass consumption to individualist consumption. Also writing in the *Journal of International Trade and Industry*, Marino Osami noted:

> In the past, consumers were happy to buy the same mass-produced products, but now they want goods that are as individualistic as possible. They want to be able to choose from a large number of possibilities.[6]

The growing appetite of Japanese consumers for imported products is reflected in the growth of Japan's manufacturing imports, most notably imports from the European Union, the US, and China. Japan's manufacturing imports increased from around $100 billion to $200 billion by 2001 (see Exhibit 8.1). Imports from the US rose from $30 billion to around $45 billion, while imports from China rose from around $5 billion to around $46 billion (Exhibit 8.2).[7]

Exhibit 8.1   Manufactured World Imports Entering Japan

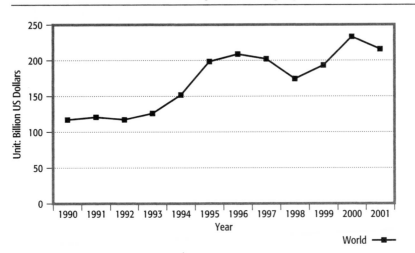

Source: Trade Statistics (Ministry of Finance)

Exhibit 8.2   Manufactured Imports Entering Japan

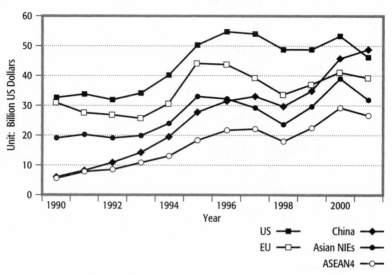

Source: Trade Statistics (Ministry of Finance)

One group of imported products popular among both younger and older Japanese women is European perfume, jewelry, and expensive designer shoes and handbags. Another product that has gained popularity among consumers is cheese. According to JETRO statistics, cheese consumption has increased from 210 tons in 1996 to 260 in 2000. A third imported product that has drawn the attention of Japanese consumers is wine. Wine import volume has increased from 147,439 klgms in 1997 to 171,833 klgms by 2001. A fourth popular product is European cars. Peugeot imports, for instance, rose from 5,000 units in 1996 to 7,000 by 2000, while Alfa Romeo imports increased from 3,000 to 6,000.[8]

In short, as Japan's markets have opened to world businesses, Japanese consumers have developed an appetite for imported products, such as designer apparel, cheese, wine, and imported luxury cars, that help them find their identity and assert their individuality.

Smaller Households

Though tradition calls for strong ties between parents and children even after marriage, Japanese household life is beginning to follow the course of other industrialized countries. Households have become smaller, sheltering

Exhibit 8.3   Changes in Household Composition

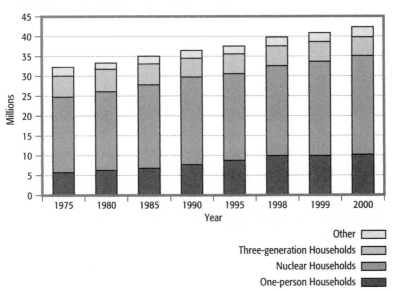

Source: Ministry of Health, Labor and Welfare

one or two instead of three generations (see Exhibit 8.3).[9] Within this trend, three segments may be identified: (1) single males and females, (2) married couples without children, and (3) married couples with children.

Single males and females

With the average marriage age shifting from the middle to the late 20s for males and from the early to the middle 20s for females, Japan is often called a "society of singles." According to the *1995 Population Census,* the percentage of singles in the age group of 25–29 years was the highest ever since the first population census of 1920, both for males (66.9 percent) and for females (48 percent). The percentage of one-person households was the highest percentage for Tokyo (16 percent), followed by the Hokkaido prefecture, the Kanagawa prefecture, the Kyoto prefecture, and the Kagoshima prefecture (10.6 percent).[10]

Married couples without children

With rising female employment and changing attitudes toward marriage, many Japanese are getting married at a later age and having fewer children.

Japan is, therefore, catching up with the "yuppy" trend experienced by America in the '80s. They eat out frequently, participate in after-hour company parties, and get together with friends on weekends. They also spend heavily on clothing, household appliances, furniture, automobiles, traveling, and other leisure activities.[11] Though both parties are working, most families still follow the Japanese tradition of the male spouse handing over his salary to the female spouse, who makes almost every consumption decision. While women maintain this privilege even after having children, their functions change dramatically.

Married couples with children

Households with children have an increased economic burden both inside and outside the household, especially families with more than one child. With more time needed for childcare, the female spouse withdraws from the labor market and allocates more time to children. With more expenses and only one source of income, male spouses must allocate more time to the market to make ends meet. Most men leave home early in the morning and come back late at night, leaving little time for children and other leisure activities. As a result, women are in charge of almost all household decisions, especially regarding spending and education.

Graying Households

The aging of Japan's population is another factor that will shape consumer trends for years to come. As is the case in other industrialized countries, Japan's population is aging, and by the year 2020, it will be one of the oldest in the industrial world. The portion of the population 65 years of age or older is expected to increase from 11.5 percent in 1989 to 24 percent in 2020. The corresponding percentages for the other industrialized countries in 2020 are 14 percent in the US, 16 percent in the UK, and 20 percent in Germany (see Exhibit 8.4).[12]

From Goods to Services

In addition to these other trends—the graying of households, the increasing labor force participation of women, the rising number of single households, and the rise of real incomes—Japanese consumers are shifting from goods to services, specifically those that improve their quality of life.

Exhibit 8.4   Japan's Graying Population: % of Total Population 65 and Over

Country	Year		
	1960	**2000**	**2030***
Japan	6.1	17.3	29.6
US	9.3	12.3	20.2
UK	11.7	15.8	28.3
Germany	10.9	16.4	27.7

* World Bank projections.
Source: *OECD in Figures,* Supplement to the OECD Observer, various issues.

Exhibit 8.5   GDP and Employment by Sector in 2002

Sector	Japan		US	
	% GDP	**% Employment**	**% GDP**	**% Employment**
Agriculture	1.7	5.1	2.4	2.6
Industry	36.1	31.7	24.9	23.1
Services	62.2	63.2	72.8	74.4

Source: OECD Observer, June/July, 2003.

Reflecting this shift, Japan's economy is being transformed from an industrial into a service economy. The service sector is now the largest sector in terms of contribution to GDP and employment, but the size of the service sector is still well below that of the US (see Exhibit 8.5). In 2002, the service sector provided for 62.2 percent of the GDP and the 63.2 percent of employment, well below the corresponding US figures of 72.8 percent and 74.4 percent. Conversely, the industrial sector of Japan is larger than that of the US, providing for 36.1 percent of the GDP and 31.7 percent of employment; the corresponding figures for the US are 24.9 percent and 23.1 percent, respectively.[13]

Within the service sector, Japan's strengths are only in community and personal services, while America's strengths are in wholesale/retail trade, hotel, finance, insurance, and real estate, as well as the sector producing government services. In 2002, community, education, health, social work, and other services accounted for 24.6 percent of the Japanese GDP, compared to a 12.7 percent contribution in the corresponding US sector (see Exhibit 8.6). Wholesale, retail trade, restaurants, and hotels contributed

Exhibit 8.6   The Contribution of Various Types of Services to GDP in 2002

Industry	Japan	US
Wholesale/Retail Trade and Hotels	11.8	17.0
Transport/Storage and Communications	6.6	6.0
Finance, Insurance, and Real Estate	19.1	29.3
Public Administration and Defense	4.6	11.0
Education, Health, Social Work, and other services	24.5	12.7

Source: OECD Observer, June/July, 2003.

11.8 percent of the GDP in Japan, compared to 17 percent of the GDP in the US. The finance insurance and real estate sectors contributed 19.1 percent of the GDP in Japan, compared to 29.3 percent in the US.[14]

From Quality to Value

In the Bubble economy, Japanese consumers were concerned only with product quality and after-sales service, not with price. As a matter of fact, low-priced products were automatically classified as low-quality products and rejected. But as the bubble burst and the Japanese economy slid into its worst postwar contraction, consumers began searching for value—quality products at affordable prices—and this has gradually changed the landscape of the Japanese market. To find these values, Japanese consumers are escaping from the traditional distribution system to discount stores and mail-order catalogs, as several financial and economic observers have noted:

> The recession is also helping shatter other myths about Japanese consumers. A few years ago it was the gospel that Japanese consumers cared only about quality and service, not price. Lowering a price often made the product less attractive. But consumers now are shunning high-priced department stores, with their legions of obsequious sales clerks, in favor of discount stores.[15]

> At the same time, Japan's consumer psychology started to change, and deflation, ruinous as it was, proved to have a hidden payoff. Shoppers demanded lower prices and got them—from entirely new retail categories such as "100 yen" shops, discount grocers, and warehouse-style department stores offering more and cheaper imported goods.[16]

Japanese consumers also find value in nontraditional retailers like Amway and Avon Products, as well as the Internet, an issue to be addressed in subsequent chapters.

More Plastic and Less Cash

For years Japanese consumers have been paying their bills in cash, taking very little in debt. But as more and more Japanese travel to the US, they are developing a taste for using credit cards and taking on debt. This is especially true of young people, who are eager to enjoy the good life sooner rather than later, as Fujiwara in "Consumer Pioneers," explained: "These young men and women want to have their needs met and desires satisfied as quickly as possible. This is a generation that seeks almost instant gratification."[17] Reflecting consumers' appetite for borrowing, the number of consumer loans has grown 1.7 times in the 1990s alone, and 50 times from the late 1960s to the late 1990s.[18] With the consumer credit market continuing to deregulate and with more consumers willing to take on debt, Japan's potential as a consumer market should be magnified, which will be rewarding to the companies that are well positioned in this market.

In short, Japan's new economy is characterized by a growing appetite for imported products that emphasize individualism, smaller and graying households, and making more use of plastic and less use of cash—all trends that shape opportunities for world businesses.

Opportunities

The Singles Market

Single households have the largest per capita spending among all consumer groups in Japan. As of 2002, single-member households had an average monthly per capita consumption of 175,048 yen ($1600).[19]

Young singles typically engage in spending sprees: shopping for imported designer clothes and jewelry in the fashion stores of Ginza; dining in western-style restaurants, coffee shops, and delis in Shibuya and Harajuku; and visiting nearby Tokyo Disneyland and taking weekend ski trips in the Nagano mountains. According to JETRO, the deli/prepared food market has increased from around 29 billion yen in 1990 to 56 billion yen by 2000.[20] As of 2001, close to 80 percent of singles in their late 20s and early 30s participated in travel excursions, and close to 86 percent participated in amusement hobbies like karaoke bars and watching movies.[21] Such periodicals as *Fortune* and *The Wall Street Journal* have reported:

> [Japan] is one of the great koans of the global marketplace: Thirteen years after the Bubble Economy burst, Japan's jobless rate hovers near an all-time high, stocks languish, and bankruptcies rage, but shoppers

still can't get enough $4,000 handbags and $1,500 shoes. The European fashion industry is counting on shoppers in the industrial world's sickest economy to keep afloat.[22]

Splurging on luxury handbags gives many consumers the illusion of wealth and helps them forget anxiety over jobs and the future, at least temporarily.[23]

Some of the beneficiaries of the growing singles market are fast-food restaurants, coffee shops, and entertainment companies. McDonald's, for instance, has opened 1,000 outlets in Japan, while Disney has admitted over 100 million people.[24] Starbucks has opened 500 coffee shops, while Tally's coffee sales have tripled.[25]

Another beneficiary of the singles market is upscale specialty retailers. US-based Tiffany has opened 28 boutiques in various locations in Japan, and Greece-based jewelry maker Follie-Follie has 62 outlets.

A third beneficiary of the singles market is high-quality clothing discount retailers, such as Fast Retailing Co., Ltd., developer of the clothing brand Uniqlo, a casual product line for consumers of all ages modeled after similar products developed by American retailer Gap, Inc.[26] In 2000, Fast Retailing's sales approached 230 billion yen ($2 billion), double the sales of the previous year, while profits approached 60 billion yen ($522 million), four times those of the previous year. Another discount retailer is Ryohin Keikaku Co., Ltd., which markets household goods under the brand name Mujirushi Ryohin.[27] One of the company's innovations is the breaking of a Japanese taboo—marketing designer shirts without plastic packaging and selling them at a discount. In 2000, the company's sales reached 105 billion yen ($913 million). A third discount retailer is Zoff, a retailer of discount fashion glasses with boutique-style stores in the busiest districts of Tokyo, Harajuku, Shibuya, and Ikebukuro.[28]

The Graying Yen: An Emerging Market

Since seniors command half of the country's wealth, the aging population is expected to give a big boost to "gray yen" spending. In 1998, they spent $220 billion on consumer goods and another $100 billion on medical care, and are expected to spend around $700 billion in 2025.[29] Elderly consumption expenditure in 2003 was 83 and 102 percent of the consumption of young couples, among the highest in OECD countries.[30]

In many respects, Japan's graying market is similar to those of other developed countries. Elderly consumers perceive old age as "a time to retire and devote one's life to hobbies," such as gardening, traveling, and fitness. According to a 1998 Management and Coordination Agency survey, 30 percent of people aged 50–73 want to live a "fuller" life, enjoying traveling and attending shows. In other respects, Japan's elderly are trendsetters, that is, they reach for new, innovative products, setting up new trends.

Acknowledging the importance of the graying yen, Japanese companies are already cashing in on the emerging market with innovative products that allow seniors to live independent and busy lives. In *The Los Angeles Times,* Evelyn Iritani noted:

> One thing Japanese companies have learned: Senior citizens want products that allow them to continue active lifestyles. As in the United States, improvements in diet and medical care mean seniors are living more independent, busy lives. They don't want to be labeled old or treated with kid gloves.[31]

Matsushita Electric, for instance, has developed "nursing care support systems," which monitor seniors' living conditions and assist them with daily routines. The Kanagawa Institute has developed the Power Assist Suit, which allows caregivers to take better care of bedridden patients.[32] NTT's DoCoMo has developed the Easy Phone, which is simply a phone that's easy to use. Iritani added:

> And whether they are selling cars, household appliances or bathroom fixtures, Japanese companies are taking the lead in developing products and services aimed at older consumers, often by embracing universal design, a concept developed in the United States a decade ago.[33]

One of the beneficiaries of the graying population is the financial service industry, particularly companies selling financial products suitable for people near or at retirement, such as fixed-income securities and annuities. In the second half of 2003, for instance, US-based Hartford Life Insurance sold $4.89 billion worth of variable annuities (a 66 percent increase over the previous year), Europe-based ING sold $2.10 billion worth of variable annuities (a 46 percent increase), while Alico Life sold $1.37 billion (a 16 percent increase).[34]

Another beneficiary is the medical products and pharmaceuticals industries. For the period 1989–1999, the number of medical care establishments increased from around 53,000 to around 68,000, while the number of establishments engaged in social insurance and social welfare activities increased from 24,000 to 37,000.[35] The market for assistive devices has increased from 7,731 devices in 1993 to 11,389 in 2000.[36] As of the early 2000s, US medical device makers held 25 percent of the country's $20 billion medical equipment market. In the pacemaker segment, Medtronic, Inc. holds a 30 percent share, while Baxter International holds a 90 percent market share in the home care market.[37] Related to this market is the nursing home business. The number of nursing homes reached 7,582 (464,000 residents) in 2001, twice as many as in 1990.[38]

In short, Japan's New Economy is dominated by smaller and older households, inhabited by consumers looking for products that allow them to find their identity and assert their individuality. They spend more on services, shop around for value, and pay more often with plastic than cash. This is especially true of the nation's singles and seniors that offer most of the opportunities for world businesses.

Endnotes

1. Andruss, "Japanese Market Ad Research," 3, 6.

2. Moore and Smith, "Taking Global Brands to Japan."

3. MITI, *Survey on the Internationalization of Enterprises (in the Distribution Industry).*

4. JETRO, "White Paper."

5. Fujiwara, "Consumer Pioneers."

6. Osami, "Trend Toward Choosiness."

7. Japanese Ministry of Finance, "Trade Statistics of Japan."

8. JETRO, *White Paper.*

9. Ministry of Health, Labor, and Welfare, *1985 Population Census,* 40.

10. Ibid., 50.

11. JETRO, "Young People More Active."

12. OECD in Figures; OECD, Paris, 2004 edition.

13. Ibid.

14. Ibid.

15. Pollack, "Myths Aside, Japanese Do Look for Bargains."

16. Bremner and Tashiro, "Is Japan Back?," 26–31.

17. Fujiwara, "Consumer Pioneers," 28.

18. MITI, "Adjustment of Consumer Agreements for Installment Sales."

19. Management and Coordination Agency, *2002 Census of Japanese Establishments.*

20. JETRO, *Japanese Market Report.*

21. Japan   "Summary results of the 2001 Survey on Tim

22. Kar

23. M   x," B1, B4.

24. M   port.

25. S   rt.

26. Takes   in sight for Fast Retailing," *The Nikkei Weekly,* July 14,

27. Kawasaki, "Bottom in Sight for Retailing," 18.

28. Ibid.

29. Kim, J. M., "How to Strike Gold from Asia's Old," 32.

30. "Japan's New Trendsetters: Elderly People Show the Way," http://jin.jic. or.jp/trends00bonbun/tj990706.html, 7/25/04.

31. Iritani, "In Japan—Elderly, Restless and Ready to Buy," C1.

32. Lytle, "Life Online: A Yen for a Hi-tech Life."

33. Iritani, "In Japan—Elderly, Restless and Ready to Buy," C1.

34. Singer, "Japanese Jackpot: How Annuities Caught On," C1.

35. Japanese Statistics Bureau, "1999 Survey on Service Industries."

36. JETRO, *Japanese Market Report.*

37. Pacific Bridge Inc., http://www.pacificbridgemedical.com.

38. Ibid.

CHAPTER 9

FOREIGN AFFILIATES IN JAPAN

- Coca-Cola entered into the Japanese market, together with the troops, as a supplier of the US army.

- Motorola forced its way in with pressure from Washington, DC.

- McDonald's joined in with the help of the shrewd entrepreneur, Den Fujita, while Denmark-based Bodum Group entered the Japanese market by tapping Osamu Taniguchi, a former Sony executive.

- McDonald's and KFC capitalized on the fast foodization trend. Tamotsu Aoki explained: "McDonald's and KFC entered as foreign companies. They did not initially target the mass market, and their entrance to the scene coincided with a trend toward the fast-foodization of Japanese eating practices."[1]

- Seven-Eleven's parent Southland Corporation entered a franchise agreement with Japanese retailer Ito-Yokado.

- German personal-care products maker Wella courted mid-level wholesalers.

- AT&T, Vodafone, and British Telecom entered the market through a joint venture with Japan Telecom Company, and P&G entered into a joint venture with Hitachi Corporation.

- Applied Materials began with a sales agreement with Kanematsu Corporation, which they eventually acquired.

- The Disney Company built a popular theme park that neither kids nor adults could resist visiting.

- Microsoft, Compaq Computer, and Apple Computer made products that were too good to be kept out of the market.

These examples highlight some of the factors that have contributed to the success of "early movers" into the Japanese market: mode of entry, brand name recognition, strategic alliances, and a willingness to adapt to the local market conditions. And as these quotes indicate, leaders of world business recognized that success would require a deeper understanding of these factors:

> . . . good American companies are very successful in Japan. . . . [They] come understanding that Japan is the world's second largest market and very lucrative. I would go to talk to the IBMs, the McDonalds, the Proctor and Gambles, the Max Factors, and the American Family Life Insurances—somebody that's in your field—and find out why they're so successful.[2]

Foreign businesses may be missing important information about how to market goods and services successfully in Japan. Specifically, foreign firms need to understand better what product strategies work in Japan. The evidence suggests that companies that understand Japan's social-cultural underpinnings are more successful at selling their products.[3]

The five sections of this chapter provide a more detailed discussion of foreign affiliates in Japan. The first four sections review the modes of entry, industry presence, performance, and competitive strategies of foreign affiliates already established in the Japanese market, while the fifth section reviews the experience of four specific companies: AFLAC Japan, Digital Equipment Corporation Japan, Pfizer Japan, and Jardine Flemming.

Modes of Entry

Though easier than two decades ago, entry to the Japanese market continues to be a tricky and expensive venture. Foreign companies seeking to establish or expand their presence in Japan continue to face demanding customers and partners and high start-up costs. Company start-up costs in Japan ranked second only to those of the UK, while setting up and maintaining an office in Tokyo costs almost twice as much as those of her industrial counterparts (see Exhibit 9.1).[4]

To overcome these constraints, some companies license their products, while others form joint ventures with local companies, acquire stakes in domestic companies, or set up wholly owned subsidiaries. Each mode of entry has advantages and disadvantages (see Exhibit 9.2).[5]

A licensing/franchising arrangement assumes a low resource commitment, but a high risk of copyright/patent infringement. Texas Instruments,

Exhibit 9.1   Start-up Costs in Major Industrial Countries in 2000

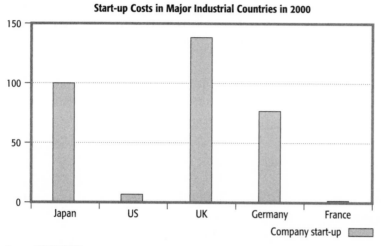

Start-up Costs in Major Industrial Countries in 2000

Source: JETRO 6/2000

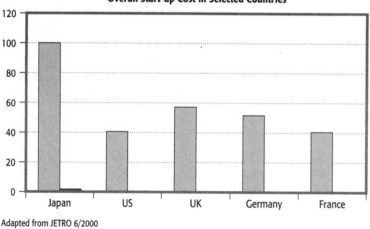

Overall Start-up Cost in Selected Countries

Adapted from JETRO 6/2000

for instance, chose to enter the Japanese market through licensing, only to find itself in a long legal battle for the infringement of its patents by Japanese competitors.★[6]

★ Licensing may further inhibit a company's future expansion. Dunhill is a case in point. The company's licensing of its products made it difficult for the company to address the growing market of single females.

Exhibit 9.2   Advantages and Disadvantages of Different Entry Strategies

	Parameters		
Entry Strategies	**Corporate Control**	**Degree of Commitment**	**Copyright/Patent Infringement Risk**
Licensing/Franchising	Low	Low	High
Joint Ventures/Alliances	Moderate	Moderate	Moderate
Wholly Owned Subsidiary	High	High	Low
Mergers and Acquisitions	High	High	Low

A joint venture or a strategic alliance that assumes a larger commitment offers better control and a lower risk of dissemination (see Exhibit 9.2). Procter and Gamble, for instance, entered the Japanese market in a joint venture with local partners, most notably Itochu Corporation. McDonald's, IBM, Apple Computer, and AT&T have also formed various joint ventures with Japanese corporations. American semiconductor maker Axcelis Technologies entered the Japanese market in a 50/50 partnership with Sumitomo Heavy Industries, which offered manufacturing and service support. American electronics distributor Arrow Electronics developed a joint venture with Tokyo electronic parts distributor Marubun Corporation. In 2001, pharmaceutical giant Roche Haas set up a 50.1 percent joint venture with Chugai Pharmaceutical Co., Ltd.

For the most part, joint ventures have been successful. In 2002, Axcelis Technologies/Sumitomo Heavy Industries commanded a solid 55 percent of the local ion market. The Roche Haas/Chugai Pharmaceuticals partnership gave the Roche Group the fifth position in the domestic pharmaceutical market and access to new products.[7]

Yet some joint ventures have turned sour, like the partnership between Borden Corporation and Meiji Milk Products Company. Under the agreement, signed in the 1970s, the Japanese partner agreed to produce and distribute Lady Borden ice cream, Borden margarine, and other Borden dairy products in the Japanese market. The relationship was working well until 1990, when import liberalization of dairy products created a serious friction between the two partners. Borden requested Meiji Milk Production Co. to distribute imported milk products made with less expensive milk, but Meiji rejected the idea because it would have meant severing its traditional ties with major domestic milk producers. As a result, the partnership was terminated and Borden had to start searching for a new partner all over again.[8]

Mergers and acquisitions require an even larger commitment between the two parties because they must overcome a number of regulatory hurdles, especially in sectors dominated by a few large companies. Mergers and acquisitions further require the blending of corporate cultures, a difficult task when the merging companies have been established in different countries. Mergers and acquisitions have been the favorable form of entry in the pharmaceutical sector, however, giving foreign companies instant access to Japan's complex approval and distribution system.[9]

A wholly owned subsidiary is, perhaps, the only way to bypass both the problems associated with product licensing and joint ventures. In exchange for a high commitment, foreign companies can have both good control of their investment and a low risk of dissemination (see Exhibit 9.2). As it turns out, a wholly owned subsidiary is the most common form of entry into the Japanese market. According to a 1999 METI survey, 68.8 percent of foreign companies doing business in Japan have established wholly owned subsidiaries, 28.6 percent have established joint partnerships, and 9.5 percent through mergers and acquisitions.[10]

The degree of foreign participation in joint ventures in Japan appears to be highly correlated with the size of the company, the nature of the product, and the length of presence in the Japanese market. Large pharmaceutical companies, including Pfizer, Ecolab, and American Home Products, all of which have been in the Japanese market since the '50s, have chosen wholly owned subsidiaries. Companies in knowledge-intensive industries like software have also chosen wholly owned subsidiaries. Smaller companies with a shorter history in the Japanese market, on the other hand, have typically chosen joint ventures (see Exhibit 9.3).[11]

In brief, foreign companies enter the Japanese market in a number of different ways: licensing, joint ventures, acquisitions of domestic companies, and wholly owned subsidiaries. Each mode of entry has its own advantages and disadvantages, and they are not mutually exclusive. Companies that want a gradual expansion should start with a licensing agreement and proceed with a joint venture or a wholly owned subsidiary. Companies that want a quick expansion should start with a domestic acquisition or with a wholly owned subsidiary, especially in industries involving patents like computers, pharmaceuticals, and chemicals.

Exhibit 9.3   Entry Mode of Selected Foreign Subsidiaries

Company	Industry	Ratio of Foreign Ownership (%)
Foseco Minsep, PLC	Chemicals	92.0
Foseco Minsep, PLC	Metals	34.0
Societe Nat. ElfAq.	Chemicals	40.0
L'Air Liquide S.A.	Chemicals	66.9
Rhone-Poulec Films	Chemicals	50.0
Legris K.K.	Metals	100.0
BASF AG	Chemicals	50.0
Henkel	Chemicals	50.0
Bayer AG	Chemicals	75.0
SMW Schneider and W	Metals	55.0
Samson AG	Machinery	49.0
Delbray Holding B.R.	Food	80.0
Kraft, Inc.	Food	100.0
Hesta AG	Machinery	50.0
Maersk Line A/S	Machinery	75.0
Sulzer Brothers Ltd.	Machinery	49.0
Ifo Sanitar AB	Ceramics	50.0
Sandivik AB	Metals	100.0
Warner-Lambert Co.	Pharmaceutical	50.0
Vista International	Food	62.5
Permawick Co., Ltd.	Chemicals	50.0
The Lubrizol Corp.	Chemicals	100.0
W.R. Grace and Co.	Chemicals	50.0
Rogers Corp.	Chemicals	50.0
Pfizer Inc.	Pharmaceutical	100.0
Merck and Co.	Pharmaceutical	51.6
Bristol-Meyers Co.	Pharmaceutical	100.0
Ecolab, Inc.	Pharmaceutical	100.0
American Home Products	Pharmaceutical	100.0
Dow Chemical	Chemicals	100.0
Great Lakes Chemical	Chemicals	50.0
Phillips Petroleum	Chemicals	50.0
Rohm and Haas	Chemicals	47.5
Grace and Co.	Plastics	51.0
Norton Co.	Ceramics	100.0
Sococo Product Co.	Paper and Pulp	45.0
Alcan Aluminum	Metals	51.0
Allied Signal	Machinery	49.0

Exhibit 9.3   (Continued)

Company	Industry	Ratio of Foreign Ownership (%)
The Steelastic Co.	Machinery	50.0
Cross and Tucker	Machinery	50.0
Eaton Corp.	Machinery	50.0
TRW Inc.	Wholesale	100
Kirkwood Industries	Wholesale	42.5
B.M.X. Products	Wholesale	100.0
Holme Ringer Co.	Shipping	100.0
Tairen Enterprise	Metals	49.0
Nedwoold Holdings	Communication	50.0
J.D. Edwards Japan K.K.	Software	100.0
PeopleSoft Japan K.K.	Software	100.0
Siebel Japan K.K.	Software	100.0
SAP Japan Co., Ltd.	Software	100.0
Manugistics Japan, K.K.	Software	100.0

Source: Statistics Office; Aichi Prefecture Administration, Nagoya, Japan (translated from Japanese); and JETRO industry surveys.

Industry Presence

Foreign companies are present in almost every sector of the Japanese economy, in particular manufacturing, real estate, commerce, finance and insurance. According to the 34th Annual Survey of Foreign-Affiliated Companies in Japan, there were 1,639 foreign affiliates: 33.0 percent in manufacturing and 67.0 percent in nonmanufacturing activities, 43.3 percent in wholesaling, 14.3 percent in services, 6.5 percent in chemicals, 6.3 percent in electric machinery, and close to 4 percent in general machinery (see Exhibit 9.4). The Kanto province was the most popular location for foreign affiliates, followed by Kinki and Chibu provinces.[12]

Performance

Expansion into the Japanese market has been very rewarding for foreign affiliates and their parent companies. In most of the sectors included in METI's 34th annual survey, foreign-affiliate productivity exceeded those of their domestic counterparts. The productivity gap was particularly large in the manufacturing sector: 13.49 percent versus 7 percent (see Exhibit 9.5).[13]

Exhibit 9.4   Distribution of Foreign Capital Companies by Industry in FY2000

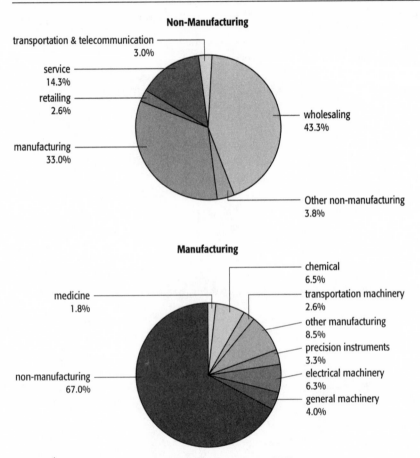

Source: 34th Survey of Trends among Foreign-Capitalized Firms, July 2001 (METI)

For the period 1996–2000, the ordinary income of foreign affiliates ranged between 4.8 and 3.7 percent, while the ordinary income of their domestic counterparts ranged between 2.5 and 1.5 percent (see Exhibit 9.6).[14]

In brief, foreign affiliates are present in almost every Japanese industry, most notably in service, and they enjoy high productivity and profit margins.

Competitive Strategy

Foreign affiliates in Japan have pursued a host of strategies. Some have deployed "unique marketing methods," while others have "catered to local community tastes" and introduced "superb products and advertising" (see

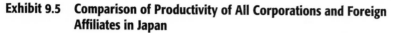

Exhibit 9.5   Comparison of Productivity of All Corporations and Foreign Affiliates in Japan

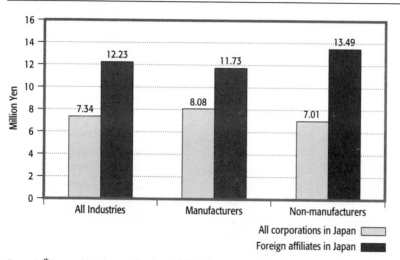

Source: 34th Survey of Trends among Foreign-Capitalized Firms, July 2001 (METI)

Exhibit 9.6   Trends in Ordinary Income to Net Sales Ratios

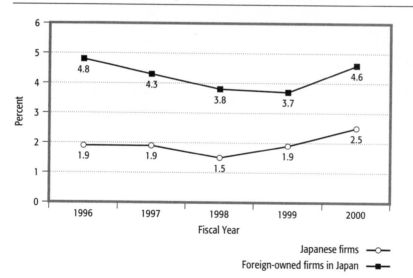

Source: 31st Survey of Trends among Foreign-Capitalized Firms, July 2001 (METI)

Exhibit 9.7).[15] Though diverse at the outset, most of the competitive, successful foreign affiliates have adopted a common three-step strategy. They have:

1. Adapted to the Japanese business practice and consumer preferences. To offer some examples, Avon, a cosmetics company, provided products

Exhibit 9.7   Foreign-Affiliate Companies: Competitive Strategies

Company	Years in Japan	Business	Strategy
GE	Early 1900s	Power generation equipment	Brand recognition; Joint ventures
Pfizer	1953	Pharmaceuticals	Set up local R&D center; Successful lobbying of Japanese regulators
Amway	1979	Detergents/Cosmetics	Unique marketing method
Avon	1983	Cosmetics	Cater to local community tastes
Baxter International	1985	Hospital supplies	Dominate growing market
BMW Japan	1979	Automobiles	Quality management; Image
Braun Japan	1962	Electric razors	Superb products and clever advertising
Castrol	1976	Automotive lubricants	Offering what market really wanted
Corning Japan	1966	Glass works	Step by step building the business
Donnelly Corporation	1986	Car mirrors	Utilizing Japan as foothold to Asia
Givaudan	1970	Fragrance/Flavors	Proposing new ideas to consumers
Japan Vilene	1960	Textiles	Emphasis on new technology
Johnson & Johnson	1980	Medical/Health supplies	Successful recruitment of local labor
Max Factor	1953	Cosmetics	A pioneer in the Japanese cosmetic industry
Monsanto	1980	Agricultural/Chemicals	Product excellence and superior marketing
Nippon Goodyear	1952	Auto tires	Brand name recognition
Nippon Lever		Consumer products	Shrewd marketing
Nippon Sherwood Industries	1970	Medical supplies	R&D pays off
Parfums Givenchy	1988	Cosmetics	A newcomer with a unique strategy
Procter and Gamble		Consumer products	R&D to overcome tough competition
Sandoz Pharmaceuticals	1973	Pharmaceuticals	Good communication with home office
Smithkline Beecham	1987	Medical	Understanding the distribution system
Apple Computer	1986	Computers	Adapting to the Japanese market
Bodum Group	1998	Coffee makers	Innovative distribution

suitable to the local needs and tastes. The German automaker, BMW, emphasized product quality and corporate image. The electric razors company, Braun, introduced "superb products," and Johnson & Johnson successfully relied on the recruitment of local labor (see Exhibit 9.7).[16]

2. Developed new products and services for the Japanese market. Cosmetics corporation Max Factor's strategy included the introduction of several new products for the Japanese market. Fragrance and flavors corporation Givaudan's relied on new products and new ideas as a vehicle for success in the Japanese market. Consumer giant Procter and Gamble has been spending heavily on R&D to introduce new products (see Exhibit 9.7).

3. Promoted products aggressively. For example, Monsanto, America's chemical giant, emphasized "product excellence and superior marketing," Nippon Lever emphasized "shrewd marketing," Braun Japan emphasized "clever advertising," while Givaudan "proposed new ideas to Japanese consumers" (see Exhibit 9.7).

In brief, foreign presence is evident in every sector of the Japanese economy, especially in manufacturing, and has been very rewarding. Profit margins of foreign affiliates surpassed those of domestic corporations. Adapting to the conditions of the local market, developing new products, and promoting them aggressively is the three-fold strategy that accounts for the success of foreign affiliates in the Japanese market, as the experience of four companies—AFLAC Japan, Digital Equipment Corporation Japan, Pfizer Japan, and Jardine Flemming—confirm.

Early Movers: Four Case Studies

The following case studies regarding AFLAC Japan, Digital Equipment Corporation Japan, Pfizer Japan, and Jardine Flemming provide insights into the barriers and problems these companies faced when starting up foreign affiliates, and reveal how they developed strategies for overcoming these obstacles to achieve success. Chosen from the four controversial industries—insurance, electronics, pharmaceuticals, and finance—the experience of all four corporations offer valuable lessons for latecomers to the Japanese market.

AFLAC Japan

For years, Japan's highly regulated insurance market—one of the largest in the world—was off limits for foreign companies, especially the smaller ones.

Exhibit 9.8   AFLAC Japan Sales Results

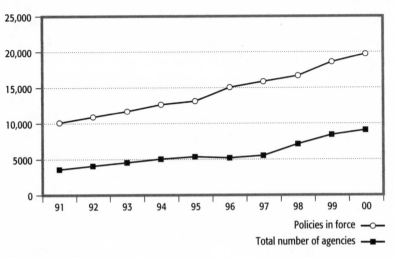

Source: Corporate Reports

In the late 1990s and the early 2000s, however, this changed. Many of the industry's regulations were lifted, paving the way for foreign insurers to enter the Japanese market. As of 2003, 25 foreign insurance firms had entered the Japanese market, and their market share increased from less than 4 percent in 1997 to 16.3 percent in 2002.[17]

One of the smaller foreign insurers benefiting from the opening of Japan's insurance industry was AFLAC. Established in 1974, AFLAC Japan is currently the largest foreign insurance provider in Japan, and the second most profitable company behind IBM and Coca-Cola. In 2000, the company had 20,000 policies in effect, handled by 9,000 agents (see Exhibit 9.8); new annualized premium sales were up 14.5 percent to 99.8 billion yen, compared with 87 billion yen in 1999, while premium income rose 7.1 to 720.8 billion, compared with 673 billion in 1999; net investment income grew 7.4 percent to 135.7 billion, compared with 126.3 billion in 1999; total revenues were 857.2 billion, up from 799.8 billion in 1999; pretax operating earnings increased 12.3 percent to 82.9 billion compared with 73.8 billion in 1999.[18] How did AFLAC manage to crack the world's largest and most heavily regulated insurance industry?

Competitive strategy

AFLAC Japan's success in the Japanese market can be attributed to a five-step strategy:

1. *Early entry.* As was the case with other successful foreign companies, AFLAC entered the Japanese market in 1974, a time when the Japanese insurance market was highly regulated. AFLAC Japan managed to obtain a license to underwrite supplemental medical insurance policies that reimbursed out-of-pocket expenses for cancer treatment.

2. *Focus on a market niche.* AFLAC Japan focused its strategy on a market niche largely ignored by domestic carriers: supplemental cancer insurance. Over time, favorable demographics and strategic agreements turned AFLAC Japan's market niche into a mass market, especially in the late 1990s when Japan's insurance market was deregulated.

3. *Innovative sales methods.* AFLAC Japan was among the first insurance companies to introduce the "insurance ladies," that is, they recruited women to sell insurance door-to-door, a program modeled after Avon's "cosmetics ladies." This method is suitable for selling personalized products and services in networked societies like Japan. AFLAC Japan was also one of the first companies to take advantage of a 1996 law that allowed insurance companies to sell policies online and by mail.

4. *Strategic alliances.* AFLAC Japan has forged a number of strategic alliances with domestic insurers, including the second largest insurer, Daichi Mutual Insurance, to operate medical and nursing services in the country.

5. *The introduction of new products.* In 2002, AFLAC Japan introduced a host of whole-life insurance products to supplement its cancer insurance products.

In short, through early entry, innovative sales methods, and successful strategic alliances, AFLAC Japan turned a market niche into a mass market and became one of the most successful companies in Japan.

Digital Equipment Corporation Japan

Digital Equipment Corporation of Japan is a wholly owned subsidiary of Digital Equipment Corporation (DEC), a major hardware/software computer maker (later acquired by Compaq Computer, part of Hewlett Packard). DEC Japan was established in 1982, 14 years after DEC established a local branch office in 1968.

DEC's entry into the Japanese market was a bumpy one. Tariff and nontariff barriers, administrative problems, and labor problems haunted her early attempts to get a foothold in the market. Patience and commitment finally paid off, however. After a sluggish performance in the '60s and '70s, DEC Japan turned in a startling performance in the '80s. Between 1980 and 1990, sales rose 25 percent annually, from 88 million yen in 1980 to 128.8 billion yen in 1990. In 1991, the company had 4,000 employees and 40 offices throughout Japan.[19]

Tariffs and quotas

When DEC first entered the Japanese market in 1968, tariff and nontariff barriers were still in place. Every single computer had to be scrutinized by MITI. In recent years, however, both tariffs and nontariff barriers have been cleared, tariffs are negligible, product certification has been simplified, and METI's attitudes have changed, giving DEC Japan better access to the Japanese market.

Customs procedures, patents, and licenses

Due to a lengthy patenting process, patent and licensing infringement have always been a problem for high-technology products in Japan. The company complained that patenting computer products was a lengthy process. It generally took four to five years for an approval, which opened the door to the risk of infringement by major Japanese competitors. When the company applied for a patent on a 70-bit mini-computer, for instance, Hitachi came out with a similar model, inviting protests by the company. In March 2001, the Japanese government introduced legislation that eased up on custom procedures, patents, and licenses.

Distribution system

DEC Japan's current distribution system consists of three channels: a trading company, sales to original equipment manufacturers, and direct sales. As the electronics industry was dominated by *keiretsu* groups, selling to original equipment manufacturers has always been a problem for DEC Japan. But as the company officers are quick to explain, breaking through *keiretsu* relations is not a problem just for foreign companies but for Japanese companies, too. Hitachi, for instance, cannot sell to Mitsubishi affiliates. Nevertheless, in an attempt to cope with the problem, the company has developed ties with Japanese affiliates, like the one with Toshiba made in 1990 regarding laptop computers.

Competitive strategy

As is the case with most foreign affiliates, DEC Japan's competitive strategy is based on three elements—adapt to local conditions, develop new products, and promote them aggressively:

1. *Adaptation to the local market conditions.* DEC Japan's adjustment to the Japanese market was marked by two significant developments in the early 1980s. In 1982, DEC Japan introduced a terminal capable of handling Kan-ji (Chinese characters), making it easier to program in the Japanese language.

   Then, in 1984, Edmund Reilly arrived in Japan as the fifth branch manager. Reilly quickly realized that Japanese companies would not buy foreign high-tech products without after-sales support: "Even in a completely open environment, many Japanese would be reluctant to buy American because they are used to a different level of support. They expect more systems integration and they expect solutions."[20] To provide these services, Reilly emphasized the recruitment and development of qualified domestic labor, especially the recruitment of college graduates, and adapted to the Japanese employment system of lifetime employment, seniority wages, and decision by consensus.

2. *New product development.* With 10 percent of sales spent on R&D and with research facilities in Japan, DEC Japan can be considered an aggressive product developer. In the 1990 fiscal year alone, DEC Japan introduced several new products, including the VAX9000 system, DEC station 5000 Model 200, VAX6000 System, and VAX 3000 Model 310; connection software products for VAX and Fujitsu large size computers; LAN video teaching material; and transaction processing software products.[21]

3. *Product promotion.* Ever since DEC Japan was established as a local company, management has taken measures to enhance the company's image as a provider of high-quality computer hardware and software products. Industry exhibits, symposia, conferences, seminars, awards, joint ventures with Japanese computer makers, and service support centers are some of the ways DEC Japan enhances its corporate image and increases sales.

New problems

In spite of spectacular sales growth, due to both external and internal constraints, DEC Japan's market share has remained steady at 3 percent of the industry. External constraints include *keiretsu* relations—an institution particularly present in the electronics industry—and the government's procurement system. DEC Japan has unsuccessfully bid for government contracts. One of the problems appears to be the "one yen" bidding practice employed by DEC Japan's competitors: Japanese computer makers, such as Fujitsu and NEC, often offer to sell hardware to the government at an extremely low price, hence the term "one yen," a door-opening policy that allows the bidder to sell other products and services to the government at a profit.

Internal constraints include her parent company's tight control and shortsighted view of the Japanese market. Profits realized by DEC Japan are returned to the parent company instead of being reinvested in the human and nonhuman resources of DEC Japan, a problem common to almost every foreign company doing business in Japan.

Despite these ongoing obstacles to growth, DEC Japan's willingness to adapt to the local conditions, new product development, and aggressive promotion turned the company into one of the early success stories of world business in the Japanese market.

Pfizer Japan

With 127 million people and the longest life expectancy among developed nations, Japan is the world's third largest market for medicines in the world. Tapping into this market has not been easy for foreign medicine makers, however, because of tariffs and quotas; custom procedures, patents, and licensing requirements; and distribution and advertising constraints. In recent years, most of these barriers of entry have been eliminated, putting this market sector more in line with other developed economies.

Tariffs and quotas

Prior to 2001, medicine imports to Japan were subject to an 18.6 percent tax, placing them at a competitive disadvantage against their domestic counterparts. After 2001, however, the tax fell to 5 percent.[22] This has helped Pfizer expand its presence in the Japanese market, achieving the number one position by 2003.

Customs procedures, patents, and licenses

Until 1998, the Japanese government believed that the Japanese body was different from the western body; therefore, they required western medicines to be re-tested in Japan. This requirement imposed enormous costs and delays to foreign companies bringing medicines to Japan. Since 1998, however, the Japanese government has allowed foreign test results to be submitted as supportive evidence for new drug approval applications. Documentation of minor product modification and sourcing, as well as customs clearance for drug products, were also simplified. Further, drug price listings and tariff calculations became transparent.[23] These changes have shorten the approval time for foreign drugs from 18 months to 12 months and helped Pfizer receive quick approval for a number of its medicines, including Viagra, Genotropin and Vfend.

Distribution system

Though free of *keiretsu* relations, Japan's pharmaceutical distribution system is quite complex, even more complex than the US system. Drugs must flow through three distribution layers before reaching the end consumer/user: first-tier wholesalers, second-tier wholesalers, and then a third tier that includes retailers, medical institutions, and hospitals. Reflecting the complexity and multiplicity of the Japanese distribution system, distribution costs are 14 to 16 percent higher in Japan than in the US.[24] This changed in October 1, 2000, making it less costly for foreign pharmaceutical companies to distribute their products in Japan.

Advertising

Some illnesses, such as psychological disorders, are taboo, so the Japanese government's medical system will not pay for medications that treat them. The government also banned advertisements that increased patient awareness of such diseases, as well as patient solicitation for clinical trials, which made it difficult for foreign companies like Pfizer to advertise its products. To overcome this barrier, Pfizer Japan partnered with the Japanese community, organizing annual symposia through which they formed partnerships between patients and pharmaceutical firms. The purpose of these partnerships was to lobby the government for the expedient approval and reimbursement of new treatments.

Competitive strategy

As with DEC Japan and AFLAC Japan, Pfizer Japan was immediately established as a Japanese company committed to the Japanese market. This commitment was reflected in the company's decision to build a research center near Tokyo to pursue research in an exciting area of medicine—immunology—making it a valuable addition to other Pfizer research facilities in Canada, France, Mexico, Scotland, and the US. The company has been further organizing workshops to assist government officials in expediting the country's lengthy product review process and in understanding western practices for licensing publicly supported discoveries to the pharmaceutical industry.

In the late 1990s, these efforts paid off, as the government began to accept data from western patient-based trials, and to allow advertisements that promoted patient awareness to certain diseases and patient solicitation for new medicine trials. The company's hot-selling drug, Viagra, was approved in just six months on US data, for example, and they were able to advertise it. Landers noted: "Now western drug companies find it quicker and easier to get their products approved in Japan. American-style drug advertising is a commonplace. (Viagra-maker Pfizer, Inc., for example has run frequent newspaper ads about erectile dysfunction, featuring soccer legend Pele.) Patients are demanding more drug information from doctors and are lobbying the government to speed up approval of pharmaceuticals from abroad."[25]

Reflecting these efforts, Pfizer Japan's position advanced from twentieth in the early 1990s to thirteenth by 1998 to first in 2003. In 2000, with the acquisition of Warner-Lambert, Pfizer Japan became the largest foreign company in Japan. For the period 1996–2000, Pfizer experienced a 60 percent growth in market share, the highest among western companies in the country, reaching 3.5 percent of the overall market.[26] This position was further strengthened with the acquisition of Pharmacia in 2003 and its 1.5 percent share in the Japanese market, turning Pfizer Japan into Japan's second largest prescription-medicine provider.

Ongoing problems

Like any other pharmaceutical company, Pfizer Japan Corporation must apply for product approval for product development and marketing for the local market. Patent approval and patent infringement is still a major obstacle for foreign pharmaceutical companies. Patent approval typically takes four to five years, but in some cases it may take as many as nine years. And while a foreign company waits for drug approval, many Japanese generic drug companies apply for their own patent on the same or similar drug.

Pfizer Japan experienced one such case of patent infringement by a Japanese corporation.[27]

Nevertheless, a long commitment to the Japanese market and a close partnership with the local community allowed Pfizer Japan to overcome the complex medicine approval and advertising process in Japan, and to become the most successful foreign pharmaceutical company in Japan.

Jardine Flemming

Jardine Flemming is a Bermuda-based holding company with offices in London, Canada, the US, Hong Kong, Australia, and New Zealand. Jardine Flemming's Japanese office provides a broad array of financial services, including investment management, corporate finance, underwriting, and banking.

Japan is one of the world's largest securities markets. Attracted by the size of the market and prospects generated by further deregulation, Jardine Flemming established its Tokyo office in 1970. As of 1990, the Tokyo office had about $3.7 billion assets under management, half of which are currently invested in the Tokyo market for Japanese clients. In 1985, in a joint venture with Yasuda Trust and Banking Company Limited, Jardine Flemming became Japan's largest foreign investment advisory firm in Japan, advising corporate clients and managing institutional and individual investment portfolios. Specifically, the company is engaged in four types of business: equities, equity derivatives (options and futures contracts), underwriting, and government bonds.

Competitive strategy

Jardine Flemming's competitive strategy is based on three elements—long-term commitment, quality service, and product development:

1. *Long-term commitment.* Having a thorough knowledge and understanding of the risk and rewards of the Japanese market, Jardine Flemming made a long-term commitment to the Japanese market: "We are under no illusions that it will require considerable tenacity, skill, and stamina to establish ourselves in this sophisticated and competitive market but, as the second largest market of this type after the United States, its potential is clear."[28]

2. *Quality services.* With 12 economists following all major economic and corporate developments of the Japanese economy and with regular

publications of industry developments, Jardine Flemming provides its clients original, quality research and investment recommendations. Jardine Flemming's full membership in the Tokyo Stock Exchange—the only membership among the Asian-based securities houses—is another vehicle for the fast and accurate execution of customers' trades.

3. *Product development.* With regulatory restrictions lifted, Jardine Flemming has been aggressive in product development. In particular, Jardine Flemming has been active in three new product areas: (1) currency options, a hedge for currency exposures; (2) guarantee return accounts; and (3) protection of capital investment.

Ongoing problems

Financial regulation and staffing are the two most important problems for Jardine Flemming. Unlike commodity trade barriers in manufacturing that have been almost completely lifted, service trade barriers, especially regulations in the financial industry, are to a great extent intact. Savings are still controlled by postal thrift outlets and the four major securities houses.

Digital Equipment Corporation of Japan, AFLAC Japan, Pfizer Japan, and Jardine Flemming are four success stories in four diverse industries. Commitment, patience, the willingness to adapt to Japanese business conditions, the development of new products, and aggressive promotion are some of the factors of their success.

As the doors of the Japanese market have opened up and business opportunities have become more visible, many foreign companies have set up or expanded their operations in the Japanese market, with IBM, Coca-Cola, and Shell Oil at the top of the list. Yet, with real estate prices high and difficulties in recruiting local personnel, doing business in Japan is still a tricky and expensive task.

To address this problem, many foreign companies have established partnerships with domestic companies. Partnerships may not always work, however, especially in high-tech sectors that involve patents. That explains why the majority of foreign companies have established wholly owned subsidiaries.

Though the presence of foreign companies is still small compared to the size of the Japanese market, it extends in every industry, especially manufacturing. Overall, foreign affiliates in Japan enjoy high profit margins, higher than those of their Japanese counterparts. Adaptation to local market conditions, new product development, and aggressive product promotion constitute the strategy for success, a strategy that will be detailed in the third part of this book.

Endnotes

1. Aoki, "Aspects of Globalization in Contemporary Japan," 72.
2. "How to Succeed in Japan's Tough But Rewarding Market."
3. Martin, D. and Herbig, P., "Marketing Implications," 172.
4. JETRO, *Japanese Market Report,* 2000.
5. Ibid.
6. Landers, "Good Medicine: Westerners Profit as Japan Opens its Market," A1.
7. Osland, Taylor, and Zou, "Selecting International Modes of Entry and Expansion," 153–161.
8. Ibid.
9. "Foreign Insurers Seek Novel Policies," 13.
10. Japanese Ministry of Finance, "Foreign Direct Investment."
11. Ibid.
12. METI, "34th Annual Survey of Trends."
13. Ibid.
14. Ibid.
15. Ibid.
16. JETRO, *The Challenge of the Japanese Market;* and various corporate reports.
17. JETRO, "A New Era."
18. AFLAC Inc., *2001 Annual Report,* 18.
19. AFLAC Inc., *2000 Annual Report.*
20. Wilder, "Finding a Place in the Rising Sun," 116.
21. Author's own interviews, August 2002.

22. JETRO, "A New Era."

23. Ibid.

24. American Chambers of Commerce in Japan, "2001 US-Japan Business White Paper," 85.

25. Landers, "Good Medicine," A1.

26. IMS HEALTH, "East Meets West: Japan Falling to Multinationals?"

27. Pfizer, *2003 Annual Report*.

28. Jardine Flemming, *Annual Report 1990*, 4.

PART III

STRATEGIES FOR WORLD BUSINESSES

The Japanese market is very competitive. Every year thousands of companies fail; only the fittest survive. Yet, as discussed in the second part of this book, many foreign companies not only survived but prospered in Japan. In every sector, from pharmaceuticals to chemicals to consumer goods, foreign affiliates enjoy brisk sales and high profit margins, a good payoff for the parent companies. What is the secret of their success? It is a three-fold strategy that I call ADP:

- *Adapt* to the Japanese consumer demands, business practices, and rules of competition,
- *Develop* new products and new ideas that cater to the needs and imagination of the consumers of a dynamic market, and
- *Promote* products and services aggressively through traditional and non-traditional marketing and distribution channels.

Part III of this book offers an intensive look at the ADP strategy. The first chapter discusses the peculiarities and specificity of Japanese consumer demands, business practices, and rules of competition that foreign firms must follow. The second chapter explains how Japanese companies design and develop new products through extensive employee participation, cost cutting, and investment in applied research and automation. The third chapter describes the Japanese advertising rules and styles, as well as the traditional and nontraditional channels of distribution.

CHAPTER 10

ADAPT TO THE JAPANESE BUSINESS CONDITIONS

For those wishing to sell to Japan, it is very necessary they make the effort to acquire as much knowledge as possible about the people they will be selling to before they attempt marketing.[1]

Japanese External Trade Organization

"I faxed more than 100 inquires to Japanese businesses last year, and I received only two responses," complained a consultant in a recent round table discussion in Athens, Greece. Does it mean that Japanese businesses were not interested in the list of products the consultant was promoting? Does it mean that Japanese companies were not interested in imports from Europe? Nobody can answer these questions with certainty. But what someone familiar with Japanese business practices can say is that informal and impersonal contacts are neither proper nor sufficient methods of initiating business relations with Japanese companies. Impersonal communication does not show enough promise and commitment to prospective customers and business partners, and therefore it is not worth responding to, at least in Japanese customers' minds. As Brent Bowers put it in *The Wall Street Journal,* to do business in Japan, one must go to Japan: "While numerous business owners wring their hands and wonder how they can possibly break into the Japanese market, some have discovered a neat trick. To sell to Japan, go to Japan."[2]

Succeeding in making a deal requires direct presence and familiarity with local sales, marketing, and management practices, especially with *nemawashi,* and the abundance of "red herrings," or bureaucracies, as numerous business experts have explained:

In order to truly succeed in Japan, a company must have a direct presence. The successful companies in our study invariably had a direct operating subsidiary with its own Japanese management and local sales marketing, manufacturing, and development capability.[3]

. . . the Japanese style of management by consensus means slow decision making and many meetings. Far less business is done by the phone here than in the United States because of the value placed on relationships. Also time-consuming is the process of *nemawashi,* or laying the groundwork, in which one wins approval for a proposal in advance of the meeting at which a proposal will be discussed. That assures the meeting will be free of confrontation, but also a waste of time.[4]

It is about navigating the abundance of red herrings on the information highway, while at the same time being able to map out macro trends, examine how they influence a particular sector, and pray that your timing at the sector level meets more than just your expectations. It has to meet your required returns too. If you are looking for an easy ride in this country, think again.[5]

Adapting to a new business environment is the key to survival and success for every company doing business in a foreign market, especially in a large and complex market like Japan.* To succeed in Japan, foreign companies must adapt to the demands and rules of the Japanese market by: (1) tailoring their products to consumer demands for high quality, informative packaging and labeling, prompt delivery, and after-sale service, and (2) following the Japanese business practices and rules of competition. The two sections of this chapter will address these two issues.

Tailoring Products to Consumer Demands

American and European car sales people are aggressive. They deploy every gimmick to acquire prospective customers, but they do not make home visits; they wouldn't go that far. Japanese salespeople, on the other hand, would visit prospective customers at home, going over car prospectuses in an effort to convince them to buy from their company. If the prospects end up buying a car from them, they will be grateful and try to keep them happy until the next purchase. Even if they don't make a sale, the salespeople will still try to nurture long-term relationships, hoping that the customers will buy from them next time.

In some respects Japanese consumers are similar to consumers of any other country. They strive to make ends meet. They are after value, good

---

* Succeeding in the Japanese market further requires the right preparation. Before introducing its dish detergent in the Japanese market, P&G, for instance, conducted a study that found that domestic products displayed little concentration. P&G came up with a highly concentrated liquid that enjoyed a smashing success. Wal-Mart studied the Japanese market for many years before making its entry. The company management, for instance, concluded that the best way to enter the market was through a joint venture with domestic retailer familiar with the peculiarities and specifics of the domestic market.

quality products at low prices, especially in the harsh times of economic downturns. Yet, in other respects, Japanese consumers are different. They have their own preferences, lifestyles, income, and spending patterns. They are obsessed with order and detail, and have a strong preference for quality products packaged with care and elegance and delivered punctually with due diligence. Additionally, Japanese consumers plan the purchase of major items well ahead of time, often spending heavily on gifts in December and July when bonuses are paid.

In open, developed economies characterized by market saturation, product quality and brand recognition are not enough to entice customers, however. This is especially the case for Japan's market, where many companies have failed to entice consumers even with brand name products. As Scalise, in "Patience holds the Key . . . ," in *Asian Chemical News,* explained: "Not all brand names do well in Japan, any more than foreign companies that decide to invest in Japan suddenly hit pay dirt. But as the successful companies have learned, doing business in Japan is not the same as doing business in Asia. It's a developed, not a developing, country with its own prospects, pride and problems, not to mention highly developed preferences."[6] Novelty and distinction found in customized domestic and imported products are therefore also essential.

Product Quality

In a society where order, detail, and perfection are a way of life, commodities are always scrutinized before being purchased. In department stores, consumers check clothes for any lose thread or little defect. In supermarkets, consumers check product labeling, packaging, and content carefully. An unclear label or unfamiliar contents are reasons to reject or even return a product. Laundry detergents of uneven crystals and canned peaches of uneven shape or size are often returned to stores.

Packaging and Labeling

Packaging has always been the "silent salesman," a representation of the product's and producer's image that attracts the customer. Whether buying or selling products, giving or receiving gifts, or making or receiving payments, packaging and labeling are more than a matter of convenience or aesthetic pleasure. They convey a message from the giver to the receiver, or from the seller to the buyer, and it is deeply rooted in the Japanese tradition, as this quote from the Japanese External Trade Organization reveals:

> Since ancient times, containers and the writing on them have been highly valued in Japan. Natural products such as wood and paper are traditional wrapping materials that continue to be popular today. In Japan, when a fee or a charge is passed from one person to another, the money is almost always wrapped first. To simply hand someone un-wrapped cash is considered to be in poor taste. . . . While serving the functions of protection, handling and convenience, packaging is also the silent salesman or the "face" of the product. Packages help to sell, which accounts for the huge time and effort that goes into its creation and the cacophony of color that fills the average supermarket aisle.[7]

Much more so than westerners, Japanese consumers view wrapping and packaging as an integral part of the product, as Martin and Herbig have documented:

> The typical Japanese consumer will refuse to accept a product that is not well wrapped. The Japanese consumer typically views packaging as much more valuable in and of itself and not in the instrumental manner of a westerner. The beauty of a product lies not only in the functional aspects but also in the appearance, size, and the like. Prod-ucts have an intrinsic value and thus should be enjoyed in their own right.[8]

Effective and protective packaging is of particular importance for food products exposed to severe humidity in the summer months. Biscuit and cracker makers, for instance, wrap each item separately before packing them in a box. Campbell Soup, asked Sud-Chemie Performance Packaging to de-velop Container Dry II humidity and moisture control bags to keep mois-ture out of products for 60 days.

Effective packaging must be supplemented by clear labeling that spells out in detail the product ingredients, as dictated by a number of rules and regulations. In the liquor industry, for instance, labeling is dictated by three laws: the Liquor Business Association Law, the Food Sanitation Law, and the Measurement Law. Imported wine must include the product name (the phrases "fruit wine" or "sweetened wine"), list of food additives, alcohol content, volume, country of origin, distributor, etc. In the mineral water industry, imported mineral water labeling is also dictated by the Food

Sanitation Law, the Measurement Law, and the JAS Law. Imported mineral water labels must also include the product name, net content, preservation method, list of ingredients, date of minimum durability, and country of origin.[9]

Failure to comply with labeling rules and regulations can result in severe fines and costly product recalls. In 2000, P&G's failure to spell out that its Pringles potato chips were made with unapproved gene-sliced technology, for instance, resulted in the recall of 800,000 units of the product.

Prompt Delivery

After negotiating for several months with Japanese importers, a Greek wine company received a fax on a Friday afternoon requesting several wine containers be delivered to the port of Piraeus early the following Monday morning.

Though isolated, this story demonstrates the importance of punctuality in Japanese business and everyday life. Being on time or early for appointments is a way of showing your respect and appreciation for the other party. Prompt product delivery is a way for sellers to show their respect and appreciation for customers, and the impetus for customers to give the seller future business.

Prompt delivery is of particular importance when it comes to purchases of major products like automobiles and appliances, where customers must be convinced about the availability of components and spare parts, as Martin and Herbig explain:

> The Japanese expect prompt service and a wide choice of items, especially for major purchases. Foreign businesses in Japan must therefore carry a large and complete inventory of replacement parts and provide trained service personnel. This aspect is especially important in the automobile industry, since many Japanese fear that buying a foreign car means they will not be able to get the necessary parts or service.[10]

Prompt delivery must be accompanied by after-sales customer service and product guarantees.

After-Sales Customer Service and Guarantees

As someone put it, "If American customers are kings, Japanese customers are gods," and they are treated as gods. In small neighborhood stores, owners welcome customers at the door with the traditional bowing greeting. In department stores, banks, and corporate offices, young women are assigned the sole task of greeting customers. In restaurants, special banners hung at the entry inform customers that the store is open for business, while the restaurant staff greets patrons with a loud *irishamsu,* or welcome.

Everywhere in Japan customers are treated not as strangers, accidental tourists who just happen to drop by, but as valuable partners in a long lasting relationship that continues with services long after a product is purchased. While western societies see after-sales services as a legal obligation, often taking the form of a written guarantee, Japanese consumers view these services as a natural part or implicit understanding in the ongoing relationship.

This treatment of customers often creates problems for foreign producers of consumer durable products, such as household appliances, who rely on limited guarantees that often expire within a year after the product is sold. To overcome the Japanese stereotype that foreign companies do not match their Japanese counterparts in after-sales support, Dell Computer, for instance, hired hundreds of full-time support staff to monitor its help-desk office, rather than outsourcing this activity.[11] British vacuum cleaner manufacturer, Dyson, switched to offering a two-year instead of one-year guarantee, and has sped up repair time to 72 hours. To provide services comparable to its peers, measuring equipment maker Faro Technologies Inc.'s subsidiary, Faro Japan Inc., located its offices in Nagoya, near the Toyota factory. Peugeot provides drivers with 24-hour roadside services and a courtesy car while the customer waits for repairs.[12]

Novelty and Distinction

With rapid technological achievements, rising incomes, and increasing foreign traveling, Japanese consumers are no longer content with quality products. They search for novel products that bring distinction and social status, often reaching for foreign products, such as designer clothes from the UK and Italy, perfumes from France, and shoes and sneakers from the US.

To sum up, to succeed in the Japanese market, foreign companies must adapt to the demands of the Japanese market, which is not just another market. Japanese consumers have their own preferences and lifestyle. They are obsessed with product quality, packaging, delivery, after-sales service, and pricing. Adapting to these demands is the first step to accessing the Japanese market. To get there, it takes more than that. It takes a commitment to the Japanese business practices and rules of competition.

Following Business Practices and Rules of Competition

For many western managers and entrepreneurs, Japanese business practices and competition sound like a scary legend: Big banks ready to finance ambitious corporate plans that stretch ten twenty, even fifty years into the future; *keiretsu* groups that have forged relationship webs that keep outsiders off the Japanese market; and s*amurai*-style management aligned with labor, ready to fight all the way to the end for market shares.

Business Practices

Understanding the business practices of foreign countries and behaving accordingly is always a difficult exercise, especially if that country is Japan. Formal introductions, long-term relationships, lengthy negotiations, after-hours gatherings in *sushi* and *karaoke* bars, and vague communication can easily turn off westerners looking for quick results.

Formal introductions

In a group-oriented society that values long-term relations, or *aisatsu,* a formal introduction by a group member is, perhaps, the only way for an outsider to develop a relationship with the group. This certainly applies to developing relationships and making deals with business groups. To find a partner, for instance, foreign companies must find either a Japanese contact or another foreign company with Japanese contacts who are willing to make the formal introductions between the two parties. Toys "R" Us, for instance, tapped McDonald's partner, Mr. Fujita, for introducing Japanese partners and for getting around the many regulatory hurdles of the retailing industry. Apple Computer turned to the Sony Corporation for assistance in finding Japanese distributors for its products, while Xerox teamed up with Fuji Corporation. Though formal introductions may open the door to a business group, keeping the door open takes continuous contact to nurture a long-term relationship.[13]

Long-term relationships

Long-term planning and long-term relationships are an integral part of the Japanese business life. David B. Montgomery, writing in *Japan and the World Economy,* stated: "One of the most notable aspects of Japanese corporations is their willingness to take a very long-term view. Freed from the tyranny of accountants by the nature of their financial structure, they are able to pursue strategies which have a long time frame."[14] Corporations develop five-, ten-, even twenty-year plans. Within those plans, relations with partners, suppliers, and customers last through both good and bad times. When the bad times come, corporations maintain their relations with suppliers, even if they can get better deals somewhere else. Large corporations also retain redundant workers and retrain them for new tasks. And when the good times come again, suppliers and workers refrain from unreasonable claims that impair the company's ability to compete in domestic and international markets.

Foreign companies can develop long-term relationships with Japanese partners by establishing representative offices, forming joint ventures, or even by establishing wholly owned subsidiaries, as discussed in the previous chapters. In all cases, the exchange of visits, business information, and gifts in addition to frequent personal communications, are necessary to preserve and strengthen a long-term relationship.

Lengthy negotiations

Business negotiation is a lengthy process in Japan, and includes three stages. In the first stage, especially when it comes to new relationships, the two parties become familiar with each other and talk about things unrelated to business. In the second stage, a business proposal is prepared and presented to the other party. The business proposal must be detailed and convey to the other party a good understanding of the market and a clear strategy for following through. In the third part, the proposal may be circulated to the members of the organization for discussion and consensus building. W. Ouchi explained the process in his book, *Theory Z:* "When an important decision needs to be made in a Japanese organization, everyone who will feel its impact is involved in making it. In the case of a decision of where to put a new plant, whether to change a production process, or some other major event, this will often mean 60 to 80 people are directly involved in the making of the decision."[15] This kind of consensus building from the bottom up, known as *nemawashi,* is quite different from committee decision making in many American corporations, where policy matters are reviewed by a group of senior members and a majority consensus is quickly reached. Discussions and negotiations in Japanese corporations are quite broad and may go on forever.

This lengthy decision-making process has often been criticized by western executives, who often want quick results to appease short-sighted stockholders. The Japanese decision-making process has merit, however. As Akio Morito describes, it makes policy implementation easier: "Once a decision is reached, whether it originally came up from the shop floor or down from the front office, it is the Japanese way for everyone to devote every effort to implementing it without the sniping and backbiting and obstructionism that are sometimes seen in some western companies and universities. It is a fine situation to be in, because everybody is doing his share of the work, but getting there can be difficult."[16] In other words, time that is lost in the decision-making process may be made up during the implementation. Consensus building may be carried out on the shop floor, off the shop floor, and even outside the company in social gatherings, such as after-hour meetings.

After hour business meetings

Work in western societies normally ends when the regular workday hours end and everybody heads home, but not in Japan. Regular time is often followed by *tsukiiai,* meaning "Japanese-style friendship activities." These informal gatherings in *sushi* and *karaoke* bars are not just for entertainment; here, the consensus-building process continues. *Tsukiiai* strengthens personal relations and gives workers and business partners the feeling of belonging together in the same group, sharing common objectives. Though such corporate gatherings are not unfamiliar to many foreign executives, the frequency, broad participation of corporate members, and nature of *tsukiiai* may, indeed, be unfamiliar, especially because they often conflict with family life.

Implicit communication

If there is one thing valued the most in business relations, especially in the US, it is explicit, direct communication. Talking straight and revealing your views are considered a virtue, even if those views and answers may be negative and hurt the other's feelings. This is not the case in Japan, however, where feelings and sentiments come before cruel rationality. Being explicit and speaking your thoughts is incompatible with Japan's group mentality, goes against group conformity, and may be considered confrontational. You cannot get far in Japan by being confrontational. You cannot break business deals by hurting people's feelings. Saying little, in long and indirect sentences that let the other party guess your meaning, is considered a far better way to communicate than short, direct sentences. This way of communication is often confusing and even disappointing to the western ear that listens in different frequencies.

Rules of Competition

In many respects, competing in Japan is similar to competing in any other country. Product quality, price, prompt delivery, advertisement, and after-sales service are some of the vehicles used to get ahead of the competition. Yet, as discussed in Chapter 2, Japan is an economy of two sectors: an anachronistic, noncompetitive sector and a modern, competitive sector. The rules of the game may vary in each sector.

In the noncompetitive sector, foreign companies must rely on partnerships and alliances with one of the internal groups to enter these markets, or they must devise creative marketing techniques that bypass the traditional promotion and distribution channels. In the modern sector, foreign companies must apply creative marketing techniques based on long-term planning rather than short-term profit. Chicashi Moriguchi, writing in *Japanese Economic Studies,* stated: "The Japanese enterprise is deliberately oriented toward secure, long-term development. Maximization of short-term profits is not an objective; profits from successful undertakings are accumulated, to be used for the development of new undertakings in the future."[17] Akio Morita goes on to explain that in long-term planning, short-term profits are sacrificed to long-term sales and market share growth: "Share of market is more important to Japanese corporations than immediate profitability. If the purchase of an expensive new piece of machinery will depress short-term profits but can be expected eventually to increase the company's share of the market, the decision will almost always be to make the investment in the long-range future of the business."[18] Market shares in major industries are widely publicized in the daily press.

Prices must be reasonable and typically change only once or twice a year, normally at the beginning or the middle of the year. Unreasonable prices or frequently changing prices are seen as a breach of the long-term trust between buyers and sellers.

Furthermore, price cuts may sever long-term relations between manufacturers and retailers. In 1965, for instance, supermarket chain Daie sold Matsushita products 20 percent below the suggested manufacturer's price. What was Matsushita's response? They refused to ship any products directly to Daie.[19] Yet, as the Japanese economy slowed in 1990s and the early 2000s, more and more retailers began choosing to discount products, even if it meant risking their long-term relations with manufacturers. And consumers are going for it, as *The Wall Street Journal* reported:

> Discount stores, selling everything from computers to eyeglasses, are springing up and attracting many new customers. Department stores, which saw an average 6.6 percent decline in 1993—the second consecutive year they registered a fall—have reluctantly joined the war. Manufacturers are cutting costs and making their products cheaper. Some are moving production bases overseas to take advantage of lower wages, and retailers are looking for ways around the nation's inefficient and expensive distribution system.[20]

In Japan's New Economy, products must have a clear image and personality. "Thanks to recent changes, largely in retail distribution, there has been an enormous proliferation of products and brands in the Japanese marketplace. Products need a clear, individual image or personality. Now, more than ever, the need to attach values to products is crucial. Agencies have to bring their global knowledge of branding to the Japanese market; some may even try to educate clients," advised Tyron Guiliani in *Asia's Newspaper for Media and Advertising.*[21]

Clearly, the first step of a successful strategy for the Japanese market is adapting to local consumer demands, business practices, and rules of competition. To pursue this objective, foreign companies must establish a direct presence in the Japanese market by forming a joint venture with a local company or establishing a wholly owned subsidiary. Once this step is taken, foreign companies must gear their products to the tastes of the Japanese consumer, making sure that products are reasonably priced, carefully packaged, and promptly delivered. In addition, foreign companies must learn how to develop and keep long-term relationships with Japanese partners, suppliers, and workers. They must also learn how to communicate and negotiate with the Japanese. After all these steps are taken and foreign companies are well established in the Japanese market, they must pursue the second step of the strategy: developing new products.

Endnotes

1. JETRO, *Japanese Market Report No. 67.*
2. Bowers, "Face to Face."
3. Morgan and Morgan, *Cracking the Japanese Market,* 101.

4. Pollack, "Think Japan Inc. Is Lean and Mean? Step Into This Office."

5. Scalise, "Patience Holds the Key," 11–12.

6. Ibid., 12.

7. JETRO, *The Wealth of Opportunity*.

8. Martin, D. and Herbig, P., "Marketing Implications," 174.

9. JETRO, *Marketing Guidebook for Major Imported Products*.

10. Martin, D. and Herbig, P., "Marketing Implications," 174.

11. Belson, "How Dell is Defying an Industry's Gravity in Japan," BU5.

12. JETRO, "Successful Investment in Japan."

13. JETRO, *Japanese Market Report No. 67*.

14. Montgomery, "Understanding the Japanese as Customers, Competitors, and Collaborators," 79.

15. Ouchi, *Theory Z*, 44.

16. Morita, *Made in Japan*, 199.

17. Moriguchi, "The Japanese Economy: The Capacity to Transform and Restructure," 5.

18. Morita, *Made in Japan*, 206.

19. Thornton, "Japan's Struggle to Restructure."

20. Porter, D., "Japan's Consumers Turn Tough," B7.

21. Tyron Guiliani, "Japan Marketers in Need of 'Branding' not 'Badging' Savvy Media."

CHAPTER 11

DEVELOP NEW PRODUCTS

But in capitalist reality, as distinguished from its textbook picture, it is not (price) competition which counts but the competition from a new commodity, the new technology, the new type of organization.[1]

Joseph A. Schumpeter

New product development has been an integral part of the emerging Japanese New Economy. In September 2003, for instance, Honda introduced its new minivan called Odyssey, targeting the vehicle market. Honda's introduction of its new minivan model followed the introduction of Nissan's minivan, Presage, in July of the same year; Mitsubishi's Grandis van in May; and Toyota's Wish minivan in January. In 2003, Nissan introduced a total of 23 new models: three for Europe, six for Japan, eight for Mexico and other Central American markets, and six for the US markets. Toyota churned out the Lexus series for middle-aged, high-income families; the Scion xB Compact for younger drivers; the Prius for the eco-car market; and the Yaris for the European market.

Development has not been confined to the manufacturing of products, however; it extends to services as well. In the insurance industry, for instance, Nippon Life has introduced "Forward," which covers product liability; Sumitomo Life has introduced *Hanebuto* ("strong bone"), which covers injuries due to osteoporosis; while Asahi Mutual Life has introduced "IM," which covers disabilities due to chronic diseases. In the financial service industry, brokerage and mutual fund companies have introduced new retirement savings plans modeled after the American 401(k) and Keogh plans.

The introduction of dozens of models for different world markets underscores Japan's transformation from a copycat, or imitator, to an innovator. In industry after industry, Japanese companies are churning out new products often developed in America—things like color TVs, VCRs, and Liquid Crystal Displays (LCD)—and in some cases, catching up and even bypassing American competitors. In the LCD screens, for instance, Japanese companies have assumed almost 95 percent of the world market. In the office equipment market, Ricoh Corporation and Canon have caught up and even bypassed American leader Xerox Corporation. As of 2002, Canon's sales of

$24 billion jumped ahead of Xerox's $16 billion, while Ricoh was following closely behind with $14.5 billion. The two Japanese companies, particularly Ricoh, were the pioneers in the digitalization of office products.[2]

In the 2003 J.D. Power and Associates ranking of top-quality cars (in terms of problems per vehicle), Japanese brand names like Lexus and Infinity occupied most of the top 20 ranks, while American models like Chevrolet and Oldsmobile occupied the bottom ranks (see Exhibit 11.1).[3] Toyota's Sienna and Lexus RX series and Honda's Acura MDX, TSX, Pilot, and CR-V were among the fastest-moving models off the dealers' parking lots.[4]

For years, creating new products has been Japan's "smart secret weapon" in competing against her American and European counterparts.[5] This means that in order to compete efficiently and effectively in the Japanese market, foreign companies must learn all about this secret weapon, which takes intensive preparation and an intellectual commitment.

Foreign companies, including AFLAC, Altera Corporation, Apple Computer, AST Research, Spectra Physics, and Dell Computer, have

Exhibit 11.1 Top Ten Automobile Brands

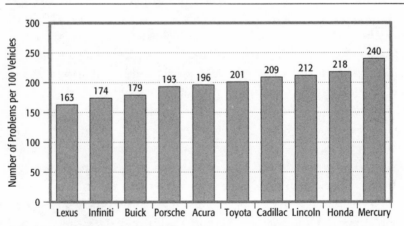

Source: Data taken from J.D Powers Associates

demonstrated such preparation and commitment by successfully introducing new products into the Japanese market. Following the introduction of software that handles Japanese characters in 1988, Apple's computer sales took off, especially the sales of its iMac Blueberry 333 MHz, which occupied the first position in 2000 (see Exhibit 11.2). Apple's market share increased from 4 percent in 1991 to 14 percent in 1994, before it returned to 5 percent in 1999 (see Exhibit 11.3).[6] But how do Japanese companies develop new products? How do their methods differ from those of western companies?

Exhibit 11.2   Apple Computer's Top-Selling Products in Japan as of 2000

Model	Rank	Market Share
iMac Blueberry 333 MHz	1st	5.4
iMac Rev B 233 MHz	2nd	3.2
iMac Tangerine 333 MHz	3rd	1.7
iMac Lime 333 MHz	4th	1.7
iMac Grape 333 MHz	5th	1.7
iMac Strawberry 333 MHz	6th	1.7
PowerMac G3 300 MHz	7th	1.4
iMac Blueberry 2663 MHz	8th	1.3
iMac DV SE 400 MHz	9th	1.3

Source: iMac News Page.

Exhibit 11.3   Apple's Market Share in Japan

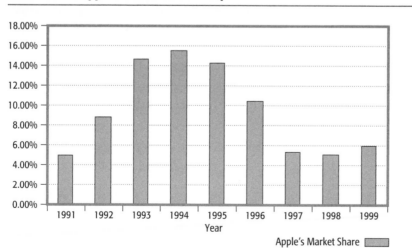

Source: iMac News Page

To address these questions, the remainder of this chapter is divided into two sections. The first section discusses product development as a competitive strategy, and the second section discusses the Japanese way of new product development and how it differs from that of western countries.

Product Development as a Competitive Strategy

As world markets become more integrated and competitive, consumers are looking for value, quality products, good services, and low prices. Consumers also look for new products that offer novelty and distinction, especially in mature markets, where fashion and faddism fade away in short periods of time, as is the case in Japan. "The faddism nature of the Japanese market means that you cannot afford to stand still or allow your brand to become staid. To the Japanese consumer, staid means boring. Successful brand managers understand the short attention span of the Japanese consumer and build this into their strategies," concluded Karl Moore and Mark Smith in "Taking Global Brands to Japan."[7]

Product development can be a rewarding strategy. Companies that manage to come up with new and different products faster than their competitors enjoy a limited monopoly power. They can either raise their market shares and even gain market leadership, or sell their products at a premium price. Sony Corporation, Intel, Microsoft, Rubbermaid, and Siemens are just a few examples of companies around the world that have successfully applied this strategy.

In today's technological universe, product development is a complex process. It requires the integration of market and technical information scattered both inside and outside the boundaries of traditional corporations. The integration of market and technical information, in turn, requires close cooperation with customers and with workers from different divisions. The use of new technologies, like flexible manufacturing and media interaction, may make this task easier and less costly than ever.

Product Development the Japanese Way

As in the US, product development in Japan starts with market research and product specification, and continues with product design, economic and engineering evaluation, and manufacturing. The Japanese product development process differs from that of the US in seven respects, however: market-driven product development; emphasis on applied research; emphasis on incremental product improvements; emphasis on early stages of product development; product development inseparable from manufacturing; cost considerations at an early stage; and extensive use of microelectronics.

Market-Driven Product Development

The best way to find out what kind of products to develop is to get close to customers, as exemplified by this quote from one of Honda's annual reports: "Honda has long been committed to manufacturing products close to the customer as a means to develop highly effective and efficient operations and quickly meet our customers' needs."[8] To offer another example of getting close to the customer, electronics companies have set up labs inside retail stores, known as "antenna stores," where product engineers and designers spend their weekends talking to consumers and repairing Louis H. Young describes:

> All Japanese companies religiously collect feedback from customers and channel it into the next generation of products. Many companies own "antenna stores"—retail shops at which product engineers work on weekends to receive direct customer feedback. To these companies, the speed with which this information is collected is more important than its statistical soundness.[9]

Some companies hire "prosumers," meaning consumers who work with producers to test out their products and make suggestions for new ones. "Prosumer staff may not be experts in manufacturing, but they have a keen consumer sense, which allows them to look at the firm's products as consumers do, helping the company to create products or offer services meeting the increasingly illusive and diverse desires of consumers." Toshiba, for instance, hires physiologists with music hobbies to work side by side with engineers, having them perform as potential customers to test their preferences.[10]

Emphasis on Applied Research

Developing new products is closely related to scientific research, especially applied research, which looks more closely at the needs of daily life, as opposed to the abstract needs of scientists in the lab. [And it is the needs of daily life that Japanese researchers address when it comes to product development, beginning from an existing product and making just marginal changes. Seiko, for example, has over 1,000 types of watches, all based on four or five models, and continues to introduce 100 different designs every month, changing only the color, case, straps. and so forth.[11]

Japan's emphasis on applied research can be attributed to two factors. The first is privately funded R&D. Close to 80 percent of Japanese R&D spending is financed by business, compared to around 70 percent in the US and 65 percent in Germany (see Exhibit 11.4). Unlike in other countries, where R&D spending is directed toward military or basic research and involves a

Exhibit 11.4   Business R&D for Selected Countries in 2000

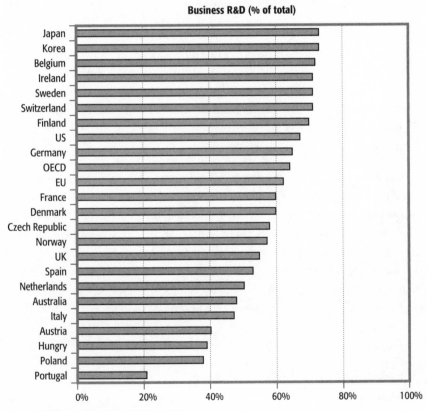

Source: OECD Economic Outlook, OECD Paris 2003

long detour before reaching commercial applications, Japanese spending is directed toward applied research, with immediate diffusion to the development of new products.[12]

The second factor is Japanese business culture. Japanese employment relations are conducive to creativity in the workplace. Teamwork, frequent job rotations, and labor transfers all facilitate the flow of information and ideas from one individual to another, from one team to another, from one department to another, and from one subsidiary to another. Thus, unlike in the West, where new ideas originate in laboratories as the product of individual effort, in Japan ideas are cultivated, recycled, nurtured, and refined in the workplace as the product of team effort, all of which contributes to the development of new products.

Emphasis on Constant Incremental Product Improvements

Continuous product improvements (*kaizen*) is an important part of product development in Japan. Toyota's Sienna minivan is a case in point. Toyota remade the vehicle by upgrading the engine power, improving gas mileage, adding an extra speed, and extending the body length, while cutting the cost by almost $1,000.[13]

The advantage of this approach is that it allows Japanese companies to bring new products to the market faster than their western counterparts, thereby expanding market shares. Moreover, the frequent introduction of new and innovative products allows Japanese companies to mass-customize their products, i.e., provide custom-made products for every possible market niche.[14]

Originating at the workplace, Japanese creativity evolves in steps rather than in leaps and bounds. It lacks the individual ingenuity and epiphany of western creativity. Japanese creativity is more adoptive to existing economic and social norms, and, therefore, easily diffused. Fujimoto, in *The Evolution of a Manufacturing System at Toyota,* described this example from Toyota:

> Toyota Motor concentrates on the manufacture of automobiles, which are an integral-architecture product. And it excels particularly in its persistent organizational learning power, what I call "evolutionary learning capability"—the key to its success in the fierce capability-building competition that is a distinctive trait of the automobile industry. Thanks to its superiority in this respect, it has been able to create an unhampered flow of design information to the production

floor, building a system for the transfer of design information onto physical media whose concentration, speed, and precision are globally without peer.[15]

Japan's orientation toward incremental rather than original forms of creativity is also rooted in the Japanese culture and philosophy. Buddhist teaching, for instance, emphasizes the importance of spiritual enlightenment of the group rather than the rational thought of the individual. In *Created in Japan,* Sheridan Tatsuno noted: "Unlike the Socratic purpose, there is no rational solution because the goal is spiritual enlightenment (*satori*) and intuitive understanding. Zen Buddhist philosophy does not place great value on rational thought alone."[16]

The adoption and recycling of existing ideas is a fact of life dictated by natural resource scarcity. Working with existing products and making everything from cars to cameras smaller is not just recycling and copying ideas; it is a drive for survival and opening up new opportunities. Tatsuno also explains: "For new products and services, the Japanese are always pursuing a variety of miniaturization strategies, which they have used as powerful tools for reducing costs and opening up entirely new markets."[17]

Japan's conservative approach to creativity is, perhaps, derived from its educational system. Japan's schools, famous for conformity and obedience, lack creativity and originality, as this commentator observed: "Despite glowing reviews by many foreign observers, Japanese schools reward conformity and obedience more than originality and initiative."[18] Conformity and obedience are carried along to the Japanese university system, where junior faculty must conform to the demands of senior faculty. "A major obstacle blocking scientific creativity in Japanese universities is the *koza* (chair) system, in which professors and lab managers in their 40s and 50s maintain absolute control over research topics and budgets."[19]

Emphasis on Early Stages

In regards to design, Japanese spend more time in the early stages of product development, while Americans spend more time in the later stages of the process. A Cranfield Institute study found that the Japanese put as much as 66 percent of the design effort into the initial, evolutionary phases, whereas western firms spend 50 percent of their effort redesigning their products at the end of the process.[20] This emphasis on the early stages of product development, also known as "phase review," also allows management to get involved and solve problems early on, as Rick Whiting explains:

> Phase review allows management to become involved early in the development process, rather than managing crises later on. The risk of waste is reduced because money and other resources are committed on a phase-by-phase basis. Periodic reviews offer milestones by which to measure core team development efforts. And because projects are nothing more than information until a prototype is built, the technique can provide tangible evidence of progress.[21]

Sony, for instance, integrates product design with shop floor production. "Sony's power in both product development and shop-floor power production has traditionally consisted of its ability to create optimal designs, in terms of component and production technology, for ultracompact products embodying clear concepts, such as the Walkman and the Handyman," stated Fujimoto in *The Evolution of a Manufacturing System at Toyota*.[22]

Emphasis on early stages further allows production engineers to work closely with manufacturing engineers, addressing manufacturing problems earlier rather than later, shortening product development cycles.

Product Development Inseparable from Manufacturing

"The difference between American and Japanese engineers is that American engineers do not want to get their hands dirty—they do not want to leave their offices and go out in the field to see how products work," an engineer for a major Japanese tire company once told me in Tokyo. Indeed, in most western countries, product development and product manufacturing are two separate processes with little communication among workers of the two departments, but not in Japan. The research and manufacturing divisions are arranged side by side, the one next to the other (see Exhibit 11.5).[23] Engineers are rotated from one division to the other, and there is a high degree of horizontal communication among departments. At the Honda Motor Company, for instance, they practice what is called the "joint boardroom,"

Exhibit 11.5   Research and Production Operations in Japan

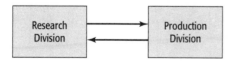

which emphasizes the difficulty and the need for such organizational arrangements.[24]

In Japan, engineers and workers are regularly reassigned from one department to another. Such practice is in sharp contrast with the American practice, where the planning department is normally above the operations department, with only occasional exchanges of experts between the two departments. Communication between departments is frequent and informal in Japan. Such a horizontal arrangement makes production flexible, and allows firms to deal with changing market and technological conditions. Production, for instance, can be switched easily from large volume to small volume and from one product to another.[25]

Horizontal communication among the members of an organization is facilitated by regular—as in daily, monthly, quarterly, and yearly—meetings of various worker groups and joint management-labor groups. Toyota, for instance, holds *obeya,* regular brainstorming meetings, where designers, engineers, marketers, and suppliers go over the details of new product development.[26] Toyota's approach is described in this example:

> In Toyota's traditional approach, in the planning phase, the chief engineer comes up with the concept, discusses it with the design groups and planning groups, and formulates a concrete plan as a result of joint discussion with those groups. With the Prius, a team of specialists from the various design, evaluation, and manufacturing functional groups sat in a big room with the chief engineer and made decisions in real time. Joining that group were not only the design engineers, but the production engineers as well so they could have discussions together.[27]

Matsushita Electric Corporation holds an annual meeting of 7,000 managers to discuss the business goals direction for the year.[28] Daily meetings are held every morning at each work site, in which workers give information about and become informed about the production schedule of the day. Daily meetings are also held at Sony Corporation, Toyota Motor Company, and the Seiko Group. As T. Kono notes:

> Corporations may try to promote horizontal communication but it is hard to ward off the drift towards bureaucratization. The divisional system is an effective way to streamline management when the company is growing but the vitality of the organization is difficult to maintain if the activities of the divisions are not coordinated. A key to successful management is to provide arrangements for horizontal links between divisions or departments.[29]

Production and research operations are highly decentralized in Japan; they are arrayed the one next to the other. The regular exchange of personnel facilitates the flow of information between the two departments, and stimulates the development of new products.

Cost Considerations at an Early Stage

In a competitive market, making good products is not enough; the price must also be right. This is why the Japanese system considers costs during the early stages of the product design process.

Early cost consideration is perhaps one of the most important differences between the Japanese and American product development processes, as Ford S. Worthy outlined in *Fortune* magazine:

> Like its famed quality philosophy, Japan's cost-management system stands western practice on its head. For example, American companies developing a new product typically design it first and then calculate the cost. If it's too high, the product goes back to the drawing board— the company settles for a smaller profit. The Japanese start with a target cost based on the price the market is most likely to accept. Then they direct designers and engineers to meet the target.[30]

In other words, American companies first develop the right product and then raise the question of cost and pricing. Products that pass the cost test proceed with manufacturing, while products that fail are returned for redesign. Japanese companies start the other way around: they explore a portfolio of products that may fit a certain cost target, and then design the products accordingly.

What is important to understand, however, is that this exercise is not just with the producer; it extends to resource suppliers and subcontractors. Producers ask subcontractors to come up with the product parts that will fit a certain cost target. Designing the right product and coming up with the right cost may not be feasible without the use of microelectronics.

Extensive Use of Microelectronics

Japan's unquestionable lead in microelectronics applications is reflected in the total factor productivity gains realized throughout the period 1979–1990. Japanese productivity rose at an average annual rate of about 2 percent, compared to a 0.2 growth rate for the United States and about 0.8 percent rate for the OECD countries. And although it lagged behind those of OECD and Finland in the 1990s, it still exceeded that of the US and Germany.[31] Japan's lead in microelectronics is also reflected in the rapid growth of the robot population. According to the 2003 *United Nations World Robotics Report,* Japan had installed close to 344,000 robots, as compared to 111,300 in Germany and 111,100 in the US.[32]

Robots and other microelectronics devices contribute to the development of new products in three ways. First, they cut waste and reduce design and manufacturing time, allowing many products to pass the cost test. Second, by improving precision, microelectronics can improve the quality of existing products. Third, by making product lines flexible, they allow companies to customize their products for different market segments.

In brief, though product development in Japan and the US both start with market research, the Japanese process: (1) is more market driven, (2) emphasizes applied over theoretical research, (3) emphasizes incremental improvements of existing products over the development of original products, (4) emphasizes early stages over later stages, (5) integrates product development and product manufacturing, (6) integrates cost considerations into design, and (7) uses microelectronics extensively.

To sum up, new product development has for years been Japan's secret competitive weapon, taking the country from a world-class imitator to a world-class innovator. American companies invented almost every breakthrough technology in the last fifty years, from transistors to color TVs, VCRs, and Liquid Crystal Displays. But it was Japanese companies that turned all of these technologies into successful products. The decentralized structure of Japanese companies that allows workers from different departments to team up and pull their skills together, their obsession with perfectionism, and a bottom-up approach to cost are some of the factors leading to Japan's success in developing new products.

Endnotes

1. Schumpeter, *Capitalizm, Socialism, and Democracy,* 21.

2. Cannon, *2002 Annual Report.*

3. JD Powers Associates, *2003 Report.*

4. Hawkins, Jr., "Finding a Car That's Built to Last," D1 and D5.

5. Worthy, "Japan's Smart Weapon."

6. iMac News Page. www.Nackasendo.com.

7. Moore and Smith, "Taking Global Brands to Japan."

8. Honda Motor Company, *2004 Annual Report,* 7.

9. Young, "Product Development in Japan: Evolution vs. Revolution," 75.

10. "Prosumers' Sniff Out Consumer Trends," 1. *The Wall Street Journal,* Oct. 30, 2003, p. A1.

11. Ibid., 75

12. Mourdoudoutas, *Adapt, Develop, Promote.*

13. Kerwin and Magnusson, "Can Anything Stop Toyota," 114–122.

14. Morimoto, *Friday.*

15. Fujimoto, 24

16. Tatsuno, *Created in Japan,* 45.

17. Ibid., 121.

18. Ibid., 264.

19. Ibid., 2.

20. Ibid., 45.

21. Whiting, "Managing Product Development from the Top."

22. Fujimoto, 24.

23. Mourdoukoutas, *Japan's Turn,* 65.

24. Whiting, "Managing Product Development."

25. Mourdoukoutas, *Japan's Turn.*

26. Kerwin and Palmeri, "Can Anyone Stop Toyota?"

27. Liker, *The Toyota Way,* 62.

28. Kono, *Strategy and Structure of the Japanese Enterprise,* 58.

29. Whiting, 29.

30. Worthy, "Japan's Smart Weapon."

31. OECD, *The Sources of Growth in OECD Countries,* 51.

32. United Nations Economic Commission of Europe, 5.

CHAPTER 12

PROMOTE PRODUCTS AGGRESSIVELY

A lot of things do not make sense to a western mind about Japan: street singing at lunch time, eating raw fish, and TV commercials, to name a few examples. Whether understanding Japanese or not, *gaijins* (foreigners visiting Japan) find it particularly hard to make sense out of the brief, vague, and sentimental TV commercials. Products rarely appear on the screen, and there is little or no explanation about the qualities of the product or the ways it serves consumer needs. Neither statistics nor comparisons to other products are provided, only black humor and vague messages beyond the comprehension of even the most sophisticated foreign marketer.

Product promotion is a complex task, especially when products have to cross borders and cultures at the same time. Concepts, images, and messages that work in one country may not work in another. This is the case when one compares American and European commercials to those of Japan. Western commercials are long, direct, logical, and emphasize the product appeal. Japanese commercials are short, indirect, sentimental, and emphasize the brand name appeal (see Exhibit 12.1).

Compounding the problem of cross-border promotion, distribution channels often place a wedge between foreign manufacturers and consumers, especially in Japan, where layers upon layers of wholesale and retail distributors tied together by long-term relations form a formidable barrier between Japanese consumers and foreign manufacturers.

Understanding the differences between Japanese and western commercials and the peculiarities and specifics of Japan's distribution system are important factors in launching a successful promotion and distribution campaign for the Japanese market, which is the subject of this chapter. The first section describes the characteristics of the Japanese promotion system, and compares it with that of western countries. The second section discusses Japan's distribution channels, and the ways foreign companies can use or bypass them.

Exhibit 12.1   Japanese Versus Western Commercials

Characteristic	Japanese	US
Duration	Short	Long
Message	Indirect	Direct
Appeal	Sentimental	Logical
Focus	Brand	Product
Statistics	No	Yes
Comparisons with competing products	No	Yes

Exhibit 12.2   History of Advertising in Japan

833	First signboard
1487	Pictorial signboards (Kamban)
1688–1704	Genroku Era–Shop curtains (Noren)
1600–1868	Edo Period–More direct forms of advertising such as handbills and ads bound into books
1868–1912	Meiji Period–Beginnings of mass media and their use in advertising. Becomes effective and inexpensive substitute for personal selling. Kohodo, the first documented advertising agency
1900	Beginnings of mass media magazines
1905	40 percent of newspaper revenues are normally being received from advertisements
1920	Large agencies such as Dentsu, Hakuhodo and Mannensha hold the largest accounts
War Period	Advertising expenditures drop due to shortages in consumer and paper goods
Post-war	Japan's economy picks up and advertising expenditures increase
1951	Invention of commercial broadcasting, a tremendous new way to promote products to consumers
1961–1970	Advertising revenues increased from $590 million (¥211 billion) to $2 billion (¥756 billion)
post-1970	Advertising revenues have increased steadily

Source: Adapted from *Kodansha Encyclopedia of Japan,* 1983, pp. 16–18.

Product Promotion the Japanese Way

Product promotion in Japan can be traced back to the first signboards in 833, the pictorial signboards in 1487, and the shop curtains in 1688 (see Exhibit 12.2). Mass-media advertising appeared much later, in the early years of the Meiji Restoration (1868–1912), when advertisements appeared in newspapers and magazines.[1]

The spread of mass-media advertising was accommodated by the proliferation of advertising agencies, buying up space in both newspapers and magazines and then selling it to advertisers, a practice eventually extended to radio and TV spots, giving advertising agencies a virtual monopoly on media access. Even today, hiring advertising agencies is the only way for advertisers to get access to mass-media advertising, still the prevailing form of advertising in Japan.

Total media advertising has risen from as little as 2,627 billion yen in 1982 to more than 5,726 billion yen in 1990 and to 6,058.1 billion in 2001. TV advertising has been the most popular form of advertisement, accounting for nearly one-third of all mass-media advertising (28.8 percent of advertising expenditures in 1990 and 34 percent in 2001). This is followed by newspaper advertising, which accounted for 24.4 percent of advertising expenditures in 1990 and 20 percent in 2001 (see Exhibit 12.3).[2]

Exhibit 12.3   Advertising Expenditures by Medium (1990 and 2001)

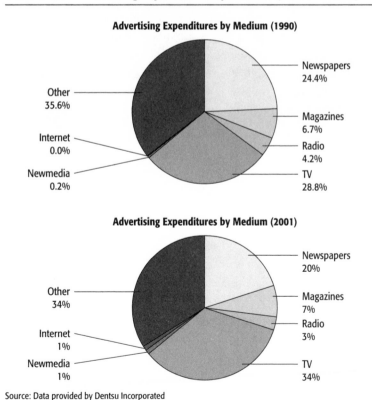

Source: Data provided by Dentsu Incorporated

But which mode of advertising is most appealing to Japanese consumers? How does it differ from the modes appealing to most western consumers? Addressing these questions, Barbara Mueller finds that the traditional "soft-sell appeal" is still strong in Japan, especially in low-level products targeting Japanese women. Messages are brief, direct, and have little relation to the advertised product. Monologues are also brief, and emphasize the brand name rather than the product.[3] The main hallmarks of the Japanese soft-sell approach include:

1. *Indirect rather than direct messages.* Western commercials are direct and explicit, making sure that viewers get the message clearly. Japanese commercials, on the other hand, are indirect and implicit, letting viewers interpret the message themselves. This approach can be attributed to the Japanese culture that values implicit rather than explicit communication. Whether at home, the office, or a public place, people rarely express their true feelings and thoughts but rather let other people guess. The most important things are never said in Japan, and Japanese commercials are no exception to this rule. They let viewers interpret the message and get the feeling of it rather than have a narrator interpret it for them. In multi-cultural, multi-racial societies like the US and EU, such commercials may be confusing and thus ineffectual, but not in a one-race, one culture society like Japan. Not only are messages indirect and implicit, they have little relation to the products advertised.

2. *Minimal relationship between ad content and advertised product.* Western commercials are logical, full of statistics and comparisons emphasizing the superiority of the advertised product over competing products. Japanese products are sentimental with no statistics and no comparisons. In the Dentsu Japan Marketing/Advertising Yearbook, T. Kishii reported: "Compared to Japanese ads, American ads make more frequent use of spokespersons and direct product comparisons, and often contain statistical figures to prove brand superiority."[4] In fact, comparative advertisement is illegal in Japan.

    In a society that values long-term relations and harmony, sentiments and feelings often come before cruel logic. As Tohru Nishikawa put it in the *Journal of Advertising Research,* "In advertising copy, too, they have a strong tendency to appeal to the dream and romanticism of life rather than stressing the function and logic of products."[5] Commercials must appeal on sentiments and feelings first, and even make sure they don't offend anyone. Viewers must feel comfortable with a product and be in the right mind to buy the product before they try to rationalize how it fits into their lives. They must also find it for themselves, instead of somebody else telling them.

3. *Brief monologues and narration with little explanation of the commercial content.* In western commercials, narration and monologues are the two most important vehicles in catching viewers' attention, but not in Japan where the most important things are never said. Nishikawa goes on to say: ". . . the Western approach to advertising, with its emphasis on detailed explanation of the brand's virtues, is not common in Japan. This may be attributed to the Japanese preference for indirect forms of expression. . . . In the Japanese culture, the more one talks, the less others will perceive him or her to be trustworthy or self-confident."[6] In Japanese ads, messages appeal to feelings rather than to reason. Monologues and narration would be too aggressive, leaving viewers with a negative impression.

4. *Humor applied to generate a bond of mutual feelings.* If the viewers' feelings are what commercials are appealing to, humor is thus a good vehicle to generate that appeal. And Japanese commercials have plenty of that. But again, it is not the kind of explicit humor that we often see in western commercials, but rather obscure black humor that a western mind would find difficult to understand and laugh about. To get a taste of the kind of humor used in Japanese ads, let us follow an example:

> A drunk businessman comes home late one night. He knocks on the door and yells, "Yoshie! I'm home!" but gets no answer. When he opens the door, he finds that the apartment is completely bare. He screams again, this time in fright and despair: "Yoshie!!" Meanwhile, Yoshie and their son are waiting for him in the kitchen of their new house. Yoshie is flabbergasted at her husband's stupidity. "He forgot we moved," she utters in disbelief. The next scene shows the man scratching his head as he makes a call from a pay telephone.
>
> Narrator: "When it comes to moving, the simpler the better. Choose Japan Transport the next time you move."[7]

5. *Famous celebrities introduced as close acquaintances or family friends.* In every country, celebrities are good marketing vehicles for reaching various

groups of viewers. A *summo* wrestling champion, for instance, is a good way to appeal to *summo* fans, and a football celebrity appeals to football fans. But unlike in western countries where celebrities appear as sponsors of a product, Japanese celebrities appear as family friends who happen to be around and relate themselves to the product. Japanese customers are fascinated with celebrities, especially foreign celebrities endorsing imported products. Dennis Hopper endorses bath tonics, Sylvester Stallone promotes food gift packages, and Whitney Houston endorses investments.

6. *Brand names supersede product names.* From Ginza to Times Square to London's Heathrow Airport, the logos of Japanese corporations are all over, and these signs cost a great deal. Why? In a country where consumers are concerned not only about the quality of a product, but also the quality and the image of the company that makes the product, commercials tend to emphasize brand names more than product names. And there is a logic behind it. David B. Montgomery explains: "Consumers in Japan associate product quality, safety, and reliability with the image of the company that produces it."[8] Large and financially stable companies are in a better position to offer after-sales service and repairs in the event that the product does not meet consumer expectations or causes injuries. But as it turns out, brand promotion is a far more efficient way of promotion rather than product promotion, especially for companies that have hundreds or even thousands of products. It costs much less to promote one brand name rather than hundreds of individual products.

7. *Short commercials of about 15 seconds.* With emphasis on brand names, with brief monologues and narration, and without comparisons and statistics, Japanese commercials are typically brief and vague. To get an idea of how brief Japanese ads are, let us follow another commercial prepared for a snack food made by Kameda Confectioners:

> The setting shows three high school students, who look like troublemakers, talking. They are actually having a serious conversation about the economy.
>
> A: "The way I see it, the only way is to lower the official rate."
>
> B: "Hey man, with you it's always the official rate, the official rate."
>
> C: "Nah. I say it's increasing domestic consumption . . ."

A: "What're ya talkin' [about]? So what happens to the balance of international payments based on profit margins from a yen-favorable exchange rate?"

Jingle: "International Snack, Kameda."[9]

In brief, to succeed in the Japanese market, world marketers must use the "soft-sell appeal." Commercials must be implicit, indirect, and sentimental, emphasizing brand names rather than products. Narration, monologues, and statistics must be kept to a minimum, and comparisons with products of competitors must be avoided.

Distribution Channels

As is the case in most countries, Japan's traditional distribution system consists of wholesalers and retailers, supermarkets, department stores, specialty/concept stores, "mom-and-pop" convenience stores, and direct mail. But unlike other developed countries where supermarkets and deep discount retailers account for the bulk of distribution, Japan's small stores account for most of the distribution. This was especially the case in the 1970s and 1980s, and explains why the distribution system has received part of the blame for the inaccessibility of Japan's markets. Layers of wholesale and retail distributors bonded together by long-term relations in a formidable web have often kept foreign products beyond the reach of Japanese consumers.* Specifically, the Japanese distribution system displays the following six features:

- A large number of small distributors and retailers. Scores of small, mom-and-pop stores crowd Japanese neighborhoods. The Large Department Law makes it difficult for the opening of supermarkets and department stores, although this barrier has decreased since the 1980s.

- Fragmentation. Exclusive contracts and franchise arrangements between wholesalers and retailers make it difficult for outsiders to get access to the system.

- Close formal and informal ties. Networks between manufacturers and wholesalers replicate the relations that existed in feudal Japan.

---

*Mourdoukoutas, P. Adapt, Develope, Promote: How to Compete in the Japanese Market, Copley Publishing Group, MA, 1995.

Manufacturers that do not belong to the network cannot get access to the distribution system.

- Strong ties between neighborhood stores and consumers. Due to the small size of Japanese apartments, consumers shop frequently and buy only a few items at a time, using neighborhood stores almost like storage outlets.

- High costs. Due to the widespread use of promissory notes, distribution and retailing costs are high, which boosts prices and limits consumption.

- Expensive guarantees. Consumer prices are further boosted by the wholesalers' buy-back guarantees for unsold commodities.

These features of the Japanese distribution system were especially evident in the 1980s, before the opening of the Japanese market to competition. Reflecting these characteristics, a 1998 MITI survey found that 39.6 percent of sales went through the wholesaler/retailer channel, 35.5 percent went through the industrial user channel, and 29.1 percent went through designated dealer channels. Most of the retailing (80 percent) was done by small retailers.[10]

Since the late 1990s, however, this has changed. In almost every product category, supermarket and discount retailers have been gaining popularity among customers at the expense of general retailers and department stores. A 2003 JETRO report stated:

The categories of retailers coming to Japan have also changed over the years. In the 1980s, luxury brands like Louis Vuitton and Hermes led the move into Japan. In the 1980s, specialty store operators with distinct lifestyle images, such as Eddie Bauer and HMV, comprised the mainstream of new entrants to the market. Most recently, Costco, Carrefour and other comprehensive retailers are beginning to claim the spotlight with their high-profile forays into the market. The overall presence of foreign retailers in Japan has expanded from the luxury product category into more everyday goods, significantly boosting market penetration of foreign brands in these areas.[11]

In the food sector, for instance, the general stores' share of the industry's sales has dropped from 44.3 percent in 1984 to 18.8 in 1999, while the supermarkets' share increased from 42 percent to 55.4 percent (see Exhibit 12.4). In the furniture industry, the share of the general retail store decreased from

Exhibit 12.4   Proportion by Expense Item and Place of Purchase

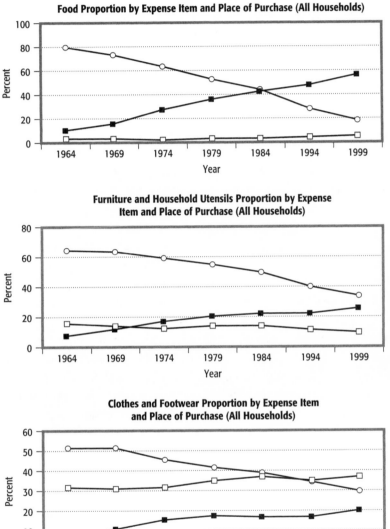

Food Proportion by Expense Item and Place of Purchase (All Households)

Furniture and Household Utensils Proportion by Expense Item and Place of Purchase (All Households)

Clothes and Footwear Proportion by Expense Item and Place of Purchase (All Households)

General retail store ─○─   Supermarket ─■─
Department store ─□─

Source: 1999 National Survey of Family Income and Expenditure

49.9 percent to 34.1 percent, while in the clothes and footwear sector, it dropped from 39.1 to 29.6.[12]

The decline in the smaller stores and the rise of supermarkets and department stores make it easier for foreign companies to bring their products to Japanese consumers, as do partnerships with domestic companies and the bypassing of traditional distribution systems.

Forge Domestic Partnerships and Alliances

Forging domestic partnerships is the conservative way to access a foreign market. Domestic partners can provide instant access to local wholesalers, distributors, and retailers, while sharing the knowledge, expenses, and risks of a new venture. Almost every foreign company has chosen this avenue, at least in the early stages of their entry into the Japanese market. Coca-Cola, for instance, established many alliances and partnerships with domestic companies, including Mitsui and Co., Mitsubishi Corporation, and Kirin Brewery Co., Ltd. General Foods established a partnership with Ajinomoto Co., Inc.; Baskin-Robbins established a partnership with Fujiya Co., Ltd.; and Buitoni formed a partnership with Kagome, a leading Japanese ketchup maker.

Domestic partnerships can pose an array of problems, however. For high-technology companies, partnerships can pose the problem of patent infringement. Texas Instruments, Digital Equipment, and AFLAC Japan all experienced patent problems with Japanese partners and competitors at one point or another, and eventually set up wholly owned subsidiaries.

Bypass Traditional Channels

As is the case in other societies, bypassing traditional distribution channels and selling directly to consumers is easier said than done. Yet a number of companies have managed to do so through consumer partnerships, direct mail, vending machines, and online sales.

Consumer partnerships

This novel idea turns buyers into sellers to other consumers in a pyramid-like scheme. Consumer partnerships work well in networked or extended family societies, where the members of a network feel obligated to assist fellow members. Introduced to Japan by a pioneer in this field, Amway Corporation, this method has been very successful. After a slow entry in the early 1980s, Amway's sales took off with 20 percent annual growth rates. With 128.6 billion yen in sales in the early 1990s, Amway was the fifth largest foreign corporation in Japan. The company had a staff of about 450 people and 500,000 distributors, with top distributors earning more than $100,000 annually.[13] By the late 1990s, Amway's early success came to a halt as the company faced a number of problems ranging from fluctuating distributor motivations to product dissatisfaction.[14]

Direct mail

In every country, direct mail is a good way to promote and distribute certain products to specific classes of consumers. Mail-order services in Japan can be traced back to the 1910s, when department stores added mail-order services to their operations. Items often sold by mail include accessories, shoes, bags, jewelry, precious metals, timepieces, eyeglasses, cameras, and life insurance policies.[15] Bags, handbags, carpets, silk scarves, neckties, and tableware are among the most popular imported items delivered by mail.[16] Franklin Mint, L.L.Bean, and Inmac K.K. are just a few examples of foreign companies that have taken advantage of direct-mail promotion and distribution. Yet, as postal rates have risen and foreign competition has intensified, selling by mail is not as easy as it used to be.[17]

Vending machines

Vending machines are everywhere in Japan—in train stations, at bus stops, on university campuses, in office buildings, on main streets, on side streets, anywhere there is space available for them. They dispense almost everything from soft drinks and alcoholic beverages to magazines, videotapes, flowers, jewelry, cameras, frozen meat, and noodle soups. As David Kilburn reported in the *Journal of Japanese Trade and Industry*: "Probably in no other country would anyone dream of filling a roadside vending machine with expensive jewelry! A high price tag is clearly no barrier to vending sales. Machines can sell expensive as well as inexpensive items."[18]

Vending machines are a quick and inexpensive way of promoting and distributing products, especially in Japan, where the traditional distribution system is inaccessible to outsiders. Machine users can use their cellular phones to pay for merchandise, while machine owners can apply state-of-the-art wireless technology to monitor inventories in remote locations, charge higher prices, and launch new product promotions.[19] According to the Japan Vending Machine Association, in 2001, there were more than 5.6 million vending machines, or about one machine for every 300 inhabitants, dispensing close to $58 billion in sales.[20] Coca-Cola, the company that virtually introduced vending in Japan, has installed 60 machines per 10,000 people, about three times as many as in the US and eight times as many as in Germany. Vending machine sales totaled $56 billion in 2000. In 1998, Coke vending machine sales accounted for 38.1% of all non-alcoholic sales in Japan.[21]

In a country obsessed with personalized service and elegant product packaging and delivery, vending machines represent a shift in retailing, as *The New York Times* writer James Sterngold reported:

> In a nation where retailing methods have been described as a reflection of people's unique character, the trend represents a deep change in habits. For generations, the formula for reaching consumers in Japan was said to require lavish attention and lots of personal service. Japan had so many small neighborhood shops, it was said, because they provided the sense of intimacy and trust consumers demanded.[22]

This shift can be traced to a number of factors: First, vending machines are an extension of the "storage space" concept behind Japan's small neighborhood stores. David Kilburn adds: "Pressure on space within stores also encourages the growth of vending. Many shops expand their sales area into the street with a lineup of vending machines."[23] Second, vending machines provide convenience to busy Japanese people. They need only a few seconds to grab a product at any time in any place. Third, Japan does not have the same problems with vandalism as other countries do, even when vending machines dispense such enticing products as beer. Kilburn notes: "Low crime levels and a high level of respect for other people's property are factors that help the industry grow."[24]

Online sales

The Internet has become an integral part of everyday Japanese life. In 2000, there were 12.5 million Internet subscribers (see Exhibit 12.5).[25]

According to the Japanese Statistics Bureau, the typical Internet user is a 30- to 34-year-old male, who uses the Internet to gather information, place orders, and make financial payments. Specifically, 12.10 percent of these Internet users made purchases based on information gathered from the Internet, 9.90 percent placed orders through the Internet, and 5.60 percent paid by credit card through the Internet (see Exhibit 12.6).[26]

Exhibit 12.5   Internet Access Modes

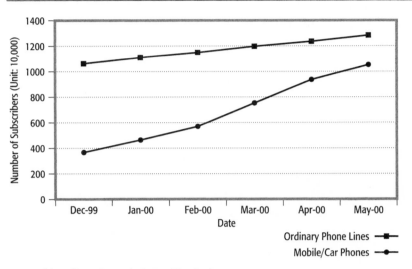

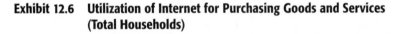

Source: Ministry of Posts, Communications, and Broadcasting

Exhibit 12.6   Utilization of Internet for Purchasing Goods and Services (Total Households)

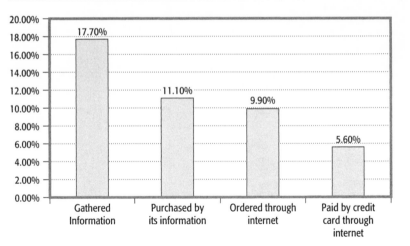

Source: March 2002 Survey of Household Economy, Statistics Bureau, www.stat.go.jp, 7/3/2003

The heavy use of the Internet by males in their early 30s makes online sales an efficient and effective medium in distributing products and services that appeal to this age group, such as books, electronic gadgets, and financial and insurance products. Sales of financial products, automobiles, and real estate are expected to grow at the fastest rate.[27]

To sum up, product promotion is the third and, perhaps, most important part of the ADP strategy. To sell their products to Japan, foreign firms must become familiar with the Japanese promotion and distribution systems. Commercials must be brief, indirect, and implicit. Monologues and narration should be kept short and have little relation to the content of the product that is being advertised, statistics should be kept to a minimum, and comparisons with competitive products should be avoided. Though designing commercials on these principles is the necessary way of appealing to the Japanese consumer, it is not sufficient.

For products to reach consumers, foreign firms must manage to work with the existing distribution system or bypass it. Alliances and partnerships with domestic companies are two common ways of working with domestic companies. Consumer partnerships, direct mail, vending machines, and the Internet are the common ways of bypassing the system.

Endnotes

1. Mourdoukoutas, *Adapt Develop, Promote.*

2. Data provided by Dentsu Incoporated.

3. Mueller, "Standardization vs. Specialization: An Examination of Westernization in Japanese Advertising."

4. Kishii, "Message vs. Mood: A Look at Some of the Differences Between Japanese and Western Television Commercials," 39.

5. Nishikawa, "New Product Development," 28.

6. Ibid., 41.

7. Ibid., 42–44.

8. Montgomery, "Understanding the Japanese as Customers," 70.

9. Ibid., 43–44.

10. MITI, *Survey on the Internationalization of Enterprises.*

11. JETRO, "A New Era in Japan's Retailing Market," 14–15.

12. Statistics Bureau, "1999 National Survey."

13. Holzinger, "Selling American to the Japanese."

14. Arnold, et al., "Amway Japan Ltd.," 2.

15. JETRO, *Mail Order in Japan,* 6.

16. Ibid., 10.

17. Shirai, "Party's Over in Mail-order Market."

18. Kilburn, "Vending Industry Keeps Growing," 20.

19. Terhune and Kahn, "Coke Lures Japanese Customers with Cellphone Come-ons," B1 and B4.

20. www.Japan-Guide.com, 1/24/2004.

21. The Coca-Cola Company, *1993 Annual Report;* photomann.com/Japan/machines, 1/31/2004; "Sales per Vending Machine Accelerates in Japan. Coke Dominates," www.beverage-digest.com/editorial/990827, 1/31/2004.

22. Sterngold, "Why the Japanese Adore Vending Machines," 1.

23. Kilburn, "Vending Industry Keeps on Growing," 20.

24. Ibid., 20.

25. Ministry of Posts, Communicaions, and Broadcasting.

26. Statistics Bureau, "March 2002 Survey."

27. "The Internet User," 3.

CHAPTER 13

FROM HERE TO THE FUTURE

We need to get away from the traditional "convoy" approach to industrial policy, which has aimed to ensure the survival even of the companies that trail the pack. Instead the focus should be on the strongest and fastest-moving companies in each field; industrial policy should aim to help these front-runners advance even faster.[1]

Corporations are frantically slashing costs and revamping their operations. Politicians are changing the rules of parliament, for example, by requiring ministers to answer their own questions instead of relying on bureaucrats to promote policy debates. Planned pension reforms are set to spread share-ownership, forcing companies to start paying attention to shareholder rights.[2]

Change is breeding confusion and fear. As individual action becomes more decisive in business, the gap between haves and have-nots is inevitably going to widen. That means Japan must grope its way quickly toward a new way of deciding public policy, one that does not require the nation to wait while bureaucrats and the LDP figure out one-size-fits-all solutions.[3]

Jonathan Sprague and Murakami Mutsuko

In the early 1980s, Japan's Old Economy created a land of paradox, a rich country with poor consumers. Japan was rich in factories that cranked out low-cost, high-quality products hard to match by other countries, including automobiles, copy machines, machine tools, and consumer electronics. She was rich in income and savings that financed the expansion of her companies around the world, most notably in the US, where the Japanese amassed American trophies—movie studios, skyscrapers, technology companies, and golf courses—one by one. And finally, Japan was rich in management systems that served as the model for the world, especially for the emerging economies of Southeast Asia.

At the same time, however, Japan was poor in living standards that lagged behind those of other industrial countries, especially those of the US and Europe. Japanese workers had little choice in where they would work and for how long. Japanese consumers had little choice as to what products they would buy, where and when they would buy, and how much they would pay for them. Japanese manufacturers, especially those belonging to *keiretsu* groups, had little choice in who they would buy materials and supplies from, who they would borrow funds from, or how they would reach their customers.

At the root of this paradox were Japan's economic institutions and policies, put in place in the mid-1950s, which emphasized production, savings, and exports over leisure, consumption, and imports, turning the country into a market sanctuary. One of these institutions was economic dualism, the parallel existence of two sectors: a modern, open commodity sector and a closed, backward commodity sector. Dualism extended to the labor sector, which included a privileged sector, where workers enjoyed lifetime employment, seniority wages, and the protection of enterprise unions, and a non-privileged sector, where workers enjoyed none of the above. Economic dualism was supported and reinforced by government activism—policies that protected and regulated domestic markets, constraining both domestic and foreign competition; keeping the price of basic products and services, such as beef, rice, citrus fruits, electricity, and telephone services, well above world prices; and nurturing a culture of workaholism and thrift.

But as it faces the future, Japan is no longer the land of paradox. The country's factories continue to churn out high-quality products and savings remain high, but they no longer finance foreign acquisitions. Japan's management is still popular, but no longer serves as a model for other countries. At the same time, Japan is an open economy with living standards that come closer to those of other industrial countries. Japanese consumers have more choices as to what, when, and where they will buy things, and how much they will pay for them, although they are missing the personal attention and touch of the neighborhood store. Japanese workers have more choices in who they will work for and for how long, but they can no longer count on lifetime employment and the generous benefits associated with it. Japanese manufacturers have more choices as to who they will buy their supplies from and how they will reach their customers, but they can no longer count on government protectionism and cozy business relations to shelter them from investor activism and hostile takeovers.

One of the drivers behind the transition from the Old Economy to the New Economy was the departure from the early policies that emphasized production over consumption, and the dismantling of the institutions that accommodated them. Trade liberalization, for instance, opened domestic markets to foreign products and competition, providing Japanese consumers with broader product choices at affordable prices. Deregulation opened up Japan's backward, inefficient sectors to both foreign and domestic competitors, lowering the prices of basic services, such as utilities and telecommunications, for both consumers and businesses.

Another driver was the business and political restructuring that transformed Japanese companies from pro-stakeholder to pro-stockholder organizations, giving stockholders a louder voice regarding the direction of their companies and elected politicians better control over the economic direction of the country.

A third driver was the prolonged stagnation of the 1990s that severed relations within *keiretsu* groups, opening certain sectors of the economy to competition.

Japan's transformation from a producer to a consumer society has eased the entry of foreign companies into the Japanese market. In the distribution sector, for instance, deregulation has eliminated several layers of middlemen, bringing foreign producers closer to Japanese consumers. In retailing, deregulation and depressed real estate prices have allowed foreign retail giants like Wal-Mart, Costco, and Carrefour to bring their discount model to the Japanese market. In the financial and manufacturing sectors, depressed equity prices have allowed foreign companies to take equity stakes in domestic competitors: Merrill Lynch in Yamaichi Securities, Shaghai Electric in Akiyama Machinery Manufacturing, General Motors in Mazda Motor Company, Suzuki in Fuji Heavy Industries, to name a few examples. In some sectors, foreign affiliates have gained significant market shares, challenging domestic competitors: Goldman Sachs has surpassed legendary Nomura Securities in mergers and acquisitions advising; Sun Microsystems, HP, and IBM have assumed leading positions in Unix servers; and IBM, Apple Computer, and Dell have all gained market shares in personal computers. In other sectors, foreign companies have been reviving their Japanese partners, for example, Ford turned around Mazda and Renault turned around Nissan.

In order to succeed, world businesses have been launching a well-orchestrated, three-fold business strategy, which I refer to as ADP: *adapt* to the Japanese business practices, consumer preferences, and constraints and rules of competition; *develop* new products and new services that cater to the needs and imagination of an ever-changing market ruled by fashion and faddism that quickly turns brand products obsolete; and *promote* products and services aggressively through traditional and nontraditional marketing and distribution channels.

In covering Japan's economic changes in more detail, this book was divided into three parts. Part I provided an overview of Japan's fading Old Economy, economic dualism, government activism, and internal and external frictions. It then explained the drivers of the New Economy: trade liberalization, deregulation, the prolonged economic stagnation that followed the burst of the economic bubble, and business and political restructuring. Part II offered a discussion of the emerging trends and opportunities in Japan's New Economy, and the ways they have benefited world businesses, particularly foreign subsidiaries. Part III laid out the three-fold ADP strategy for competing in the Japanese market.

Looking into the future, Japan's New Economy is expected to be a tale of two worlds: The first world will be a world of true democracy, where individual citizens rather than government bureaucrats and corporations shape the destiny of the country; where the economically free Japanese people will decide what to buy, and where and when to buy it; where opportunities will release the creativity and ingenuity of the Japanese people, leading to new products, processes, and business models; and where Japan will live in harmony and reciprocity with its trade partners. At the same time, Japan's New Economy will create a second world, where individuals and businesses must learn to live with the risks and uncertainties associated with a more open, individualistic society, subject to the whims of market forces that create wide swings in prices, wages, and employment; where the Japanese people must learn to master the risks and uncertainties that affect their lives; where Japanese workers must learn to live without lifetime employment, seniority wages, and union protection, and instead earn bonuses determined by market forces; where managers must learn to survive in a world of active investors, corporate raiders, and hostile takeovers that make their jobs and lavish perks ever more uncertain; and where business owners must learn to live with the constant threat of new competitors and the prospect of bankruptcy.

At times, the two worlds will coexist in harmony with each other, especially in times of economic expansion. Most Japanese people will be willing to accept growing risks and uncertainties as the price to pay for a more open, liberal society. At other times, the two worlds will collide with each other, especially during economic contractions. The Japanese people will be divided into winners and losers, with winners giving their support to the New Economy and the opportunities it creates, and with losers giving their support to the Old Economy and the many regulations that protected their lives.

Among the winners will be young entrepreneurs, who can now pursue new business opportunities in less regulated, open markets. Among the losers are expected to be the country's legendary bureaucrats who have already tried to "step on the brakes" to many of the changes brought about by the New Economy. As Ushio Chujo wrote in *The Nikkei Weekly:* "A major factor slowing the deregulation process is that both industry and the bureaucracy have been protected by and benefited from regulation and have persistently resisted giving up their vested interest."[4] These bureaucrats will be joined by domestic retailers, wholesale and retail distributors, and *keiretsu* groups that have also seen their power eroding under the New Economy.

One of the challenges of the Japanese policy makers will be to balance these dueling forces that provide support for the New Economy and the centrifugal forces that provide support for the Old Economy, by eliminating the confusion and fear brought about by the New Economy. Policy makers must further address several demographic challenges: the record low birthrates (1.39 children per couple in 2000) that are expected to cut Japan's population by 50 percent by the end of the twenty-first century, down to 125 million in the early 2000s; the shrink of the labor force from 70 percent to 55 percent of the population by 2050; and the explosion of the senior citizen population, which is expected to increase from 15 percent in 2000 to 30 percent by 2050.[5]

A tale of two worlds, the New Economy is a mixed blessing for world businesses. On the one hand, an open, liberal economy is expected to lower the cost of entry and expansion of world businesses into the Japanese market. On the other, an open, liberal economy is expected to invite the entry of new competitors into the Japanese market, thereby intensifying the competition and eliminating market rents. This means that Japan's New Economy leaves no room for comfort and complacency, especially among the early movers that enjoyed an advantage over the latecomers. To survive and prosper, world businesses must constantly destroy and create their own businesses, coming up with radically new products and processes and turning market niches into mass markets, as is the case in every competitive market.

Endnotes

1. Takahiro, "A Twenty-first Century Strategy for Japanese Manufacturing," 20–25.

2. Sprague and Mutsuko, "Japan's New Attitude."

3. Ibid.

4. Chujo, "For Japan Deregulation is Inevitable and Necessary."

5. Yim, "Gender Gap," 12–13.

BIBLIOGRAPHY

Abe, N., A. Ishibashi, and M. Naito. "Japan Inc. Finally Bolsters Efforts to Snag Foreign Direct Investment." *The Nikkei Weekly* (June 9, 2003): 3.

Abecasis-Phillips, J. *Doing Business in Japan*. Chicago: NTC Business Books, 1994.

Abramovitz, M., and P. A. David. "Convergence and Deferred Catch-Up: Productivity Leadership and the Waning of American Exceptionalism." *Growth and Development: The Economics of the 21st Century*. Edited by R. Landau Taylor and G. Wright. California: Stanford University, 1995.

"A Closer Look: Tax Reform (editorial)." *Nikkei Weekly* (June 24, 2002): 3.

Addison, J., and A. Castro. "The Importance of Lifetime Jobs: Differences Between Union and Nonunion Workers." *Industrial Relations Review* 40, no. 3 (April 1987).

AFLAC Inc. *2000 Annual Report*. Columbus, Ga, 2001.

AFLAC Inc. *2001 Annual Report*. Columbus, Ga, 2002.

American Chambers of Commerce in Japan. *Trade and Investment in Japan*. 1991.

American Chambers of Commerce in Japan. *Trade and Investment in Japan: The Current Environment*. 2003: 5.

American Chambers of Commerce in Japan. "2001 US-Japan Business White Paper." 2002: 1, 17.

American Chambers of Commerce in Japan, "2001 US-Japan Business White Paper." 85.

Andruss, P. L. "Japanese Market Ad Research." *Marketing News* 34, no. 22 (2002): 3, 6.

Anonymous. "The Turnaround at Nissan Motors." *Strategic Direction* 17, no. 11 (November/December 2001): 25.

Aoki, M. "Toward an Economic Model of the Japanese Firm." *Journal of Economic Literature* 28 (March 1990): 1–27.

Aoki, T. "Aspects of Globalization in Contemporary Japan." *Many Globalizations.* Edited by Peter L. Berger and Samuel P. Huntington. New York: Oxford University Press, 2002: 72.

Arayama, Y., and P. Mourdoukoutas. *The Rise and Fall of Abacus Banking in Japan and China.* Esport, CT: Quoum Books, 2000.

Arnold, D., J. Quelch, Y. Fujikawa, and P. Reinmoller. "Amway Japan Ltd." *Harvard Business Online* (Feb. 11, 1999): 2.

Audretsch, D. *The Market and the State,* New York: New York University Press, 1989.

Bank of Japan. *Balance of Payment.* Tokyo, 2001: 12.

Bank of Japan. "Bank of Japan Comparative Statistics." Tokyo, 1992.

Barsony, A. "Co-operation with the Dynamic Asian Economies." *The OECD Observer* 168 (February/March 1991).

Baum, J., and L. de Rosario. "Japan in Asia: The Sumo Neighbour, Unequal Partners." *Far Eastern Review* (February 21, 1991).

Becker, G. "Why Europe Is Drowning in Joblessness." *Business Week* (April 8, 1996).

Belson, Ken. "How Dell Is Defying an Industry's Gravity in Japan." *The New York Times* (Dec. 8, 2002).

Berger, M. "Renaissance: the Making of the Japanese Corporation." *Business Week* (July 11, 1994).

Bergsten, C., and W. Cline. *The United States-Japanese Economic Problem.* Washington, D. C.: Institute for International Economics, 1987.

"A Big Bundle of Hot New Exports (cover story)." *Business Week* 1 (1991).

Blustein, P. "WTO Negotiations May Hold Key to Bush's Legacy of Free Trade." *The Washington (D. C.) Post,* July 28, 2002.

Borrus, M. "Chip Wars." *California Management Review* 30 (1988): 64–70.

Bowers, B. "Face to Face." *The Wall Street Journal,* January 1992.

Bremmer, B., Ch. Dawson, K. Kerwin, and C. Palmeri. "Can Anything Stop Toyota?" *Business Week* (November 17, 2003): 45.

Bremner, B. and H. Tashiro. "Is Japan Back?" *Business Week* (June 14, 2004): 26–31.

Browdy, D. "The Invention that Got Away." *Technology Review* 94 (1989): 42–51.

Brown, C., and M. Reich. "Developing Skills and Pay through Career Ladders: Lessons from Japanese and US Companies." *California Management Review* 39, no. 2 (1997).

Burbone, L. "Import Barriers: An Analysis of Time-Series Cross-Section Data." *OECD Economic Studies* 11 (Autumn 1988).

Burrows, P. "In Search of the Perfect Product." *Electronic Business* (June 17, 1991).

Butler A. "Trade Imbalances and Economic Theory: The Case for the U.S.–Japan Trade Deficit." *Federal Reserve Bank of St. Louis* (March/April 1991).

Cannon. 2002 Annual Report. Tokyo, 2003.

Carliner, G. "Patterns in Japanese and American Trade." Presented at the International Symposium on Current Policy Issues in the United States and Japan, in Tokyo, Japan, October 21–22, 1985.

Caves, R., and M. Uekusa. "Industrial Organization." *Asia's New Giant: How the Japanese Economy Works.* Edited by Hugh Patrick and Henry Rosovsky. Washington, DC: The Brookings Institute, 1982.

Chiang, H. C., and P. Mourdoukoutas. "The Revival of the US Productivity: Is it for Real?" *Current Politics and Economics of the US* 1, no. 2/3 (1995): 1.

Christopher, R. *Second to None: American Companies in Japan.* New York: Fawcett Columbine, 1982.

Chu, Ch. "Japanese Mindset—The Roots of Today's Japanese Business Culture." *Business Credit* (July/August 1992).

Chujo, U. "For Japan Deregulation is Inevitable and Necessary." *The Nikkei Weekly* (March 13, 1995).

The Coca-Cola Company. *1993 Annual Report.* Atlanta, Ga: CocaColla Corporation, 1994.

Cohen, A. "Japan in Transit: Modeling the Japanese Corporation." *Management Japan* 6, no. 2 (Autumn 1993): 54.

Cole, R. "Work and Leisure in Japan." *California Management Review* (Spring, 1992): 53.

Cole, R. E. *Work, Mobility and Participation: A Comparative Study of American and Japanese Industry.* Berkeley: University of California Press, 1979.

Compilation of Fair Trade Commission. "Regulations and Decisions Relating to Multi-level Sales," 1994.

Cooper, W. "Japan–U.S. Trade: The Structural Impediments Initiative." *Current Politics and Economics of Japan* 1, no. 1 (1991): 25.

Corker, R. "The Changing Nature of the Japanese Trade." *Finance and Development* 28, no. 2 (June 1991).

Corning Company. www.corning.co.jp. Accessed May 4, 2004.

Curtis, G. (editor), *The United States, Japan, and Asia: Challenges for U.S. Policy.* New York: W. W. Norton & Company, 1994.

Cushman, D., S. Haynes, and M. Hutchison. "U.S.–Japanese Trade and the Yen-Dollar Exchange Rate." *Southern Economic Journal* 56 (1989): 98.

Czinkota, M., and J. Woronoff. *Unlocking Japan's Markets: Seizing Marketing and Distribution Opportunities in Today's Japan.* Boston, Massachusetts: Charles E. Tuttle Company, 1991.

De Silva, N. "Hashimoto Faces Mammoth Task to Drag His Nation Out of Economic and Social and Social Morass." *Hong Kong Standard* (Jan. 11, 1996).

Defoe, L. "Firm Finds Japan Hungry for Mail-order Catalogues." *The Business Journal Serving Greater Sacramento* 3, no. 2 (1987): 48.

Dekle, R. "The Japanese 'Big Bang' Financial Reforms and Market Implications." *Journal of Asian Economies* 9, no. 2 (Summer 1998): 237–249.

DiBenetto, A., M. Tamate, and R. Chanban. "Developing Creative Advertising Strategy for the Japanese Market Place." *Journal of Advertising Research* (January/February 1992): 97.

Doi, N. "Aggregate Export Concentration in Japan." *Journal of Industrial Economics* (UK) 39, no. 4 (June 1991): 434.

Doi, N. "The Efficiency of Small Manufacturing Firms in Japan." *Small Business Economics* 4 (1992): 29–35.

Dore, R. *Flexible Rigidities.* California: Stanford University Press, 1986.

Dore, R. "Japan in Recession." *Dollars and Sense* 192 (March–April 1994).

Douglas, S. P., and C. S. Craig. "Achieving Success in the Japanese Market." *Japan and the World Economy* 2 (1990).

Economic Planning Agency Bureau (editor). *A Modern-Day Open-Market, Free-Guild Policy: Deregulation and Economic Rejuvenation.* Tokyo: Ministry of Finance Printing Office, 1994.

Eisenstodt, G. "Confucius or Marx?" *Forbes* (December 4, 1995).

European Commission (Unit of relations with Japan). *Note for the Attention of the Members of the 113 Committee* (DEPUTIES) 113 (November 25, 1994).

Ferguson, N. "Global Firms Battle through Japanese Markets." *International Financial Review* 21, no. 6 (June 2002): 69–73.

Fingleton, E. *Blindsided: Why Japan is Still on Track to Overtake the US by the Year 2000*. Boston, MA: Houghtom MIffin Co., 1995.

Flamm, K. "Making New Rules." *The Brookings Review* 2, no. 2 (Spring 1991).

Flath, D. "Why Are There So Many Retail Stores in Japan?" *Japan and the World Economy* 2 (1990): 368–386.

Flath, D. *The Japanese Economy*. New York: Oxford University Press (2000).

"Foreign Insurers Seek Novel Policies (editorial)." *Nikkei Weekly* (May 12, 2003): 13.

Forman, G. "The Hidden Dangers of Industrial Policy." *The Wall Street Journal* (March 1, 1993).

Frank, R. H. and R. M. Hutchens. 1993. Wages, Seniority, and the Demand for Rising Consumption Profiles. *Journal of Economic Behavior and Organization* 21, no. 3: 251–276.

Fukoda, A., and S. Hirota. "Main Bank Relationships and Capita Structure in Japan." *Journal of Japanese and International Economics* 10 (1996).

Fujimoto, T. *The Evolution of a Manufacturing System at Toyota*. New York: Oxford University Press (1999).

Fujiwara, M. "Consumer Pioneers." *Journal of International Trade and Industry* 3 (1990): 10.

Genay, H. "Japan's Corporate Groups." *Federal Reserve Bank of Chicago* 20 (1990).

Guiliani, T. "Japan Marketers in Need of 'Branding,' Not 'Badging' Savvy Media." *Asia's Newspaper for Media and Advertising* (October 31, 2003).

Golub, S. "Is Trade Between the United States and Japan Off Balance?" *Finance and Development* (September 1994).

Gonenc, R. "A New Approach to Industrial Policy." *The OECD Observer* 187 (April-May 1994).

Grein, A., C. Craig, and H. Tanak. "Integration and Responsiveness: Marketing Strategies of Japanese and European Automobile Manufacturers." *Journal of International Marketing* 9, no. 2 (2001): 19–50.

Guth, R. "Eroding Empires: Electronics Giants of Japan Undergo Wrenching Change." *The Wall Street Journal* (June 20, 2002): 1.

Guth, R. "Survival of the Slimmest in Japan." *The Wall Street Journal* (January 31, 2003): B5.

Guth, R. "Family Ties: Japanese Giant Fights to Keep Control of Fast-Growing Unit." The Wall Street Journal (Dec. 18, 2001): A1

Hall, C. "Project on the Globalisation of Economic Activity and SME Development: Japan." *OECD,* Paris, 1995.

Hall, R. "The Importance of Lifetime Jobs in the U.S. Economy." *The American Economic Review* 72, no. 4 (1982): 716–24.

Halliday, J. *A Political History of Japanese Capitalism.* New York: Pantheon Books, 1975.

Hamani, A. "The Characteristics of Labor Disputes and their Settlement in Japan." *Social and Cultural Background of Labor of Labor Management Relations in Asian Countries,* proceedings of the 1971 Asian Regional Conference on Industrial Relations in Tokyo, Japan.

Hamilton, D. "Japan Struggles to Follow US in Telecommunications." *The Wall Street Journal* (February 14, 1996).

Hamilton, D. "Japanese Voters Turn from Reformers, Delivering Win to Liberal Democrats." *The Wall Street Journal* (October 21, 1996).

Harumi, Y. "The Lifetime Employment System Unravels." *Japan Quarterly* (October–December 1993).

Hashimoto, M. "Bonus Payments, On-the-Job Training, and Lifetime Employment in Japan." *Journal of Political Economy* 87, no. 5 (1979): 1086–1104.

Hashimoto, M., and J. Raisian. "Employment Tenure and Earnings Profiles in Japan and the United States." *American Economic Review* 75, no. 4 (1985): 720–736.

Hawkins, Jr., L. "Finding a Car That's Built to Last." *The Wall Street Journal* (July 9, 2003): D1 and D5.

Heita, K. "Japanese Economic Revolution versus the Western Experience (Part 1)." *Journal of Japanese Trade and Industry* 4 (1994).

Henkoff, R. "New Management Secrets from Japan." *Fortune* (November 27, 1995).

Hfheinz, P. "One Currency, Many Voices: Issues That Still Divide Europe." *The Wall Street Journal* (January 2, 2002): A2.

Hickok, S. "Japanese Trade Balance Adjustment to Yen Appreciation." *Federal Reserve Bank of New York Quarterly Review* 14, no. 3 (Autumn 1989).

Higuchi, Y. "A Comparative Study of Japanese Plants Operating in the US." Association of Japan Statistics Meeting at Nanzan Univ., Japan, 1987: 10.

Hirose, T. "Hollowing Out: Can New Growth Replace Japan's Pruned Industries?" *Nikkei Weekly* (January 16, 1995).

Hiroy, Y. "Re-examining Corporate Governance in Japan." *Journal of Japanese Trade and Industry* (March/April 2003).

Holloway, N. "Soul of Inefficiency: Counting the Cost of Japanese Trade Barriers." *Far Eastern Economic Review* (December 22, 1994).

Holloway, N. "Strong in One Way, Weak in Another." *Far Eastern Economic Review* (June 8, 1989).

Holzinger, A. G. "Selling American to the Japanese." *Nation's Business* (October 1990).

Honda Motor Company (Japan), *2004 Annual Report*. Tokyo, Japan, 2004.

Hoshi, T., and A. Kashyap. *Corporate Financing and Governance in Japan*. Cambridge, MA: The MIT Press, 2001.

"How To Succeed In Japan's Tough But Rewarding Market." *Forbes* (January 6, 1992).

"How to Succeed in the Japanese Market." *Tokyo Business Today* (July 1990).

Hulten, C. *Productivity Growth in Japan and the United States*. Chicago: The University of Chicago Press, 1990.

IMF. *Japan, Economic and Policy Developments*. 1998.

IMS HEALTH. "East Meets West: Japan Falling to Multinationals?" htpp://www.ims-global.com/insight/news-story/0109. Accessed April 9, 2003.

International Monetary Fund. *Japan, Economic and Policy Developments.* Washington, DC: International Monetary Fund, 2002.

International Monetary Fund. *World Economic Outlook.* Washington DC: International Monetary Fund, 1993.

"The Internet User and On-line Commerce in Japan." Tokyo: Japan Economic Institute, 2002.

Iritani, E. "In Japan—Elderly, Restless and Ready to Buy." *Los Angeles Times* (August 24, 2003): C1.

Itoh, M. *The Japanese Economy Reconsidered.* London: Palgrave, 2000.

Iwami, M. "What Is 'Japanese Style' Management?" *Management Japan* 21, no. 1 (Spring 1992).

Jacobs, L., and P. Herbig. "Japanese Product Development Strategies." *Journal of Business and Industrial Marketing* 13, no. 2 (1998): 132–154.

Jannosuke, M. *Contemporary Politics in Japan.* Berkeley: University of California Press, 1995.

"Japan Aging Quicker Than Thought (editorial)," Nikkei Weekly (February 4, 2002).

The Japan Company Handbook 1979–1990, Tokyo: Toyo Keizei, 1991.

Japanese Ministry of Finance. "Export and Import Statistics." 2004.

Japanese Ministry of Finance. "Foreign Direct Investment in Japan." November, 2002.

Japanese Ministry of Finance. "Trade Statistics of Japan" www.customs. go.jp. Accessed 3/25/2002.

Japanese Statistics Bureau. "Summary Results of the 2001 Survey on Time and Leisure Activities." September 2002.

Japanese Statistics Bureau. "1999 Survey on Service Industries." November 2001.

Jardine Flemming, *Annual Report 1990.* Hong Kong: Jardine Flemming, 1998.

JETRO. *The Challenge of the Japanese Market.* 1990.

JETRO. "8th Survey on Attitudes of Foreign Companies Towards Direct Investment in Japan." March 2003.

JETRO. "Focus Japan." www.jetro.go.jp. Accessed Dec. 10, 2002.

JETRO. *Japanese Market Report.* Tokyo, 2000.

JETRO. *Japanese Market Report No. 67* (March 2003).

JETRO, *Japanese Market Report.* 2004.

JETRO. "A New Era in Japan's Retailing Market." *Invest in Japan* 2 Special Edition (2003): 14–15.

JETRO. *Mail Order in Japan* 77 (March 1990): 6.

JETRO, *Marketing Guidebook for Major Imported Products.* 1990.

JETRO. *Meeting the Challenge: The Japanese Kaisha in the 1990s.* 1993: 36.

JETRO. *The 9th Survey on Attitudes of Foreign-Affiliated Companies Toward Direct Investment in Japan.* Feb. 2004.

JETRO. "Successful Investment in Japan." www3.jetro.go.jp/iv.cybermall. Accessed 5/20/04.

JETRO. *TRADESCOPE* 14, no. 4, (April 1995): p. 15.

JETRO. *The Wealth of Opportunity.* 1989.

JETRO. "White Paper on International Trade 2001." www.jetro.go.jp/it/e/pub. Accessed April 17, 2002.

JETRO. "Young People More Active but Dependent Longer." www.dec.ctu.edu.vn/ebooks/jetro/5.2.html. Accessed July 15, 2003.

Johnson, C. *Japan: Who Governs The Rise of the Developmental State.* New York: Norton and Co., 1995.

Johnson, C. *MITI and the Japanese Miracle.* San Francisco: Stanford University Press, 1982.

Joint Congressional Committee. "The Japanese Market: How Open Is It?" 101st United States Congress, sess J841–14, 1989–90: 44.

Kano, C. "Recession Chic." *Fortune* (September 29, 2003): 52.

Kanrei, T. "Japan's Trade Surplus: Look at the Quantum Figures." *KKC Forum* 2 (July 1994).

Katsuto, U. "Downsizing, Japanese Style." *Japan Echo* 21, Special Issue (1995).

Katz, R. *Japan, the System That Soured: The Rise and Fall of the Japanese Economic Miracle.* Armonk, New York: M. E. Sharpe, 1998.

Kawada, H. "Workers and Their Organizations." *Japanese Business Organizations.* Edited by K. Ouchi and J. Levine. Tokyo: Ochanomizu Shobo, 1973.

Kawakita, T. "Is the Japanese Labor Market Dual Structured?" *Japan Labor Bulletin* (August 1, 1992).

Kawasaki, T. "Bottom in Sight for Retailing," *The Nikkei Weekly* (July 14, 2003): 18.

Kazuo, Y. "A Dose of Deregulation to Buoy Business." *Japan Echo* 21, no. 4 (Winter 1994): 15.

Kerwin, K., and P. Magnusson. "Can Anything Stop Toyota?" *Business Week* (November 17, 2003): 114–122.

Kilburn, D. "The Sun Sets on Japan's Lifers." *Management Today* (September 1993).

Kilburn, D. "Vending Industry Keeps Growing." *Journal of Japanese Trade and Industry* 4 (1991): 20.

Kilburn, D., and S. J. Hill. "Creatively Cracking Through the Ad Clutter." *Advertising Age* (December 10, 1990).

Kim, J. M. "How to Strike Gold from Asia's Old." *Far Eastern Economic Review* 166, no. 29 (July 2003): 32.

Kim, S. B. "Modus Operandi of Lender-Cum-Shareholder Banks." Federal Reserve Bank of San Francisco (1990).

Kinoshita, T. "An Open Asia." *Look Japan* (March 1992).

Kishii, T. "Message vs. Mood: A Look at Some of the Differences between Japanese and Western Television Commercials." *Dentsu Japan Marketing/Advertising Yearbook* (1988). Tokyo: Japan, Dentsu, 1987.

Koike, K. "Japanese Workers in Large Firms." *Keizai Kagaku* 26, no. 1 (1978).

Koike, K. "Workers in Small Firms and Women in Industry." *Keizai Kagaku* 27, no. 1 (1980).

Kojima, K. "An International Perspective on Japanese Corporate Finance." *RIEB Kobe University Discussion Paper*, No. 5 (March 1995).

Komatsu, R. *Kigyobetsu Kumiai no Keisei [Development of Enterprise Unionism].* Tokyo: Ochanomizu Shobo, 1971.

Komiya, M. "The Japanese Computer Industry: An Industrial Policy Analysis." *Information Society* 6, no. 1, 2 (1989).

Komiya, R., M. Okuno, and K. Suzumura. *Industrial Policy of Japan.* Tokyo: University of Tokyo Press, 1984.

Kono, T. *Strategy and Structure of the Japanese Enterprise.* New York: Sharpe, 1985.

Koretz, G. "In Japan Small is Beautiful." *Business Week* (March 4, 1996).

Krugman, P. "America in the World Economy: Understanding the Misunderstandings." *Japan and the World Economy* 7 (1995).

Krugman, P. "The Myth of Asia's Miracle." *Foreign Affairs* (November/December, 1994).

Landers, P. "Good Medicine: Westerners Profit as Japan Opens Its Drug Market." *The Wall Street Journal* (December 2, 2002).

Landers, P. "Rare Proxy Battle Aims to Redress Japan Capitalism." *The Wall Street Journal* (May 13, 2002): A1 and A12.

Lawrence, R. "Imports in Japan's Closed Markets or Minds?" *Brookings Papers on Economic Activity* 2 (1987).

Lewis, J. "Western Companies Improve upon Japan's Keiretsu." *The Wall Street Journal* (December 12, 1995).

Liker, K. J. *The Toyota Way: 14 Management Principles from the World's Greatest Manufacturer.* New York: McGraw-Hill, 2004.

Lin, C.A. "Cultural Differences in Message Strategies: A Comparison Between American and Japanese TV Commercials." *Journal of Advertising Research* (July/August 1993).

Lincoln, E. *Arthritic Japan: The Slow Pace of Economic Reform.* Washington, DC: The Brookings Institution, 2001.

Lincoln, E. *Japan's Unequal Trade.* Washington, DC: The Brookings Institution, 1990.

Lincoln, J. "Employee Work Attitudes and Management Practice in the U.S. and Japan: Evidence from a Large Comparative Survey." *California Management Review* (Fall 1989).

"Loan Crisis Makes Clear the Need to Overhaul Finance Ministry (editorial)," *Nikkei Weekly* (February 19, 1996).

Lynn, et. al. "Engineering Careers, Job Rotation, and Gatekeepers in Japan and the United States." *Journal of Engineering & Technology Management* 10, no. 1, 2 (June 1993).

Lytle, J. M. "Life Online: A Yen for a Hi-tech Life." *The Guardian* (September 11, 2003).

Maki, A. "Personal Savings Rate." *Keio Business Review* 26 (1991): 3.

Makido, T., S. Kimoura, and P. Mourdoukoutas. "IT and Competitive Advantage: the Case of Japanese Manufacturing Companies." *European Business Review* 15, no.5 (2003): 307–311.

Management and Coordination Agency. *Census of Japanese Establishments.* Tokyo, 1985.

Management and Coordination Agency. *Census of Japanese Establishments.* Tokyo, 2002.

Management and Coordination Agency. *2002 Census of Japanese Establishments.* Tokyo, 2003.

Markoff, J. "Auction Sites In Japan Fear Move to Limit Online Sites." *The New York Times* (February 6, 2002).

Martin, N. "An Original Copier: Ricoh Leads the Industry with Advanced Digital Office Machines." *Barron's* (January 6, 2003).

Martin D., and P. Herbig. "Marketing Implications of Japan's Social-Cultural Underpinnings." *Journal of Brand Management* 9, no. 3 (2002): 179–89.

Marubeni Corporation. *Corporate Annual Report.* 2004.

Matsushita Electric Industrial Company. *2002 Annual Corporate Report.* Tokyo. 2002.

Mazda Motor Co. *Corporate Annual Report.* 2004.

McDonald's. 2003 Annual Report. Oak Brook, IL, 2004.

McDufflie, J., and T. Kochan. "Do US Firms Invest Less in Human Resources? Training in the World Auto Industry." *Industrial Relations* 34, no. 2 (April 1995).

McInerney, F., and S. White. *Beating Japan.* New York: Truman Talley Books/Dutton, 1993.

Mckinney, J. "Degree of Access to the Japanese Market: 1979 vs. 1986." *Columbia Journal of the World of Business* (Summer 1989): 53–60.

Melloan, G. "How Japan's Goblin's Spook Wall Street." *The Wall Street Journal* (March 10, 1996).

Melloan, G. "The Japanese Give Hashimoto a Low-Confidence Vote." *The Wall Street Journal* (October 21, 1996).

METI. *Adjustment of Consumer Agreements for Installment Sales*. 1999.

METI. *1994 Census of Commerce*. 1995: 20.

METI. "The 34th Annual Survey of Trends Among Foreign Capitalized Firms in Japan." Tokyo, 2002.

METI. "The 35th Survey of Foreign Affliates in Japan." 2002.

METI. *2002 Economic and Industrial Policy Forward-Looking Structural Reform Toward Self-Sustained Growth*. 2001.

METI. *White Paper*. Tokyo, 2002.

METI. *White Paper*. Tokyo, 2004.

Minister of Foreign Affairs. *Diplomatic Bluebook*. 1990.

Ministry of International Affairs and Communications. *Annual Report on Family Income and Expenditure Statistics Bureau*. 2002.

Ministry of Health, Labor, and Welfare. *1985 Population Census*.

Ministry of Posts, Communicaions, and Broadcasting. Publication Name. Tokyo, 2003.

Minton-Eversole, T. "Working for a Japanese Company." *Journal of Training and Development* (March 1993).

MITI. "Adjustment of Consumer Agreements for Installment Sales." Tokyo, 2002.

MITI. *Outline of Small and Medium Enterprise Policies of the Japanese Government*. 1995.

MITI. *Survey on the Internationalization of Enterprises (in the Distribution Industry)*. January/February 1989.

MITI. *White Paper on Trade*. 1988.

MITI. *White Paper on Trade*. 1990.

"MITI's Vision for the 1990s (cover story)." *Journal of Japanese Trade and Industry* 5 (1990).

MOFA. "Japan's Approach to Deregulation." www.Mofa.go.jp/j-info/japan/regulate. Accessed January 2, 2002.

Moffett, S. "Going Gray: For Ailing Japan, Longevity Begins To Take Its Toll." *The Wall Street Journal* (February 11, 2003): A1 and A12.

Moffett, S. "The Japanese Paradox." *The Wall Street Journal* (September 23, 2003): B1, B4.

Moffett, S. and P. Dvorak. "Asian Fusion: As Japan Recovers, An Unlikely Source Gets Credit: China." *The Wall Street Journal* (May 4, 2004): A1, A12.

Montgomery, D. B. "Understanding the Japanese as Customers, Competitors, and Collaborators." *Japan and the World Economy* 9 (1997): 537–551.

Morgan, J., and J. Morgan. *Cracking the Japanese Market: Strategies for Success in the New Global Economy.* New York: Free Press, 1991.

Moore, K., and M. Smith. "Taking Global Brands to Japan." The Conference Board, www.conferenceboard.org/worldwide/. Accessed May 21, 2004.

Mori, K. "The Place of Foreign Workers in a Graying Society." *Economic Eye* 13, no.1 (Spring 1992).

Moriguchi, C. "The Japanese Economy: The Capacity to Transform and Restructure." *Japanese Economic Studies* (Spring 1990).

Morimoto, *Friday.*

Morita, A. "A Critical Moment for Japanese Management."

Morita, A. *Made in Japan.* New York: Weatherhill, 1987.

Morita, A. "Partnering for Competitiveness: The Role of Japanese Business." *Harvard Business Review* (May/June 1992).

Mourdoukoutas, P. *Adapt, Develop, Promote: How to Compete in the Japanese Market.* Massachusetts: Copley Publishing Group, 1995.

Mourdoukoutas, P. "Economic Barriers for Foreign Affiliates in Japan." *International Journal of Manpower* 13, no. 9 (1992).

Mourdoukoutas, P. *Japan's Turn.* Lanhan, MD: Univeristy Press of America, 1993.

Mourdoukoutas, P. *The Rise and Fall of Abacus Banking in Japan and China.* Westport, Connecticut: Quorum Books, 2000.

Mourdoukoutas, P, and S. Papadimitriou. "Do Japanese Companies Have a Strategy?" *European Business Review* 98, no. 4 (1998): 227–234.

Mourdoukoutas, P., and U. Roy. "Job Rotation and Public Policy: Theory and Applications of Japan and the USA." *International Manpower Journal* 15, no. 6 (1994).

Mroczkowski, T., and M. Hanaoka. "Continuity and Change in Japanese Management." *California Management Review* (Winter 1989).

Mueller, B. "Standardization vs. Specialization: An Examination of Westernization in Japanese Advertising." *Journal of Advertising Research* (January/February 1992).

Naito, M. "Chipmakers Seek Synergy in Union." *Nikkei Weekly* (June 24, 2002).

Nakagawa, T., and H. Matsuzaka. "Employment and Wages." *Basic Research in Wages*. Edited by Ichiro Nakayama. Tokyo: Tokyo University Press, 1956.

Nakamoto, M. "Manufacturing: The Japanese Art of Performance." *Financial Times* (May 18, 2004): 12.

Nakamura, A. "Nissan Enters Luxury Minivan Fray with Remodeled Presage." *Japan Times* (June 27, 2003).

Nanjo, S. "Government Finances Past and Present." *Economic Eye* (Spring 1995).

Nasar, S. "The Risky Allure of Strategic Trade." *The New York Times* (February 28, 1993).

Neff, R. "Why Hashimoto Has to Hang Tough." *Business Week* (January 27, 1997).

"New Paradigms in the Japanese Labor Market," *Focus Japan* 21, no. 4 (April 1994): 2.

Ng, C. S.V., and S. G.Yip. "Japan's Coming Competitive Renaissance." *Strategy and Business* 34 (Spring 2004): 46–56.

Nikkei Sangyo Shiburn. (June 15, 1989): 12.

Nishida, K. "Social Relations and Japanese-Style of Management: Internal and External Ittaika-Mode Relations of Japanese Enterprises." *Japanese Economic Studies* 12 (1984).

Nishikawa, T. "New Product Development: Japanese Consumer Tastes in the Area of Electronics and Home Appliances." *Journal of Advertising Research* (April/May, 1990).

Nishinarita, Y. "An Overview of Japanese Labor–Employer Relations from the 1870s to the 1990s." *Hitobashi Journal of Economics* 36 (1995).

Noble, G. "Japan in 1992: Just another Aging Superpower?" *Asian Survey* (January 1993).

Noland, M. "Japanese Trade Elasticities and the J-Curve." *Review of Economics and Statistics* 71 (February 1989).

"No. of Foreign Students Tops 110,000." *Japan Today* (Dec. 4, 2004): 1.

Noriaki, K. "Japanese Employment and Labor Laws in Transition." *Journal of Japanese Trade and Industry* 4 (1997).

OECD. "1994 Economic Survey of Japan." 1995.

OECD. *The Development of Industrial Relations Systems.* 1977.

OECD. *Economic Outlook.* 1988.

OECD. *Industrial Policy in OECD Countries.* 1989.

OECD. *Industrial Policy in OECD Countries.* 1993.

OECD. *Layoffs and Short-Time Working in Selected OECD Countries.* 1983.

OECD. *OECD Economic Observer.* 1992.

OECD. *OECD Economic Observer.* Paris. 2004.

OECD. *The Sources of Growth in OECD Countries.* 2003: 51.

Ohashi, I. "A Comparison of the Labor Market in Japan and the United States." *Japanese Economic Studies* (Summer 1983).

Ohkusa, Y., and S. Ohta. "An Empirical Study of the Wage–Tenure Profile in Japanese Manufacturing." *Journal of the Japanese and International Economies* 8, no. 2 (June 1994): 174.

Onishi, N. "Japan Discovers Dark Side of Consumerism" *Houston Chronicle* (September 21, 2003): 33.

Oishi, N. "Subcontractor Attrition Eroding Economic Base." *The Nikkei Weekly* (April 4, 1992).

Oishi Sh. "The Bakuhay System in Nakane." *Tokugawa Japan: The Social and Economic Antecedents of Modern Japan.* Edited by Chie and Oishi from translations by Conard. Tokyo: University of Tokyo Press, 1990: 213–231.

Ono, T., "Buy-back Plan Lifts Hitachi, Backfires on Sony," *Nikkei Weekly* (May 12, 2003): 12.

Ono, T. "Shut Out: As Slide Drags On, Japan Inc. Sacrifices Its Youngest Workers." *The Wall Street Journal* (December 19, 2001): A1 and A10.

Osami, M. "Trend Toward Choosiness." *Journal of International Trade and Industry* 3 (1990).

Osland, Taylor, and Zou. "Selecting International Modes of Entry and Expansion." *Marketing Intelligence and Planning* 19, no. 3 (2001): 153–161.

Ostrom, D. "The Keiretsu System: Cracking or Crumbling." *Japan Economic Institute Report* 14 (April 7, 2000).

Ostrom, D. "'A New Economy'? Yes, But with a Difference," *Tokyo Business Today,* November 2000, Table 3.

Ostrom, D. "Trends in Japanese Trade with the Middle East." Presented at the Conference on Japan and the Middle East, June 1, 1990: 1–17.

Ouchi, W. *Theory Z.* Boston: Addison-Wesley Publishing Co., 1981.

Overton, B. "Japanese Market is Ripe for Picking." *Target Marketing* (February 1991).

Ozawa, I. *Blueprint for a New Japan: The Rethinking of a Nation.* Tokyo: Kodansha International, 1994.

"Pacific Aisles: Wall-Mart's Foray Into Japan Spurs A Retail Upheaval (editorial)," *The Wall Street Journal* (September 19, 2003): A1, A6.

Pacific Bridge Inc. http://www.pacificbridgemedical.com. Accessed on May 17, 2004.

Patrick, H., and H. Rosovsky (editors). *Asia's New Giant: How the Japanese Economy Works.* Washington, DC: The Brookings Institution, 1976.

Pension Fund Association. "The Behavior of Domestic Investors." *Japan Economics Weekly* (May 21, 2004): 10.

Pfizer. *2003 Annual Report.* New York, 2004.

Pollack, A. "Japan Cites U.S. Demands in Collapse of Auto Talks." *The New York Times* (May 7, 1995).

Pollack, A. "Japan's Companies Moving Production to Sites Overseas." *The New York Times* (August 29, 1993).

Pollack, A. "Myths Aside, Japanese Do Look for Bargains." *The New York Times* (February 24, 1994).

Pollack, A. "Think Japan Inc. Is Lean and Mean? Step Into This Office." *The New York Times* (March 20, 1994).

Pollack, A. "Japan Inc.'s Dying Bit Players." *The New York Times* (May 8, 1995).

Porter, D. "Japan's Consumers Turn Tough." *The Wall Street Journal* (March 28, 1994): B7.

Porter, M. *The Competitive Advantage of Nations.* New York: The Free Press, 1990.

Porter, M., H. Takeuchi, and M. Sakakibara. *Can Japan Compete?* Cambridge, MA: Perseus Publishing, 2000.

Powell, B., and H. Takayama. "Scenes from a Bust." *Newsweek* (1992).

Prestowitz, C. "Getting Japan to Say Yes." *The Washington (D.C.) Post* (January 31–February 6, 1994).

Prime Minister's Office. *Index of Business.* Tokyo, 2000.

Prime Minister's Office. *White Paper on National Lifestyle.* Tokyo, 2000.

"Profits Net Shareholders Dividends." *The Nikkei Weekly* (June 9, 2003): 4.

"Prosumers Sniff Out New Trends." *The Wall Street Journal* (October 30, 2003).

Raskin, A. "How to Bulletproof Your Product (Hint: Take to Japan)." *Business 2.0* (September 2003): 54.

Reed, S. "Japan: The Banking Scandal Could Hamstring Hashimoto." *Business Week* (February 5, 1996): 65.

Reichheld, F. *The Loyalty Effect.* Massachusetts: Harvard Business School, 1996.

Reid, T. R. "Lifestyles of the Rich and Funless." *The Washington Post Weekly* (November 18–24, 1991).

"Remarks by US Trade Representative, Micky Kantor." *The New York Times.* (February 24, 1994): 17.

Ryuichiro, M. "Why Bureaucrats Don't Serve the Public Interest." *Japan Echo* 23, no. 3 (Autumn 1996).

Ryutaro, H. "Directions for the Future of the Japanese Economy." *Journal of Japanese Trade and Industry* 3 (1995).

Sakai, K. "The Feudal World of Japanese Manufacturing." *Harvard Business Review* (November/December 1990).

Sakai, K. "Japan Unveils Plan to End Banking Crisis That Could Clear the Way from Failure." *The Wall Street Journal* (June 9, 1995).

Sakai, K. "Many Japanese Companies to Report Losses." *The Wall Street Journal* (February 21, 1996).

Sakai, K. "Japan's Tokai Bank Sets Big Write-Off in Bid to Put Industry Crisis Behind." *The Wall Street Journal* (February 29, 1996).

"Sales per Vending Machine Accelerates in Japan. Coke Dominates." www.beverage-digest.com/editorial/990827. Accessed 1/31/2004.

Sanger, D. "How Washington Inc. Makes a Sale." Business Section of the *The New York Times* (February 19, 1995).

Sanger, D. "Japan's Bureaucracy: No Sign It's Losing Any Power." *The Wall Street Journal* (February 27, 1994).

Sapsford, J. "Japan's Bureaucrats Balk at Curbing Clout." *The Wall Street Journal* (December 26, 1996).

Sapsford, J. "Tokyo Hits a Wall with Economic Plans." *The Wall Street Journal* (June 28, 1995).

Sato, K. "Can Japan Really Change? What Are the Problems?" *Journal of Japanese Trade and Industry* 1 (1995).

Sato, Y. "Work Organization and Job Quality of Small- and Medium-Sized Enterprises (SMEs) in Japan." *Keio Business Review* 32 (1996).

Saxonhouse, G. "What Does Japanese Trade Structure Tell Us about Japanese Trade Policy?" *Journal of Economic Perspectives* 7 (Summer 1993).

Scalise, P. "Patience Holds the Key. . . ." *Asian Chemical News* (January 13–19, 2003): 11–12.

Schumpeter, J. *Capitalism, Socialism, and Democracy.* New York: Harper & Row, 1976: 21.

Seiko, Y. "Changing Japanese Society and the Consciousness of the Young." *Journal of Japanese Trade and Industry* (January/February 2002).

"Shellshocked by the Yen, Japanese Companies Still Find Ways to Cope, (cover story)", *New York Times* (April 18, 1995).

Shimada, H. "Japanese Capitalism: The Irony of Success." *Economic Eye* 13, no. 3 (August 1992).

Shinposha, T. K. *The Japan Company Handbook 1979–1990.* Tokyo Japan: Toyo Keizai, 1991.

Shinposha, T. K., and K. K. Soran. *The Japan Economic Journal* (Tokyo: 1990): 26.

Shirai, T. "A Theory of Enterprise Unionism." *Contemporary Industrial Relations in Japan.* Edited by Taishiro Shirai. Madison: Wisconsin University Press, 1983: 117–143.

Shirai, T. "Party's Over in Mail-Order Market." *The Nikkei Weekly* (February 14, 1994).

Shirouzou, N. "Japan Tightens Ties to Affiliates." *The Wall Street Journal* (February 11, 1999): A19.

Shiseido. *Company Annual Report.* Tokyo. 2001.

Silk, L., and T. Kono. "Sayonara, Japan Inc." *Foreign Policy* 93 (Winter 1993).

Singer, J. "Goldman Again Tops List of M&A Advisers in Japan." *The Wall Street Journal* (January 17, 2003): A11.

Singer, J. "Hostile Treatment: With '80s Tactics, U.S. Fund Shakes Japan's Cozy Capitalism." *The Wall Street Journal* (April 15, 2004).

Singer, J. "Japanese Jackpot: How Annuities Caught On." *The Wall Street Journal, Eastern Edition* (June 4, 2004): C1.

Singer, J. "Under Siege: Foreigners Threaten Nomura's Dominance of Japanese Markets." *The Wall Street Journal* (January 8, 2002): A1.

Singer, J., and M. Fackler. "In Japan, Adding Beer, Wine to Latte List." *The Wall Street Journal* (July 14, 2003).

Smith, R. "MEF launches Promotion to Win Back Japanese Market." *Feedstuffs* 74, no. 5 (February 4, 2002): 9

Smitka, M. "Business Relations: Auto Parts Sourcing in Japan." *Current Politics and Economics of Japan* 3, no. 4 (1993).

Smitka, M. "Making Japan Cheaper for the Japanese." *The New York Times* (August 1993).

SONY. "Sony to Reveal Restructuring Plan." *Tech Web* (Oct. 22, 2003).

Sprague, J., and M. Mutsuko. "Japan's New Attitude." *Asia Week* 26 (October 20, 2000): 1.

Spencer, W., and P. Grindley. "Sematech after Five Years: High Technology Consortia and US Competitiveness." *California Management Review* (Summer 1993).

Starbuck's. *2003 Annual Report.* Seattle, WA, 2004.

Statistics Bureau. "March 2002 Survey of Household Economy." www.stat.go.jp. Accessed on 7/3/2003.

Statistics Bureau. "1999 National Survey of Family Income and Expenditure." Tokyo: Ministry of Internal Affairs and Communication, 2000.

Statistics Bureau. *Statistical Handbook of Japan.* Ministry of Internal Affairs and Communications, 1993.

Sterngold, J. "Making Japan Cheaper for the Japanese." *The New York Times* (August 8. 1993).

Sterngold, J. "The Men Who Really Run Fortress Japan." *The New York Times* (April 10, 1994).

Sterngold, J. "Why the Japanese Endure Vending Machines." *The New York Times* (January 4, 1994).

Stewart, D. "The Threat to Japan's Economy is Japan, not China." *Asia Times Online* (August 26, 2002).

Susumu, N. "Japanese Politics: A Ship of Fools." *Japan Echo* (Autumn 1995).

Tabb, W. *The Postwar Japanese System: Cultural Economy and Economic Transformation.* New York and Oxford: Oxford University Press, 1995.

Tajima, Y. "Catering to the Needs of a Diversifying Market." *Economic Eye* (1991).

Takahiro, F. "A Twenty-first Century Strategy for Japanese Manufacturing." *Japan Echo* (February 2004): 20–25.

Takashi, F. "Japanese Companies Move Away from Seniority-based System." *Journal of Japanese Trade and Industry* (January/February 2002).

Takashi, F. "Deregulation Dawdle." *Far Eastern Economic Review* (September 29, 1995).

Takashi, I. "Changing Japanese Labor and Employment System." *Journal of Japanese Trade and Industry* 4 (1997).

Takeo, N. "Toward a New Japanese-style System." *Journal of Japanese Trade and Industry* 4 (1997).

Takeshi, T. "Japan's Current Reforms and Lessons from History." *Journal of Japanese Trade and Industry* (January/February 2003).

Takeuchi, K. "Does Japan Import Less than it Should? A Review of Literature." *Asian Economic Journal* (September 1989).

Tallman, E., and J. Rosenbersweig. "Investigating U.S. Government and Trade Deficits." *Federal Reserve Bank of Atlanta* (May/June 1991).

Tatsuno, S. *Created in Japan*. New York: Harper-Collins Publishers, 1992.

Terazono, E. "Success has Whittled Away MITI's Powers." *Financial Times* (December 6, 1994).

Terhune, C., and G. Kahn. "Coke Lures Japanese Customers with Cell Phone Come-Ons." *The Wall Street Journal* (September 8, 2003): B1 and B4.

Thornton, E. "Japan's Struggle to Restructure." *Fortune* (June 28, 1993).

Tischler, L. "Carlos Ghosn Shifts the Once-Troubled Automaker into Profit Overdrive." *Fast Company* 60 (2002): 80.

Tomihira, M., and H. Asami. *Access to Nippon*. Tokyo: Tokyo University Press, 1994.

Toga, M. "94 Auto Imports Raced to Record High." *Nikkei Weekly* (January 16, 1995).

Toru, H. "After Eden: Japanese Politics Wandering in the Wilderness." *Japan Echo* 23, no. 2 (Summer 1996).

Toyota Motor Company. *1992 Annual Report*. Toyota City, Japan, 1992.

Toyota Motor Company. *2003 Annual Report*. Toyota City, Japan, 2003.

Toyota Motor Company. *Outline of Toyota*. Toyota City, Japan, 1997.

"Trends in Diversification of Employment Types." www.mhlw.go.jp/English. Accessed 1/30/05.

Tsuru, S. *Japan's Capitalism: Creative Defeat and Beyond*. Cambridge, Massachusetts: Cambridge University Press, 1993.

Tsuruaka, D. "Japan in Asia—Look East and Up: Malaysia Embraces Japan as Its Economic Model." *Far Eastern Economic Review* 151 (March 28, 1991).

Ueda, K. "Yen's Appreciation Won't Solve Problem of Trade Imbalance" *The Nikkei Weekly* (May 24, 1993).

Uematsu, T. "Wakon Yosai, the Ideology of the Japanese Economic Development." *Kobe University Economic Review* 39 (1993).

United Nations Economic Commission of Europe. Geneva. Oct. 17, 2003: 5.

Vickery, G. "The Patterns of Industrial Policy." *The OECD Observer* 191 (December 1994—January 1995).

Vietor, R. *Globalization and Growth: Case Studies in National Economic Strategies.* Mason, Ohio: South West, 2005.

Voss, B. "Rising to the Occasion." *Journal of Business Strategy* (September–October 1991).

Watanabe, C., and Y. Honda. "Inducing Power of Japanese Technological Innovation—Mechanisms of Japan's Industrial Science and Technology Policy." *Japan and the World Economy* 3 (1991).

Watanabe, C., and Y. Honda. "Japanese Industrial Science and Technology." *Japan and the World Economy* 4 (1992).

Whiting, R. "Managing Product Development from the Top." *Electronic Business* (June 17, 1991).

Wilder, C. "Finding a Place in the Rising Sun." *Computer World* 25 (May 20, 1991): 116.

Williams, M. "Revolving Door: Many Japanese Companies Ran Amok While Led by Former Regulators." *The Wall Street Journal* (January 19, 1996).

Wood, C. *The End of Japan Inc.* New York: Simon & Schuster, 1994.

The World Bank. *World Tables.* 1988–89 and 1991 editions. Washington, DC.

Worthy, F. "Japan's Smart Weapon." *Fortune* (August 12, 1991).

WuDunn, S. "Japan's Vaunted Bureaucrats, the Real Power Behind the Throne, Are Under Siege." *The New York Times* (May 5, 1996).

Xillinx. *Annual Report.* 2004: Y.

Yamada, M. "Japan's Vending Machines Want to Talk to You." *The Industry Standard* (April 2, 2001).

Yim, S. "Gender Gap." *Harvard Business Review* 22, no. 1 (Winter 2000): 12–13.

Young, L. H. "Product Development in Japan: Evolution vs. Revolution." *Electronic Business News* (June 17, 1991): 75.

Yuji, G. "Don't Blame the Unmarried Breed." *Japan Echo* (June 2002): 54–66.

Yusuke, F. "Preserving What is Good in Japanese Management." *Japan Echo* 21, Special Issue (1995).

Zaun, T. "Shifting Gears: Mazda Nears Turnaround." *The Wall Street Journal* (December 31, 2002): A11.

Zoltan, A. "Small Business Economics: A Global Perspective." *Challenge* 35 (November/December 1992).

INDEX

1999 Census of Commerce, 80
1985 Plaza Accord, 4, 5, 71, 84, 110
1995 Population Census, 127
1988 Trade Act, 3, 41, 49
2003 United Nations World Robotics Report, 184

A

Abecasis-Phillips, John AS, 7
absence from Japan, cultural importance of physical presence, 161
account and trade surpluses in old and new economy, 50–52
accounting companies, inaccessibility, 6
acquisitions and mergers, foreign companies, 141
Acura, 174
adapting to Japanese business conditions
    main discussion, 161–172
    ADP strategy, defined, 159
    after-hour meetings, 169
    business negotiations, 168, 169
    customer focus. See customer focus
    delivery of product, 165
    direct communication, 169
    fax correspondence, 161
    formality of introductions, 167
    guarantees on products, 165, 166, 194
    impersonal and informal correspondence, 161
    implied meaning in communication, 169
    long-term planning and long-term relationships, 167, 168
    novelty and distinction of products, 166
    packaging and labeling, 163–165
    physical presence in Japan, 161
    product quality, 163
    quick results, 168, 169
    rules of competition, 170, 171
Adjimoto General Foods, 114
ADP strategy
    main discussion, 145–147, 159–172
    adapting. See adapting to Japanese conditions
    defined, 159
    development. See developing new products
    promotion. See promotion of products

advertising
    agencies, 189
    See also promotion of products
AFLAC, 10, 80, 174
AFLAC Japan, 107, 138, 153, 156, 196
    case study, 147–149
after-hour meetings in Japanese business, 169
agents and agencies
    advertising, 189
    insurance, 148
aging trends in Japan's markets, 128, 132, 133
agricultural products, deregulation of Japanese economy, 74
Aichi Steel Works, 17
AIG, 91
aisatsu, 167, 168
Ajinomoto Co., Ltd., 196
Akio Morita, 19, 169, 170
Akiyama Machinery Manufacturing, 5, 112–113, 205
ALCOA, 110
Alfa Romeo, 126
Alico Life, 133
Altera Corporation, 174
amakundori, 85
American Chambers of Commerce, 4, 6, 30, 111
American Chambers of Commerce in Japan (ACCJ) survey, 111, 112
American Family Life Insurance, 138
American Home Direct, 80
American Home Products, 141
Amway Corporation, 130, 196–197
Andruss, Paula Lyon, 123
Annual Survey of Foreign-Affiliated Companies in Japan
    23rd, 111
    34th, 143
antenna stores, 177
Aoki, Tomotsu, 137
Aoshima, Ken, 100
Apple Computer, 119, 137, 140, 167, 174–175, 205
Applied Materials, 2, 7, 110, 117, 119, 137
applied research for new products, 177, 178
arbaito, 28
Arrow Electronics, 140
Asahi Mutual Life, 173
Asian Chemical News, 163

Asian-Pacific trade and investment, 115, 116
Asia's Newspaper for Media and Advertising, 171
AST Research, 174
AT&T, 80, 119, 137, 140
attorneys, foreign trade inaccessibility, 6
audits, mandatory, 94
automobiles and automobile companies
    deregulation of Japanese economy, 74
    in economic dualism, 3, 8
    garages, deregulation, 79
    purchase of US-manufactured auto parts, 5
Avon, 130, 145–147
Axcelis Technologies, 140

B

baby boom, aging trends in Japan's markets, 128, 132, 133
Bank of Japan, 4, 71, 82, 83, 102, 104
Bank of Tokyo, 85
Bank of Tokyo-Mitsubishi Ltd., 91
banking
    deregulation, 77, 78, 84–86
    finance companies, 3, 143
Baskin-Robbins, 196
Baxter International, 134
Beating Japan, 7
Bentsen, Lloyd, 51
bibliography, 207–230
Blue Print for a New Japan, 75
BMW, 1, 147
Bodum Group, 117, 137
bonds and securities, 78, 94, 155
bonuses for employees, 25
Borden Corporation, 110, 141–141
Bowers, Brent, 161
brands
    distinction and social status, 166
    labeling and packaging messages, 163–165
    name recognition, 137, 192
    new products, 175
    promoting products by brand names vs. product names, 192
    trends and opportunities, 123, 125
Braun, 147
breakthrough products, 118, 119
breweries, deregulation, 79
British C&W, 80
British Telecom, 137

Bubble economy
  main discussion, 82–84
  competition in post-Bubble
    economy, 89, 101
  defined, 6
  introductory information, 2,
    7, 13
  prices and spending, 130, 131
  shifting economic priorities, 70
Buddhist teachings, 180
builders. See construction
  companies
Buitoni, 196
bulletproofing, 118
bureaucratic involvement in
  business. See government
  activism
Bush, George H.W., 57, 75
business and political
  restructuring, 89–101
business meetings, after-hours, 169
business strategies
  main discussion, 2, 145–147,
    159–172
  ADP strategy, defined, 159
  advertising. See promotion of
    products
  cultural adaptation. See
    adapting to Japanese business
    conditions
  product development. See
    developing new products
buyback guarantees for unsold
  commodities, 194
bypassing traditional distribution
  channels, 196

C
Campbell Soup, 164
Can Japan Compete?, 35
Canon, 19, 27, 30, 89, 97, 173
Carrefour, 2, 109, 113, 194, 205
cars. See automobiles and
  automobile companies
Carter, Jimmy, 3
Carter administration, 57
celebrities promoting
  products, 192
cell phones
  popularity with senior
    population, 133
  vending machine interface, 197
certification of products, 72
Chamber of Commerce survey,
  4, 30
Chanel, 123
Charles Schwab Co. Ltd., 80
Chevrolet, 174
childless couples, trends, 127, 128
children, in Japan's markets, 124,
  126–128
Christopher, Robert, 7
Chrysler, 13, 15, 75
Chugai Pharmaceutical Co., 5, 95,
  112, 140
Chujo, Ushio, 207
Chuo Trust, 85
Citibank, 80
class actions, 94
Clifton, Bill, 39, 51, 57
Coach, 123
coal liquefaction research, 45–47

Coca-Cola, 1, 137, 148, 156,
  196, 198
collective bargaining, 24, 26
commercials
  length, 192
  See also promotion of products
commodity markets and
  economic dualism, 16–20
communication barriers,
  overcoming
  developing new products,
    horizontal communication,
    181, 182
  explicit, direct
    communication, 169
  impersonal and informal
    correspondence, 161
Compaq Computer, 110, 137, 149
comparison of products in
  advertising, 190
Competitive Advantage of Nations,
  The, 40, 118
competitive strategy
  domestic sector's limited
    competition in economic
    dualism, 16–18
  rules of competition in
    Japan, 170
  See also business strategy;
    deregulation of Japanese
    economy
Competitiveness of Chinese Products
  in the Japanese Market, 96
computers
  Computer Aided Design
    (CAD), 91
  foreign industry in Japan,
    137–141, 146, 148–152, 205
  help-desk outsourcing, 166
  IT practices, old vs. new
    economy, 91, 92
  MITI and technological
    advances, 45–47
  new products, 174, 175
  robots, 184
  Trade and Competitiveness Act
    of 1988,"Super 301" section, 3
  See also wireless technology
Confucianism, 22
consensus building and
  government activism, 42, 43
construction companies
  in economic dualism, 3
  foreign trade inaccessibility, 6
consumer. See customer focus
consumer economy. See
  deregulation of Japanese
  economy
consumer partnerships, 196
"Consumer Pioneers," 131
consumer spending
  Bubble Economy, 130, 131
  credit cards, 124, 131
  disposable income in Japan,
    115, 116
  food, furniture, and clothing,
    table of comparisons, 195
consumerism in economic
  dualism, 3
contracts
  employment, contractual and
    noncontractual, 20–29

government procurement
    contracts, 152
  between wholesalers and
    retailers, 193
convenience
  convenience stores, 80, 98, 193
  packaging, 164
  seniors, products attractive
    to, 133
  vending machines, 197, 198
cooperation between business and
  government, 37, 38
copyright and patent
  infringements, 138, 139, 196
Corning, Inc., 110, 119
corporate objectives in old and
  new economy, 93–96
Costco, 15, 109, 110, 113, 194, 205
costs
  cost of living in Japan, 3, 64
  developing new products, 183
  distribution channels, 194
  high cost of local labor, 6
  promotion of products, 189
  startup costs, 138, 139
Cracking the Japanese Market, 7
Created in Japan, 180
creative destruction of industry, 38
creativity in workplace, 179, 180
credit card spending trends,
  124, 131
crime
  vandalism, 197, 198
  yakuza, 78, 84
cross-functional teamwork, 89
cultural adaptation. See adapting
  to Japanese business
  conditions
currency
  foreign currency regulation, 38
  yen. See yen
customer focus
  customer service, 130, 165, 166
  developing new products,
    162–166, 177, 178
Czinkota, Michael, 7, 118

D
Daiei, 77, 170
Daikyo Sekiyu, 41
DaimlerChrysler, 94
daimyo, 17
David Kilburn, 198
de Silva, Neville, 101
debt financing, 95
DEC. See Digital Equipment
  Corporation (DEC)
delivery of products, 165
Dell Computer, 166, 174, 205
Denso Corporation, 92
Dentsu Japan
  Marketing/Advertising
  Yearbook, 190
department stores
  distribution channels, 193
  Large Department Store Law,
    15, 77, 193
  vs. warehouse and discount
    stores, 130, 171
deregulation of Japanese economy
  main discussion, 69–86
  agricultural products, 74

automobiles and parts, 74
banking, 77, 78, 84–86
bonds and securities, 77, 78
breweries, 79
distribution system, 72, 76
domestic consumption, 71
expansionary monetary and
    fiscal policy, 71
financial system, 77, 78
garages, 79
government procurement,
    72, 79
hours of work, reduction, 70,
    71, 82
import quotas, 74
insurance, 74, 77, 78
interest rates, 77, 78
introductory matters, 8
nontariff trade barriers
    (NTB), 74
oil imports, 79
procurement, 72, 79
product standards and
    certification systems, 72
protectionism, lifting, 72
retail, 76
tariffs, 72, 73
taxis, 79
telecommunications, 79
Trade and Competitiveness Act
    of 1988, 3
yen, value of, 71
See also old vs. new economy;
    open Japanese markets
design emphasis in product
    development, 180, 181
designer products
    trends and opportunities in
        Japan's markets, 125
    See also brands
developing new products
    main discussion, 173–185
    adapting to Japanese business
        conditions, 162–166
    ADP strategy, 159
    applied research, 177, 178
    brands, 175
    breakthrough products,
        118, 119
    as competitive strategy, 176–178
    consumer focus, 162–166
    continuous product
        improvements, 180
    cost and price
        considerations, 183
    creativity in workplace, 179
    customer focus, 162–166,
        177, 178
    customer needs, 177, 178
    early design emphasis, 180, 181
    feedback from customers, 177
    horizontal communication,
        181, 182
    incremental creativity, 180
    market-driven, 177, 178
    microelectronics
        applications, 183
    original forms of creativity, 180
    "phase review", 180, 181
    product perception, 175
    productivity, 183, 184
    "prosumers", 177

research, 177, 178
research and manufacturing
    proximity, 181
robots, 184
tailoring products to consumer
    demands, 162–166, 177, 178
testing ground, Japan as,
    117, 118
Diamond Lease Co., 91
Digital Equipment Corporation
    (DEC), 1, 10, 119, 138, 153,
    156, 196
    case study, 149–152
direct mail as distribution
    channel, 197
directness in communication, 169
discount stores, 130, 171
Disney Company, 132, 137
Disneyland, Tokyo, 131, 132
disposable income in Japan,
    115, 116
distinction and social status
    associated with products, 166
distribution channels in Japan
    main discussion, 193–200
    bypassing traditional
        channels, 196
    consumer partnerships, 196
    contracts and franchise
        arrangements between
        wholesalers and retailers, 193
    costs, 194
    deregulation of Japanese
        economy, 72, 76
    direct mail, 197
    domestic partnerships, 196
    economic dualism, distribution
        companies in, 3
    online, 198–200
    pyramid-like consumer
        partnerships, 196
    relationships between
        wholesalers and retailers, 193
    supermarkets and discount
        retailers, 194–196
    unsold commodities, buyback
        guarantees for, 194
    vending machines, 197, 198
DoCoMo, 133
Doing Business with the Japanese, 7
domestic consumption
    deregulation of Japanese
        economy, 71
    See also consumer spending
domestic partnerships as means of
    distribution, 196
Dore, Ronald, 41, 42, 98–99
Douglas and Craig, 19
dualism. See economic dualism
DuPont, 119
Dyson, 166

E

e-commerce, online sales as means
    of distribution, 198–200
Easy Phone, 133
Ecolab, 141
economic dualism
    main discussion, 15–35
    bonuses, 25
    commodity markets, dualism in,
        16–20

contractual and noncontractual
    employment, 20–29
defined, 13
domestic sector's limited
    competition, 16–18
exports, 3, 18–20
foreign businesses, effect of
    dualism on, 30, 31
hoarding of labor, 26
introductory matters, 3, 8
labor and employment, 3,
    15–35
lifetime employment, 21, 22
Occupied Japan, 23, 24
seniority wages, 23, 24
training and retraining, 26
unions, 24, 25
wages and compensation, 20–29
Eddie Bauer, 194
elderly, aging trends in Japan's
    markets, 128, 132, 133
Electrical Appliances and Material
    Control Law, 74
electronic companies
    in economic dualism, 3
    See also computers
Electronic Data Exchange
    (EDI), 91
employees. See labor and
    employment
energy conservation research,
    45–47
enterprise unions. See unions
equity financing, 95
Europe
    European Union (EU), 50–52,
        59–61, 190
    strategic alliances, 94
Evolution of a Manufacturing System
    at Toyota, The, 179, 181
exclusive contracts between
    wholesalers and retailers, 193
expansionary monetary and
    fiscal policy
    deregulation of Japanese
        economy, 71
expenses. See costs
explicit communication in
    Japanese culture, 169
exports
    economic dualism policies, 3,
        18–20
    government activism, 38–40
    shifting economic priorities, 4,
        53–55
extended families and pyramid-
    like consumer
    partnerships, 196

F

Fackler, M., 117
Fair Trade Commission (FTC), 17
families
    household size, trends, 124,
        126–128
    and pyramid-like consumer
        partnerships, 196
Faro Technologies, 166
Farrel, Tom, 174
Fast Retailing Co., Ltd., 132
fax correspondence in Japanese
    culture, 161

FDI (foreign direct investment), 112
feedback from customers in product development, 177
finance companies, 3, 143
   banking deregulation, 77, 78, 84–86
   foreign trade inaccessibility, 6
Financial Times, 90
Flexible Rigidities, 41
Focus Japan magazine, 99
Follie-Follie, 132
food
   Food Sanitation Law, 164–165
   household consumer spending, 195
Forbes, 174
Ford, 5, 13, 15, 75, 94, 112, 114, 205
foreign affiliates in Japan
   main discussion, 137–158
   AFLAC Japan, case study, 147–149
   competitive strategies of affiliates, 144, 145
   computer companies, 137–141, 146, 148–152, 205
   copyright/patent infringements, 138, 139
   Digital Equipment Corporation Japan, case study, 149–152
   early movers into Japanese markets, 137, 147–157
   economic dualism, 30, 31
   government activism, effect of, 47
   high startup costs, 138, 139
   industries present, 143
   Jardine Flemming, case study, 155–157
   joint ventures and strategic alliances, 140
   licensing/franchising arrangements, 138, 139
   mergers and acquisitions, 141
   modes of entry, 138–142
   performance of affiliates, 143
   Pfizer Japan, case study, 152–155
   wholly owned subsidiaries, 141
foreign currency regulation, 38
foreign direct investment (FDI), 112
foreign trade inaccessibility
   accounting companies, 6
   construction companies, 6
   financial companies, 6
   legal services companies, 6
   retail stores, 6
   trade barriers, 2–4
formality in Japanese business culture
   correspondence, 161
   introductions, 167
   wholesalers and retailers, 193
Fortune magazine, 131, 183
franchises
   arrangements between wholesalers and retailers, 193
   foreign affiliates in Japan, 138, 139

Franklin Mint, 197
freeters, 98
fringe benefits, 24, 26
FTC (Fair Trade Commission), 17
Fuji, 167
Fuji Bank, 85
Fuji Heavy Industries, 5, 95, 112, 205
Fujimoto, 179, 181
Fujita, Den, 137, 167
Fujitsu, 89, 91, 151
Fujitsu-Hitachi, 39
Fujiwara, 125, 131
Fujiya Co., Ltd., 196

G
gaijins, 187
Gap, Inc., 110, 113, 132
garages, deregulation, 79
Garten, Jeffrey, 39
GE, 90
GE Capital Corporation, 91
General Electric, 40
General Foods, 196
General Motors, 5, 13, 15, 75, 94–95, 112, 205
General Railway Signal, 40
Genotropin, 153
geothermal energy research, 45–47
Ghosn, Carlos, 89
Givaudan, 147
Glaxo Holdings, 1–2, 119
Global Hub, 91
Globalization and Growth: Case Studies in National Economic Strategies, 95
GM. See General Motors
Goldman Sachs, 114, 205
government activism
   main discussion, 35–48
   close cooperation between business and government, 37, 38
   continuity and consistency of policy, 44, 45
   creative destruction of industry, 38
   export promotion, 38–40
   foreign businesses, effect of activism on, 47
   foreign currency regulation, 38
   influence by government on Japanese companies, 40–42
   MITI and technological advances, 45–47
   protection of domestic industry, 43, 44
   signaling, 40
   social consensus, 42, 43
government procurement, deregulation, 72, 79
Grandis minivan, 173
grow or perish policy, 64
guarantees in Japanese business, 165, 166, 194
Guiliani, Tyron, 171
Guth, 89

H
han, 17
Handyman, 181

harmony as advertising requirement, 190
Hartford Life Insurance, 133
Harvard Business Review, 17
Hashimoto, 101
Hata, 101
Heckscher-Ohlin model of comparative advantage, 52
help-desk outsourcing, 166
Hermes, 113, 194
Hewlett Packard, 114, 119, 149, 205
Higuchi, Professor, 26
Hino Motors Ltd., 91
Hitachi Corporation, 89, 91, 93, 137, 150
HMV, 194
Hokkaido Takushoku Bank, 85
"hollowing out," 96
Honda, 15, 27, 30, 75, 95, 123, 173, 174, 177, 181–182
Hong Kong Standard, 101
Hopper, Dennis, 192
Hosokawa, 69, 71, 101
hours of work
   meetings after hours, 169
   reduction, 70, 71, 82
Houston, Whitney, 192
Houston Chronicle, 117
H&P. See Hewlett Packard
human resources. See labor and employment
humor in advertising, 191
hydrogen energy research, 45–47

I
IBM, 1, 35, 110, 119, 138, 140, 148, 156, 205
IDC, 80
Idemitsukosan, 41
IKEA, 113
iMac Blueberry, 174
image of company in product promotion, 192
impersonal communication, 161
implied meanings in communication, 169
imports
   desire for imported products, trends, 124, 125
   old *vs.* new economy, imports in, 55, 56
   quotas, deregulation, 74
   shifting economic priorities, 4, 5, 6
indirectness of communication, 169
individualist consumption trends, 125
industrial policy of Japan. See government activism
Infinity, 174
influence by government on Japanese companies. See government activism
informality. See formality in Japanese business culture
Information technology practices in old and new economy, 91, 92
infringement of patents and copyrights, 138, 139, 196

ING, 133
Inmac K.K., 197
innovation
  open Japanese markets, 118, 119
  See also developing new
     products
inshin-denshin, 21
Institute for International
  Economics, 73
insurance
  deregulation of Japanese
     economy, 74, 77, 78
  economic dualism, 3
  foreign companies in Japan, 143
Intel, 176
interest rates, deregulation, 77, 78
International Monetary Fund
  (IMF), 74
Internet sales as distribution
  channel, 198–200
interpersonal relationships in
  Japanese culture, 167, 168
inventory control, state-of-the-art
  vending machine
  technology, 197
irishamsu, 166
Iritani, Evelyn, 133
Isuzu Motors, 5, 91, 95, 112
Isuzu Real Estate Co., 91
IT practices in old and new
  economy, 91, 92
Ito, 7
Ito-Yokado, 137
Itochu Corporation, 140
Itoh, 7

J
Jagawa, 91–92
Japan, Inc., 13, 35
Japan and the World Economy, 167
Japan Corporate Plan, 5
Japan Echo, 40
Japan Telecom Company, 137
Japan Transport, 191
Japanese Big Bang, 78
Japanese Economy Reconsidered, 7
Japanese External Trade
  Organization, 161, 164
Jardine Flemming, 10, 107,
  138, 147
  case study, 155–157
JD Power and Associates, 174
JETRO, 71, 93, 96, 99, 109, 126,
  131, 194
Johnson & Johnson, 147
joint ventures and strategic
  alliances, 140
Journal of Advertising Research, 190
Journal of International Trade and
  Industry, 125
Journal of Japanese Trade and
  Industry, 197
jusen, 84

K
Kagome, 196
Kaifu, 102
kaizen, 179
Kameda Confectioners, 192–193
Kan-ji, 151
Kanagawa Institute, 133

Kanematsu Corporation, 137
Kanto Autoworks, 17
Kantor, Mickey, 51
Kao, 118
karaoke, 167, 169
Kasumigaseki, 102
Kato, 92
Kawada, 25
Kazuo, 40, 66, 86
KDD, 79
keiretsu, 16, 17, 18, 70, 76, 77, 79,
  91, 94, 150, 152, 153, 167,
  204, 205, 207
Keynesian stimulus policies, 102
KFC, 137
Kilburn, David, 197
kimonos, 1
Kirin Brewery Co., Ltd., 76, 196
Kishii, T., 190
Kobe Steel, 110
Kodak, 118
Koito, 15
Koizumi, 102
Komatsu, 25
Kono, T., 182
koza, 180

L
labeling and packaging messages,
  163–165
labor and employment
  collective bargaining, 24, 26
  cross-functional teamwork, 89
  economic dualism, 3, 15–35
  employee bonuses, 25
  fringe benefits, 24, 26
  high cost of local labor, 6
  hoarding workers, 26
  hours of work. See hours
     of work
  Labor Mobilization Law, 22
  lifetime employment, 21, 22,
     25, 97, 98
  outsourcing. See outsourcing
  part-time and temporary, 28
  seniority wages, 23, 24
  training and retraining, 26
  unions. See unions
  wages, 6, 20–29
  workday. See hours of work
Labor Mobilization Law, 22
Lady Borden ice cream, 140
land. See real estate
Large Department Store Law, 15,
  77, 193
LDP Party, 101, 102
Le Moulin de la Galette, 84
legal services companies, 6
Leica, 133
leisure, attitudes toward, 7
Les Noces de Pierrette, 84
Lexus, 173, 174
licensing/franchising
  arrangements, 138, 139
lifetime employment, 21, 22, 25,
  97, 98
Liquor Business Association
  Law, 164
L.L. Bean, 197
logic as goal in promoting
  products, 190

long-term objectives
  long-term planning and long-
     term relationships in Japanese
     culture, 167, 168
  old vs. new economy, 93–96
L'Oreal, 119
Los Angeles Times, The, 133
Louis Vuitton, 115, 123, 194

M
machine tool companies in
  economic dualism, 3
magazine advertising. See
  promotion of products
magnetohydrodynamic energy
  research, 45–47
Management and Coordination
  Agency, 133
management practices in old vs.
  new economy, 89–104
manufacturing
  affiliates present in Japan, 143
  offshore relocation of
     traditional manufacturing
     operations, 96
  proximity to research, 181
  shift from goods to services,
     124, 128, 129
Mark Smith, 176
market-driven product
  development, 177, 178
market fluctuations in economic
  dualism, 3
market sanctuary. See old vs. new
  economy
Marketing News, 123
marketing products. See
  promotion of products
Martin and Herbig, 165
Marubeni Corporation, 93
Marubun Corporation, 140
Matsushita, 170
Matsushita Electric, 91, 99,
  133, 182
Max Factor, 138, 147
Mazda, 5, 93, 94, 112, 114, 205
McDonald's, 123, 132, 137, 138,
  140, 167
McDonell and Douglas, 40
McInerney, Francis, 7
McKinney, 74
Measurement Law, 74, 164, 165
Medtronic, Inc., 134
meetings, after-hours, 169
Meiji Milk Products Company,
  140–141
Meiji Restoration, 37, 123, 188
MEITI. See Ministry of Economy,
  Trade and Industry
mergers and acquisitions, 141
Merrill Lynch, 205
Microsoft, 137, 176
Ministry of Economy, Trade and
  Industry, 5, 17, 80, 84, 141,
  143, 150
Ministry of Finance, 84,
  102, 104
Ministry of International Trade
  and Industry, 5, 17, 45–47,
  54, 77, 102, 110, 111, 124,
  150, 194

MITI. See Ministry of
International Trade and
Industry
Mitsubishi, 17, 76, 94, 150,
173, 196
Mitsubishi Bank, 76
Mitsubishi Electric, 76, 91
Mitsubishi Heavy Industries, 76
Mitsubishi Oil, 76
Mitsubishi-Oki, 39
Mitsubishi Real Estate, 76
Mitsubishi Trading Company, 91
Mitsubishi Trust, 85
Mitsubishi Warehouse, 76
Mitsui, 17, 90, 196
Mitsui Engineering and
Shipbuilding Company, 19
Mitsui Trust, 85
Moffett, Sebastian, 99
mom and pop stores, 193–200
Monsanto, 147
Montgomery, David B., 167, 192
Moore, Karl, 123, 176
Morgan, James, 7
Morgan, Jeffrey, 7
Morgan Stanley, 114
Moriguchi, Chicashi, 170
Morinaga Milk Products
Company, 110
Morningside, 5, 112
Motorola, 1, 35, 137
Mueller, Barbara, 190
Mujirushi Ryohin Co., Ltd., 132
Murayama, 101
Mutsuko, Murakami, 203

N
Nagasone, 69, 102
Nakamoto, Michyo, 90
National Advisory Committee on
Semiconductors, 41
NEC, 89, 110
NEC-Toshiba, 39
negotiations in Japanese business
culture, 168, 169
neighborhood stores, 193–200
nemawashi, 161–162, 168
nenpo-seido, 100
Nestle, 1, 7, 110, 114
new economy. See old *vs.* new
economy
New Insurance Business Law,
78, 80
new products. See developing new
products
New York Times, The, 97, 198
newspaper advertising. See
promotion of products
niatsu, 95
Nihon Keizai Shimbun survey, 93
Nike, 110
Nikkei, 82, 83, 104
Nikkei Weekly, The, 207
Nintendo, 110
Nippon Lever, 147
Nippon Life, 173
Nippon Trust, 85
Nishikawa, Tohru, 190, 191
Nissan, 75, 89, 94, 95, 114, 115,
173, 205
Nissan-Renault, 95
Nixon administration, 55

Nomura Holdings Inc., 93
Nomura Securities, 113, 205
noncontractual employment,
20–29
nontariff trade barriers (NTB), 74
Norihiko Shirouzu, 91
Norimitsu Onishi, 117
novelty of products, 166
NTT (telecom company), 54, 79,
80, 133

O
obeya, 182
Occupied Japan, 23, 24
Odyssey minivan, 173
OECD (Organization for
Economic Co-operation and
Development), 53, 98, 99,
117, 119, 129, 132, 178, 183
office equipment companies in
economic dualism, 3
offshore relocation of traditional
manufacturing operations, 96
oil imports, 79
Okabe, 92
old *vs.* new economy
main discussion, 13–106
account surpluses, 50–52
auditing, 94
bonds and securities, 94
business restructuring, 89–101
class actions, 94
corporate objectives, 93–96
cost of living in Japan, 64
Cross-Functional Teams, 89
debt financing, 95
equity financing, 95
European strategic alliances, 94
European Union trade deficit,
50–52, 59–61
exports, 53–55
friction with trade partners and
citizens, 49–67
grow or perish, 64
Heckscher-Ohlin model of
comparative advantage, 52
hollowing out, 96
imports, 55, 56
introductory discussion, 2, 6, 7
IT (Information technology)
practices, 91, 92
long-term objectives, 93–96
management practices, 89–104
offshoring, 96
political restructuring, 101–104
prosperity standards, 64
protectionism, 17
Ricardian model of
comparative advantage, 52
short-term objectives, 93–96
stockholders of corporations,
93–96
strategic alliances, 94
technology gap model, 52
Total Quality Control, 89
trade patterns, 52, 53
trade structure, 53–56
trade surpluses, 50–52
U.S. in Japan's old economy.
See United States trade
deficit
U.S. strategic alliances, 94

See also Bubble Economy;
deregulation of Japanese
economy; economic dualism;
government activism
Oldsmobile, 174
online sales as distribution
channel, 198–200
Ono, 98
open Japanese markets
main discussion, 109–119
Asian-Pacific trade and
investment, 115, 116
disposable income in Japan,
115, 116
foreign direct investment
(FDI), 112
innovation, 118, 119
product development and
testing ground, Japan as,
117, 118
opportunities. See trends and
opportunities in Japan's
markets
organized crime *(yakuza),* 78, 84
originality
open Japanese markets, 118, 119
See also developing new
products
Osami, Marino, 125
Ouchi, 168
outsourcing
help-desk operations, 166
offshore relocation of
traditional manufacturing
operations, 96
Ozawa, 75

P
packaging and labeling messages,
163–165
part-time and temporary
employment, 28
patent and copyright
infringements, 138, 139, 196
Pelé, 154
Pension Fund Association, 94
personal relationships in Japanese
culture, 167, 168
Peugot, 126, 166
Pfizer, 1, 10, 107, 110, 141, 154
Pfizer Japan, 138, 147, 156
case study, 152–155
P&G, 117, 118, 119, 137, 138, 140,
147, 165
Pharmacia, 154
phase review, defined, 180, 181
phones. See cell phones
Picasso, 84
Pickens, T. Boone, 15
Pizza Express, 113
Plaza Accord of 1985, 4, 5, 71,
84, 110
political restructuring
government activism. See
government activism
old *vs.* new economy,
101–104
Porter, Michael, 35, 40, 118
Portrait of Dr. Gachet, 84
Power Assist Suit, 133
Prada, 124
Presage minivan, 173

presence in Japan, cultural
importance of physical
presence, 161
prices
Bubble Economy, 130, 131
new product price
considerations, 183
real estate, 5
trends, 130
vending machines, 197
Pringles potato chips, 165
Prius, 173, 182
Procter and Gamble. See P&G
procurement, deregulation, 72, 79
product development. See
developing new products
product quality. See quality
product standards and certification
systems, 72
productivity in Japanese culture,
61, 183, 184
promotion of products
main discussion, 187–202
ADP strategy, 159
brand names, 192
brand names *vs.* product
names, 192
celebrities, 192
comparative advertising, 190
expenditures, 189
harmony as advertising
requirement, 190
history of advertising in
Japan, 188
humor, 191
soft-sell approach, 190
vending machines, 197
prosperity
in economic dualism, 3
old and new standards, 64
"prosumers," defined, 177
protectionism in old economy, 43,
44, 72
See also old *vs.* new economy
pyramid-like consumer
partnerships, 196

Q
quality
product quality in Japanese
culture, 130, 163
Total Quality Control, 89

R
Raskin, Andy, 118
Raytheon, 40
R&D. See research
Reagan, Ronald, 3, 49
real estate
foreign real estate companies
in Japan, 143
land scarcity, 64
prices, 5, 6
zoning laws, 16
Reich, Robert, 39
Reilly, Edmund, 151
relationships
aisatsu, 167, 168
wholesale and retail
relationships, 193
remote locations, technology to
monitor inventories in, 197

Renault, 89, 94, 95, 115, 205
Renewal Party, 101
research
developing new products,
177, 178
MITI and technological
advances, 45–47
proximity to
manufacturing, 181
retail
main discussion, 193–200
costs, 194
deregulation of Japanese
economy, 76
foreign trade inaccessibility, 6
vending machines, 197, 198
wholesalers' buyback guarantees
for unsold commodities, 194
See also distribution channels
in Japan
Ricardian model of comparative
advantage, 52
Ricoh Corporation, 173–174
robots, 184
Roche Group, 5, 95, 112, 140
Roche Haas, 140
Rolex, 123
Rubbermaid, 176
Ryohin Keikaku Co., Ltd., 132
Ryoshin Leasing Corporation, 91

S
sacred treasures (lifetime
employment, seniority wages,
and enterprise unions), 25,
97, 98
Saito, Ryoei, 84
Sakai, Koniyasu, 17
Sakakibara, 35
samurai-style management, 167
Sanger, David, 39
Sanyo, 89–90
Sato, 7
satori, 180
savings and productivity
differentials, United States
trade deficit, 61
Scalise, 163
Schumpeter, Joseph A., 173
Scion xB Compact, 173
Second Meiji Restoration, 123
*Second to None: American Companies
in Japan,* 7
securities, 78, 94, 155
Seiko, 178, 182
Seiyu, 5, 90, 95
semiconductor research, 45–47
seniority in work force, 23–25,
97, 98
seniors, aging trends in Japan's
markets, 128, 132, 133
service
customer service, 130, 165, 166
service economy, 124, 128, 129
Seven-Eleven, 137
Shanghai Electric, 5, 112, 205
Shell Oil, 156
Shibuya Station, 116–117
Shimada, 25
Shirai, 24
Shiseido, 90
Shu Uemura, 119

Siemens, 176
Sienna minivan, 174, 179
Silva, Neville de, 101
Singer, Jason, 94, 113, 117
single people, trends, 127, 131, 132
small and medium enterprises
(SMEs), 2, 19, 36
Smith, Mark, 123
social status and brand labels, 164
soft-sell promotion of
products, 190
software
Computer Aided Design
(CAD), 91
software production
MITI and technological
advances, 45–47
See also computers
solar power research, 45–47
Sony, 19, 30, 89, 90–91, 93, 97,
137, 167, 176, 181, 182
Sony Minokamo Corporation, 92
Southland Corporation, 137
space concerns
land scarcity, 64
vending machines, 198
Spectra Physics, 174
spending patterns. See consumer
spending
Sprague, Jonathan, 203
spring offensive, 24
Stallone, Sylvester, 192
standards and certification
systems, 72
Starbucks, 117, 123, 132
startup costs for foreign companies
in Japan, 138, 139
Sterngold, James, 198
stocks, bonds, and securities, 78,
93–96, 155
stores
main discussion, 193–200
Large Department Store Law,
15, 77, 193
warehouse and discount stores,
130, 171
See also distribution channels in
Japan; retail
strategic alliances
foreign affiliates in Japan, 140
old *vs.* new economy, 94
Strategic Direction magazine, 95
Structural Impediments Initiative
(SII), 3
subsidiaries, wholly owned, 141
Sud-Chemie Performance
packaging, 164
Sumitomo, 17
Sumitomo Bank, 85
Sumitomo Heavy Industries, 140
Sumitomo Life, 173
summo, 192
Sun Microsystems, 114, 205
"Super 301" section of Trade and
Competitiveness Act of 1988,
3, 49
supermarkets and discount
retailers, 194–196
Survival of the Slimmest in Japan, 89
sushi, 123, 167, 169
Suzuki Motors, 5, 95, 112, 205
Syntex Corporation, 119

T

Takeshita, 102
Takeuchi, 35
Taking Global Brands to Japan, 176
Tally's, 132
Taniguchi, Osama, 137
tariffs and trade barriers, 2–4, 13, 63, 72, 73
tatami, 1
Tatsuno, Sheridan, 180
taxis, deregulation of Japanese economy, 79
TDK, 91, 100
technology
    MITI and technological advances, 45–47
    old *vs.* new economy, technology gap model, 52
    robots, 184
    See also computers; wireless technology
teiki sayo, 22
telecommunications
    advertising. See promotion of products
    cell phones. See cell phones
    deregulation of Japanese economy, 79
Temporary Act for the Specially Designated Industries, 38
Teradyne, 40, 117
Teradyne Corporation, 117, 119
Texas Instruments, 138–139, 196
T.G.I. Friday's, 113
Theory Z, 168
three sacred treasures (lifetime employment, seniority wages, and enterprise unions), 25, 97, 98
Tiffany, 132
time
    long-term planning and long-term relationships, 167, 168
    old *vs.* new economy, long-term objectives, 93–96
    quick results in Japanese business culture, 168, 169
Tokai Bank, 85
Tokyo Disneyland, 131, 132
Tokyo Marine and Fire Insurance Co., Ltd., 76, 80
Tokyo Stock Exchange, 156
Toshiba, 91, 150, 177
Total Quality Control, 89
Toyota, 15, 17, 26, 27, 30, 75, 91, 92, 95, 123, 166, 173, 174, 179, 182
Toyota Automatic Loom Works, 17
Toys "R" Us, 7, 15, 80, 110, 167
Trade Act of 1988, 41
Trade and Competitiveness Act of 1988, 3
trade barriers, 2–4, 13, 74
trade partners, friction, 49–66
trade structure in old *vs.* new economy, 52–56

trade surpluses, 3, 50–52
trade unions. See unions
training, workforce, 26
Transformation of the Japanese Economy, 7
trends and opportunities in Japan's markets
    main discussion, 2, 123–136
    aging population, 128, 132, 133
    brands, 123, 125
    childless couples, 127, 128
    children, 124, 126–128
    consumer economy. See deregulation of Japanese economy
    credit card spending, 124, 131
    designer products, 125
    family and household size, 124, 126–128, 127
    imported products, desire for, 124, 125
    individualist consumption, 125
    product quality, service, and price considerations, 130
    shift from goods to services, 124, 128, 129
    single people, 127, 131, 132
    spending. See consumer spending
    successful brands, 123
tsukiiai, 169
Tsurumaki, Tomonori, 84
Tyson, Laura, 39, 51

U

Under Siege, 113
Uniden, 96
unions, 24–26
    three sacred treasures (lifetime employment, seniority wages, and enterprise unions), 25, 97, 98
Unlocking Japan's Markets: Seizing Marketing and Distribution Opportunities in Today's Japan, 7, 118
unsold commodities, buyback guarantees, 194
U.S. Army, 137
U.S. Congressional report, 76
U.S. Department of Commerce, 5
U.S. strategic alliances, 94
U.S. trade deficit
    main discussion, 50–52, 56–59
    savings and productivity differentials, 61
    sources of Japan's trade surplus, 61–67
    tariff and nontariff barriers, 63
    Yen, value of, 63
utility companies in economic dualism, 3

V

van Gogh, 84
vending machines as distribution channel, 197, 198

Vfend, 153
Viagra, 153, 154
Vietor, Richard H. K., 95
Virgin Megastores, 80
Vodafone, 137

W

wages and compensation, 6, 20–29
Wal-Mart, 2, 5, 6, 90, 95, 109, 113, 205
Walkman, 181
Wall Street Journal, The, 39, 91, 94, 98, 99, 113, 114, 117, 131, 161, 171
warehouse and discount stores, 130, 171
Warner-Lambert, 154
Wella, 137
White, Sean, 7
Whitehall, 102
Whiting, Rick, 181
wholesale
    main discussion, 193–200
    wholesalers' buyback guarantees for unsold commodities, 194
    See also distribution channels in Japan
wholly owned subsidiaries, 141
wireless technology
    cell phones. See cell phones
    vending machine state-of-the-art technology, 197
Wish minivan, 173
workday. See hours of work
workforce. See labor and employment
World Federation of Trade Unions, 25
World War II, 22
Woronoff, Jon, 7, 118
Worthy, Ford S., 183
WTO, 79

X

Xerox Corporation, 167, 173–174
Xilinx, Inc., 117

Y

yakuza, 78, 84
Yamaichi Securities, 205
Yaris, 173
Yasuda Trust and Banking Co. Ltd., 155
yen
    deregulation of Japanese economy, 71
    foreign currency regulation, 38
    United States trade deficit, 63
Young, Louis H., 177
Yucata, 1

Z

Zaun, Todd, 114
Zen Buddhist philosophy, 180
Zoff, 132
zoku giin, 102
zoning laws, 16

ABOUT THE AUTHOR

Holding a Ph.D. degree from SUNY at Stony Brook, Professor Panos Mourdoukoutas began his career at the State University of Pennsylvania, and continued at Long Island University in New York, Nagoya University in Japan, and at the Economic University of Athens. Professor Mourdoukoutas has represented Greece in the United Nations, traveled extensively throughout the world, and lectured in a number of universities, including Kobe University, Tokyo Science University, Keimung University, Saint Gallen University, Duisburg University, and the Beijing Academy of Science. He is the author of several articles presented in academic and business conferences and published in professional journals and magazines, including *Barron's* and *Edge Singapore*. He has also published several books, including *The Global Corporation: The Decolonization of International Businesses*, *China Against Herself: Imitation or Innovation in International Businesses*, *The Rise and Fall of Abacus Banking in Japan and China*, *Banking Risk Management in a Globalizing Economy*, *Strategy ADP: How to Compete in the Japanese Market*, *Collective Entrepreneurship in a Globalizing Economy*, *Nurturing Entrepreneurship: Institutions and Policies*, and *When Greece Turned into Little Japan*. In 2001, he received the Literati Club Award for the Highly Commended Author.

ABOUT TEXERE

Texere, a progressive and authoritative voice in business publishing, brings to the global business community the expertise and insights of leading thinkers. Our books educate, enlighten, and entertain, and provide an intersection where our authors and our readers share cutting edge ideas, practices, and innovative solutions. Texere seeks to cultivate, enhance, and disseminate information that illuminates the global business landscape.

www.thomson.com/learning/texere

About the typeface

This book was set in 10.5/14pt, Bembo.

Library of Congress
Cataloging-in-Publication Data

Mourdoukoutas, Panos.
　The new, emerging Japanese economy : opportunities and strategies for world business / by Panos Mourdoukoutas.
　　p. cm.
　ISBN 0-324-20712-3
　1. Japan—Economic conditions—1989- 2. Japan—Economic policy—1989- 3. Free enterprise—Japan. 4. Consumption (Economics)—Japan. 5. Globalization—Economic aspects—Japan. 6. Corporations, Foreign—Japan. 7. Japan—Foreign economic relations. 8. Competition, Unfair—Japan. I.
Title.
HC462.95.M683 2005
337.52'009'051—dc22

　　　　　　　　　　　　　　　　　2005015676